What is the relationship between women and the welfare state? How do women reconcile paid work and family responsibilities? These questions are of central political concern to nearly all Western industrialized countries and have provoked considerable scholarly disagreement. In this timely book, Dr Arnlaug Leira presents both a theoretical and an empirical analysis of the relationship between women's lives, employment practices and childcare provision.

Focusing upon the social construction of motherhood in Scandinavia, Arnlaug Leira shows how, contrary to common perceptions, there is no shared model of welfare policies and women's work. Instead, the position in Norway is significantly different from that in Sweden and Denmark. The author then presents an ethnographic analysis of the lives of working mothers in Norway. She details the complexity of the strategies by which women cope and support one another in combined earning and childcare in a situation where state provision is limited.

From her empirical material, Dr Leira convincingly argues for a theoretical approach that treats women as both earners and carers rather than, as has been the tendency, viewing them as either mothers or active in paid work. She also highlights some of the key processes in the gendering of welfare state citizenship, the hierarchy of work forms that accords primacy to wage-work, the presumption that caring is to remain predominantly a private responsibility, and the gendered division of labour.

Welfare states and working mothers will be widely read by students and specialists of sociology, social policy and administration, political science and women's studies. It will also be of interest to policy makers, social workers, teachers and nursery school workers.

Welfare states and working mothers

Welfare states and working mothers

The Scandinavian experience

Arnlaug Leira

Research Director, Institute for Social Research, Oslo

CAMBRIDGE
UNIVERSITY PRESS

Published by the Press Syndicate of the University of Cambridge
The Pitt Building, Trumpington Street, Cambridge CB2 1RP
40 West 20th Street, New York, NY 10011-4211, USA
10 Stamford Road, Oakleigh, Victoria 3166, Australia

© Cambridge University Press 1992

First published 1992

Printed in Great Britain by Woolnough Bookbinding Ltd.
Irthlingborough, Northants.

A catalogue record for this book is available from the British Library

Library of Congress cataloguing in publication data
Leira, Arnlaug.
  Welfare states and working mothers: the Scandinavian experience/
Arnlaug Leira.
    p.   cm.
Includes bibliographical references and index.
ISBN 0 521 41720 1 (hardback)
1. Working mothers—Scandinavia.   2. Childcare services—
Scandinavia.   3. Welfare state.   4. Working mothers—Norway.
I. Title.
HQ759.48.L45   1992
306.874′3′0948—dc20   91-36797   CIP

ISBN 0 521 41720 1 hardback

For my sisters in kin and spirit –
and for my son

Contents

List of figures	*page*	x
List of tables		xi
Preface and acknowledgements		xiii
List of abbreviations		xiv
1 Introduction		1
2 Models of motherhood		12
3 Welfare states and working mothers: the Scandinavian experience		41
4 The collectivization of childcare		64
5 Mothers, markets and the state		97
6 Modes of mothering		132
7 Carer state and carer careers		161
Notes		178
References		185
Index		197

Figures

2.1 The childcare economy   *page* 37
5.1 Combinations of childcare and employment in
    employed-mother families   99

Tables

2.1 Institutional differentiation of childcare and corresponding
     carer careers   *page* 38
2.2 Carer careers   39
3.1 The division of day-care running costs in Denmark, Norway and
     Sweden in 1987   51
3.2 Pre-school children in state-sponsored day care by age and form
     of care, 1989   55
4.1 Children in state-sponsored day care, 1970, 1975, 1980, 1985,
     1990   92
5.1 Data on Norwegian women, 1960 and 1990   98
5.2 Women's labour force participation rate, 1973 and 1988,
     Denmark, Norway, Sweden, United Kingdom   105
5.3 Part-time employment in 1986, Denmark, Norway, Sweden,
     United Kingdom   105
5.4 Unemployment rates by sex, 1975, 1983, 1985. Denmark,
     Norway, Sweden, United Kingdom   106
5.5 Married mothers in employment by age of youngest child, 1976,
     1980, 1985, 1990   109
6.1 Mothers' employment and childcare   135
6.2 Combinations of earning and caring: dual-earner families, 1973
     and 1985   136

Preface and acknowledgements

This book draws upon several years of research dealing with women's organization of everyday life. During this work I was intrigued by the complex efforts involved in reconciling the competing demands of wage-work and caring for young children. Since the 1960s new forms of motherhood have been established in Scandinavia by the women who took up employment whilst their children were still of pre-school age. Contrary to conventional wisdom, my research shows that these motherhood 'experiments' were not whole-heartedly supported by the state. This book tells a much more multifaceted story than the one contained in the legend of the interventionist welfare state.

My work concerning the relationship between the working mothers and the welfare state has been greatly facilitated by the generous help and support of many individuals and institutions. Of basic importance are the contributions of the numerous women whom I have interviewed in the course of my research on women's work and care. Without listing their names, I am deeply indebted to them all.

Several persons have read earlier versions of different chapters. I have much appreciated the helpful suggestions of Julia Brannen, Anne Lise Ellingsæter, Helga Maria Hernes, Aud Korbøl, Siri Nørve, Anne-Lise Seip, Clare Ungerson, Cato Wadel and Caroline Woodruffe.

It is a pleasure to acknowledge the valuable discussions with Joan Acker, Kerstin Bohm, David Morgan, Birte Siim, Hildur Ve, Karin Widerberg and Kari Wærness. What might remain of errors of fact or judgement is, of course, my own responsibility.

My thanks also to the Norwegian Research Council for Science and the Humanities for the financial support that allowed me to take time off for concentrated writing and for the pleasant task of turning a dissertation into a book.

The Institute for Social Research in Oslo has provided an excellent work environment. Special thanks to Ingebjørg Wesche for her efficient and good-humoured dealings with me and my manuscript.

Abbreviations

Besl. O.   Beslutning fattet av Odelstinget (decisions made by the section of Parliament in which legislation is introduced)

FAFO   Fagbevegelsens institutt for forskning og utredning (The Norwegian Trade Union Centre for Social Science and Research)

INAS   Institutt for sosialforskning (Institute for Applied Social Research)

Innst. O.   Innstilling til Odelstinget (recommendation to the Odelsting from one of the parliamentary committees)

Innst. S.   Innstilling til Stortinget (recommendation to the Parliament from one of the parliamentary committees)

ISF   Institutt for samfunnsforskning (Institute for Social Research – ISR)

NAVF   Norges allmennvitenskapelige forskningsråd (The Norwegian Research Council for Science and the Humanities)

NIBR   Norsk institutt for by- og regionforskning (The Norwegian Institute for Urban and Regional Research)

NOS   Norges offentlige statistikk (Norway's public statistics)

NOU   Norges offentlige utredninger (Norwegian official reports)

Ot. forh.   Odelstingets forhandlinger (the proceedings of the section of the Parliament in which legislation is introduced)

Ot. prp.   Odelstingsproposisjon (proposition for new legislation or for amendments of existing legislation)

SCB   Statistiska Centralbyrån (Central Bureau of Statistics of Sweden)

SØS   Samfunnsøkonomiske studier (Social and economic studies)

SSB   Statistisk Sentralbyrå (Central Bureau of Statistics of Norway)

St. meld.   Stortingsmelding (report prepared by one of the government ministries for the national assembly)

1 Introduction

What is the relationship between women and the welfare state? A central issue in feminist discourse from the 1970s on, this question has provoked considerable scholarly disagreement and widely differing opinions. Examining in particular the welfare state organization of social reproduction, the relationship between women and the welfare state has been pictured in terms of both a 'patriarchy' (e.g. Eisenstein 1979) and a 'partnership' (e.g. Siim 1984). In the international literature the assignment of caring to women is often assumed to contribute importantly to the structurally inferior situation of women in modern welfare states, and is interpreted as an expression of patriarchal domination (Eisenstein 1979; Frazer 1987). Scandinavian research, on the other hand, commonly offers a more positive interpretation. Hernes (1982; 1984) points to the possibility of alliances being formed between women and the welfare state. Siim (1984) even argues that around issues of human reproduction a partnership was established between women and the welfare states in Denmark and Sweden in which the state acknowledged the dual obligations of mothers to wage-work and childcare.

The relationship, however, is more complex than what is conveyed in the conceptualization as either 'patriarchy' or 'partnership', as I shall show by examining how the welfare state relates to working mothers. Different welfare states have adopted distinctly different approaches in this regard (see e.g. Kamerman and Kahn 1981). Even within Western Europe there is no uniform set of motherhood policies (Leira 1987a; Moss 1988). Recent research shows the relationship as ambivalent, shaped by mutual dependence as well as contradictions (Ruggie 1984; Haavind 1987; Sassoon 1987).

Taking the changing social construction of motherhood in Scandinavia as a starting point, my analysis examines the relationship between the welfare state and women. The research explores questions of central concern in social science theory as well as in the planning of social policy: the relationship between welfare state policies and everyday

1

practices, between the welfare state and its citizens, the complex intertwining of the public and the private, the relationship between structure and agency. The book develops from a theoretical discussion of such opposites, supplemented with empirical investigations.

The welfare state and everyday life

One contrast is captured in my juxtaposition of welfare state policies and everyday practices. It is important, I argue, to bring these together in the same discussion, since studies of the state, which conventionally focus on the former, tend to minimize the importance of individual actors, whereas more ethnographic studies, which deal with everyday life, often exclude the influence of state policies. Furthermore, the combination of the two perspectives, the 'macro' and the 'micro', shows the intermix of public and private resources in the complicated 'jigsaw puzzle' of working mothers' everyday organization. The everyday perspective is essential, I maintain, if we are to understand the restructuring of motherhood and its implications not only for women as mothers and minders, but also for the welfare state. The dual perspective also shows the dependence of the formal welfare state services on an informal, 'hidden' or 'shadow' service system, developed to accommodate the vital needs of the very young. This informal economy of caring demonstrates the effects of individual agency in generating structural change. Examining the welfare state from 'the grassroots', from the mothers' point of view, raises questions as to the interpretation of the welfare state, not only in terms of patriarchy or partnership, but about the character of state interventionism.

Empirically, my argument is brought out in an analysis of mothers' employment and the provision of childcare services for wage-working mothers' children. This analysis shows that the image of the expansive Scandinavian welfare state needs to be supplemented: in the development of what I have termed 'the employed-mother family', women play a central part as change agents.[1]

Welfare state intervention in childcare and mothers' (and family) economy has produced significant changes in everyday mothering and family life. This involvement of the state has been highly controversial, welcomed as well as contested. Therefore, focusing on these aspects of motherhood change and on the concomitant conflicts yields interesting insights into the relationship between the state and the mothers: which images or models of motherhood were projected and promoted by welfare state policies? and which ones were shown in mothers' practices?

Considering that economic activity or 'production' in a wider sense, and childcare, an activity of undisputed importance in social reproduction, are essential to society, a look at the welfare state approach to mothers' economic and caring practices elucidates general processes structuring the relationship between the welfare state and women, indeed between the welfare state and its citizens.

Motherhood is crucial to an analysis of the social construction of gender, and to the economy of the welfare state as well. Even though not all women personally experience motherhood, hardly any woman in present-day welfare states is unaffected by its potentiality, and most women actually do become mothers. Considering, too, that the gender-differentiated family is a central characteristic of welfare state design, an investigation of welfare state motherhood also sheds light on the welfare state approach to women more generally.

Motherhood concepts

Motherhood is a multidimensional concept. Motherhood refers to biological processes and cultural symbols, to the individual experience of being a woman parenting and to the social construction of women as mothers. Motherhood is moulded by the interplay of gender and generations and by political institutionalization. Often perceived as a private affair, welfare state policies increasingly demonstrate the importance of motherhood to the public domain. Focusing on motherhood as a social construction, my examination barely touches on the biological aspects of motherhood and on the emotional qualities of the mother–child relationship.

Welfare state influence on mothers' lives is multifaceted and complex. The processes of change affect single mothers and married ones differently. They also have different consequences for mothers across social class, as well as across ethnic and socio-cultural background. My study does not deal with all dimensions of welfare state motherhood nor with the mosaic of consequences of welfare state policies experienced by mothers. I aim at clarifying the welfare state reconstruction of motherhood as manifested in two basic aspects, economic provision and primary socialization and care. Accordingly, I take mothers' economic activity and their childcare commitments as the concrete activities through which I examine the relationship between the state and mothers.

As an analytical tool I introduce the concept that motherhood has both earner and carer aspects. The 'earner' aspects refer to mothers' economic activities and material provision, the 'carer' aspects to primary socialization, nurturing and rearing. I use the term 'model' to help identify the changes in the structural design of motherhood, as seen in the changing relations between two important elements: the carer and the earner aspects. By this conceptualization of motherhood, I emphasize the necessity of breaking down or transcending the models of 'work' and 'family' that ignore or marginalize the interrelationship of production and social reproduction, of labour market organization and labour restitution, socio-cultural reproduction and care of children.

Conceptualizing Scandinavian mothers of young children as both providers and nurturers highlights an empirical fact neglected in much sociological theorizing of the family. Thus my concept of mothers as earners and carers differs from that presented in much of the mainstream theoretical literature, ranging from the structural-functionalism of Parsons to the domestic labour debate of the 1970s, in which caring is identified as the essential element in the social construction of motherhood, while the economic activities of the mothers are often overlooked. The interrelationship of 'work' and 'care' needs to be addressed in social theory, I contend. My discussion of mothers as earners and carers elaborates on the considerable research and reformulations of the concepts of 'work' and 'care' in Anglo-American, particularly British, and Scandinavian sociology in recent years (e.g. Leira and Nørve 1977; Wadel 1977; Wærness 1982; Graham 1983; Pahl 1984; Ungerson 1987; Finch 1989; Leira 1989). Thinking about mothers as both earners and carers allows for a more detailed examination of motherhood change. For example, the post-World War II period has seen a far-reaching structural transformation of the labour market and of family patterns in the Western industrialized societies. This empirical regularity demonstrates the need for a reconsideration also of the motherhood concepts.

Looking at the welfare state from a motherhood perspective draws attention to and raises questions about the ways in which the welfare state relationship to the family is interpreted in social theory. Examining the welfare state from a motherhood perspective, which are the predominant features? Is it the public take-over of functions that formerly belonged to the private sphere of the family? Or, does the image of the actively interventionist state need qualification? What is the role of the state as initiator or instrument of family and motherhood change? And what is the part played by mothers?

Without underestimating the significance of childcare and primary socialization, I argue the importance of thinking about motherhood in a way which captures central features of the welfare state motherhood experience, which does not underplay the material or

economic provider aspects of motherhood but includes central aspects
other than caring in the motherhood analysis.

Citizen mothers

Conceptualizing mothers as earners and carers and as citizens of the
welfare state I analyse (i) the welfare state policies instituted to
accommodate the mothers who combine earning and caring commitments and (ii) the mothers' approaches to motherhood as evidenced in
their economic activity and childcare arrangements. This analysis shows
that the remaking of motherhood is generated by welfare state policies
and by mothers' everyday practices.

More specifically my study discusses the following questions: What
policies did the welfare state adopt as regards (i) childcare provision, (ii)
mothers' economic activity? What are the 'models' or 'images' of
motherhood contained in and promoted by welfare state policies? And,
how do the motherhood models evidenced in mothers' practices correspond to those instituted by the welfare state? How do mothers approach
childcare and economic provision? What are mothers' everyday coping
strategies? In order to examine the relationship between the welfare
state and women more closely, this analysis of the making of
motherhood, I shall maintain, has to be set within a broader framework
which makes explicit the different ways in which the welfare state has
dealt with economic provision and caring, respectively: As activities of
individuals, how are caring and earning integrated into the welfare state
benefit and entitlement system? Which social rights do earning and
caring give access to? What do caring and earning entail in a citizenship
perspective? Is there such a thing as citizen the carer?

Thus I take the relationship between the welfare state and mothers in
Scandinavia as my main case in elucidating some general aspects of the
relationship between the state and citizens. Starting with T. H.
Marshall's classic studies of citizenship, and elaborating on the debate
about citizenship raised recently within international feminist research
(e.g. by Hernes 1988; Pateman 1987b; and also Lister 1990), I discuss
the compatibility of citizenship as a system of equality (in principle) with
gender as a system of inequality. I go on to analyse three assumptions
basic to the welfare state design; and of central importance in producing
a gendering of welfare state citizenship: the hierarchy of work forms
that accords primacy to wage-work; the presumption that caring is to
remain predominantly a private responsibility; and the gendered division of labour.

The empirical analysis of the relationship between the welfare state and the mothers as earners and carers also calls attention to contradictions inherent in the welfare state design. Looking at mothers highlights the fact that, in the welfare state citizenship, caring was not integrated on a par with earning. The motherhood analysis serves to clarify the different citizen status accorded to earners and carers. Contrasting the employment-related and caring-related entitlements offered by the Scandinavian welfare states, I show that welfare state benefits are structured according to a general set of premises in which formal employment is more favoured than informal caring. In interplay with the gendered division of labour this differentiation produces a gendering of citizenship.

The analysis displays state policies as inconsistent and ambivalent. For example: economic policies encouraged the economic provider aspects of motherhood, but did not provide sufficient childcare. In employment policies and in family policies as well, the everyday childcare problems of employed mothers (and fathers) remained a private concern to a considerable extent. The ensuing internal inconsistency of welfare state policies created a structural incompatibility between labour market and family organization. This problem was largely left to the individual mother (and family) to manage.

Looking at the mothers and the state, I do not assume that these are social actors with equal power to introduce social change. I do want to underline, however, that the 'models' of motherhood which emerge from my study, encompassing both carer and earner aspects, are products of welfare state policies as well as of mothers' coping strategies in everyday life. The empirical evidence from which my argument is developed therefore contains both examinations of institutional differentiation generated by policy decisions at state level and also analyses that deal with individual interactions and inter-household exchange. Caring and earning, and the relation between them, will change as state intervention, the economy and mothers' everyday practices dictate. The narrative therefore explores several processes: the modernization of motherhood, as seen in the practices of the mothers who joined the formal labour market and added ordinary wage-work to their other responsibilities; the collectivization of childcare, which refers to the introduction of state-sponsored schemes for early childhood education and care; and the development of informal labour markets to cater for the children of the employed mothers.

The Scandinavian setting

The making of motherhood in the Scandinavian welfare states calls attention to comprehensive changes in the division of labour in society.

I have focused on two of these processes: the increasing state intervention in primary socialization and care, and the exodus of the mothers
to the labour market.

Drawing upon a Scandinavian data-set I find the Norwegian welfare
state approach to mothers all the more interesting as it differs
distinctly from the policies of Denmark and Sweden. My findings do
not picture the Norwegian welfare state as actively interventionist
with regard to the employed-mother family. Accordingly, I question
the assumption commonly made about a common Scandinavian
model in reproduction policies. My study demonstrates that general
statements concerning the Scandinavian welfare states need qualification.

Discussing recent trends in the development of the Scandinavian
welfare states, Wolfe (1989) argues that the welfare states in the region
are in the process of creating a new social experiment, a welfare state
in which both women and men work, while the children are accommodated in public day care. However, it is important to observe that the
Scandinavian states are not special in this respect, but advanced.
Important as the local context is for shaping strategies and policies, the
Scandinavian 'experimenting' with the relationship between the welfare state and mothers is but one example of general processes of
profound social change occurring throughout the Western industrialized world.

Examining the relationship between the welfare state and women, I
focus on the motherhood model which in terms of numbers is
becoming the most important in Scandinavia, the one represented by
the employed mother. Thinking about mothers as both earners and
carers, and conceptualizing the social construction of motherhood as
shaped by welfare state policies as well as in everyday life, has
necessitated a multidimensional approach.

Empirically I draw upon my own research concerning welfare state
motherhood, utilizing Scandinavian, and particularly Norwegian, material. I utilize different types of data: public records, national statistics,
survey data, ethnographic material and in-depth interviews. The
empirical material was collected through a series of projects that I
carried out over the last eight to ten years dealing with women's work
and childcare. The ethnographic material and the interviews stem from
my earlier fieldwork. By analysing public records and policy documents, and by re-analysing surveys in the perspective of motherhood
change, I have 'created' data for my study. In different ways these
data, when analysed, show the multifaceted making of motherhood,
the creation of new opportunity situations – and, more indirectly, the

fading of old ones – by way of political decision-making as well as in everyday practices.

Outline of the book

My interest in the relationship between the welfare state and mothers originated in a study of inter-individual and inter-household exchanges and expanded into institutional differentiation. Structural change, I found, was produced by state policies but also by everyday activities in complex interrelationships. I present the work in the reverse order of research, starting with the state, where my investigations ended, and ending where I set out, with the everyday practices.

In *chapter 2* I present the theoretical framework within which my study is set – the conceptual and methodological reflections. Starting with a discussion of different perspectives on motherhood in the theoretical literature, I argue for an approach that conceptualizes mothers as both earners and carers and as citizens of the welfare state. This approach calls attention to the contradiction inherent in the welfare state design of citizenship that does not include 'carer' on the same basis as 'worker'. I examine the contradiction as expressed in the gendering of citizens' rights. A responsibility to provide care for very dependent persons defines both motherhood – indeed, womanhood in general – and the welfare state. Discussing the problems with the conceptual-ization of care as societal activity, as demonstrated in the recent theoretical discourse, I present a model of institutional differentiation that interlinks welfare state motherhood policies and mothers' everyday practices.

In *chapter 3* I introduce the empirical investigations of motherhood change by examining the policies concerning working mothers and childcare in Scandinavia. The intention is not to make a strictly comparative analysis, but to look in some detail at similarities and differences when it comes to mothers' employment and childcare by contrasting the evidence from Norway with that of Denmark and Sweden.

The chapter presents my analysis of comprehensive empirical mat-erial which I collected for the Council of Europe Social Research Fellowship Programme, 'Forms of Child Care', as a member of the Programme Study Group (see Thayer et al. 1988). I was generously assisted in interviews and correspondence with representatives of the government administrations in charge of early childhood education and care in Denmark, Norway and Sweden (Leira 1987a). I also drew upon national statistics, legislation, guidelines and instructions for day-care provision prepared by the central authorities of the three countries, policy proposals and plans, much of it supplied by the government representatives mentioned above. Data concerning mothers' employment and childcare arrangements I later up-dated and supplemented.

The data-sets utilized show pronounced structural similarities between the three countries. Yet, when it comes to welfare state intervention in meeting employed mothers' demands for childcare, the idea of a Scandinavian model is modified by the Norwegian case. Why Denmark and Sweden endorsed mothers' employment whereas Norway did not is not explained in my study. However, I offer some hypotheses and indicate possibilities for further research.

In *chapter 4* I explore the political history of early childhood education and care in Norway, a set of policies that entailed a comprehensive change in the carer aspects of motherhood. Other sets of state policies, for example the child benefit and the mother-and-child services, reach out to more mothers, yet they do not hold a similar importance, I contend. Only the programmes concerning early childhood education and care introduced new models of motherhood. As such, not surprisingly they were controversial. Precisely such controversies help to expose the different family and motherhood models supported by different 'actors' participating in the political process in the decades preceding day-care legislation.

My examination covers the period 1945–85, and is both narrative and analytical. The analysis is based on policy documents from the period 1945–75, including some of the important documents from the following decade. I use the reports of government-appointed committees instructed to deal with issues concerning early childhood education and care, the reports and recommendations of the Ministries in charge of day care for pre-school children, the reports and discussions of parliamentary bodies, and the texts of different proposals for a Day Care Act. My perspective and interpretation differs from those of other studies in that I focus on early childhood education and care as evidence of change in the state's relationship to mothers, and on the explicit and implicit motherhood models contained in state policies.

The main issue of the chapter is how the welfare state policies define the division of responsibility for childcare between the public and the private spheres, and draw the boundaries between the state (local and central government) and the mothers; obviously, universally oriented policies project other images of motherhood than do selective ones. Primarily I deal with two sets of questions that are of special importance to mothers: whether state-sponsored day care was to be available to all children or just a few, and whether state responsibility was to encompass all children actually cared for in extrafamilial arrangements, or to be restricted to those accommodated in state-sponsored services only. How were welfare state policies developed? by what measures? and for whom? Which model of motherhood did the policies promote, the employed or the domesticated mother?

Analysing the objectives of day-care policies and the means instituted towards reaching the stated aims, and adding to the document analysis an examination of the actual development of provisions, I underline the ambivalence in national policies as regards which motherhood model to support or promote.

Chapter 5 examines the political discourses that are of special importance as regards the welfare state policies towards working mothers in Norway. I turn to the changes in the earner aspects of motherhood, and the welfare state response to mothers who combine earning and caring activities. I make use of various sources: census data, labour market statistics and surveys of childcare arrangements. The policy documents utilized in chapter 4 are used in this chapter as well. On the basis of censuses, labour market statistics and surveys I give an overview of the main trends in women's, and particularly mothers' employment in the post-war period. Drawing upon my analysis of the political history of early childhood education and care, I explore the political institutionalization of the concept of the employed mother and discuss the role of the welfare state in promoting or supporting this family form. The employed mothers signalled a profound restructuring of the labour market and of the family, processes in which the welfare state acted only indirectly as initiator or instrument of change.

To document how mothers managed to combine earning and caring commitments when welfare state provision failed, I have made use of my earlier re-analysis of responses to questions concerning employed mothers' (and fathers') childcare arrangements included in nationwide, representative surveys (Leira 1985). Utilizing this material I have given an outline of informal childcare markets and estimated the importance of such arrangements in the overall childcare structure as well as in women's employment. I also demonstrate how the 'informal economy' or informal service system developed for care provision differs from the informal economies generated within other sectors of the economy. The informal childcare markets show how mothers managed to expand their economic activities and take up new forms of motherhood without the help of state-sponsored day care. The informal childcare economy also calls attention to the considerable ambivalence of the welfare state towards the models of motherhood represented by the employed mothers.

In *chapter 6* I turn from welfare state policies concerning mothers as earners and carers to mothers' making of motherhood as demonstrated by their combined employment and childcare commitments. I focus on the strategies mothers have developed to allow for both earning and caring, and particularly on the self-made arrangements between mothers and childminders. In earlier chapters I have documented the relative importance of such arrangements in the overall childcare structure while in Chapter 6 the everyday processes that generate an informal childcare economy are analysed. The chapter utilizes survey data concerning mothers' employment and childcare and material from interviews with mothers and minders from my previous projects. Observations and in-depth interviews with mothers and minders from an ethnographic study carried out in an urban neighbourhood provide important material for the chapter (Leira 1983; 1987b).

On the basis of survey data, I present a rudimentary typology of mothers' approaches to the earner and carer aspects of motherhood. Aspects of the mother–minder relationship are illustrated through my interview data. Focusing on mothers' daily life within one local setting, as in the ethnographic study, shows the making of motherhood in everyday practices. This study does not, of course, represent the 'average' approach to motherhood, nor the character of the 'average' mother–minder relationship. However, it does illustrate the influence of welfare state policies on mothers' everyday life as well as the influence of women's everyday practices in structural change.

In the *concluding chapter*, I return to some of the issues raised in the Introduction, in particular to questions concerning the character of the welfare state relationship to women who combine earning and caring commitments. Drawing upon the recent discourses on gender and caring in modern welfare states, I examine the interplay of three processes: the welfare state definition of public versus private responsibility for caring, the differentiation of work forms in the welfare state system of entitlements and benefits, and the gendered division of labour.

My analysis shows the welfare state relationship to women as 'Janus-faced'. Although contributing to women's decreased economic dependence on individual men, the welfare state nevertheless upholds men's privileged position in the labour market and in the welfare state reward system. This ambivalence I portray as a 'patriarchal partnership'.

2   Models of motherhood

Introduction

The theoretical literature presents different perspectives on mothers, and commonly emphasizes childcare, rearing and nurturing as the defining characteristics of motherhood. Like women in most societies, mothers in the welfare state provide material resources and care. The big transition in the industrialized world is that mothers have to leave their children for part of the time in order to provide materially. The welfare states in Scandinavia have accelerated these changes in mothers' childcare and economic activity. The emergence of what I have termed 'the employed-mother family', that is families in which mothers take on all or some of the responsibility for economic provision, calls attention to an interrelationship of work and care in individual experience and institutionalized in society. This interrelationship social analysis needs to address. Introducing the concept that motherhood has both earner and carer aspects, the carer aspects referring to primary socialization, maintaining and rearing and the earner aspects to economic provision, the first of the following sections contrasts my conceptualization of motherhood with the conventional wisdom in the social sciences, which pictures mothers primarily as carers.

The employed mother moreover provides a perspective on citizenship that reveals an important premise of the welfare state design, namely the different status attributed to earners and carers. Conceptualizing mothers as earners and carers and as welfare state citizens highlights what the theoretical debate often neglects, that in welfare state citizenship 'carer' was not included on the same basis as 'worker'. The second section examines this contradiction, that entails a gendering of citizenship, and shows the welfare state relationship to women as ambivalent.

The complexities in this relationship are clearly evidenced also in employed mothers' schedules, and particularly in their everyday provision for childcare, in which motherhood as a personal, individual

12

experience is interconnected with motherhood as institutionalized in the welfare state. Theoretically and methodologically it is worth observing that the mediation between the child's vital need for care and nurturing on the one hand, and on the other available resources produced by family members or by outside agencies such as relatives, friends, shadow labour markets or state-sponsored services is evidenced in women's everyday schedule more than in men's. Caring for children creates an interlinking between an emotional, individual and private sphere, and the public domain that exposes the 'public'–'private' distinction as hazy, as mothers commonly commute between public and private arenas and authorities, and integrate resources provided by formal and informal, public and private agencies in the management of everyday life.

The complexities of care as manifested in daily life necessitate a clarification at the conceptual level. In the penultimate section I consider the recent discourses about caring in the theoretical literature and then present my typology of institutional differentiation, derived from my analysis of working mothers' everyday childcare arrangements. As I go on to show in the following chapters, the institutional differentiation results from welfare state intervention, which is well known. An added theoretical point is that individual agency and everyday activities are important elements in structural change.

Mothers as earners and carers

The employed-mother family illuminates how the concept of the role-differentiated family, as portrayed in functional social theory (e.g. see Parsons 1955; 1960) or in the domestic labour debate (e.g. Seccombe 1974; Dalla Costa and James 1975), no longer holds for women, though it may do so for men. Conceptualizing motherhood (and fatherhood) in terms of both economic provision and caring commitments presents a different perspective on parenthood and family life from the one contained in the concept of the 'isolated nuclear family' as developed in particular by Parsons (1955; 1960). This 'nuclear family' is characterized by a pronounced division of labour between the parents: father is the economic provider of the family; mother is the home-maker and carer-parent. I shall discuss Parsons' theorizing of the family and motherhood/parental roles, not because I find it a particularly useful guide in presenting family patterns in Scandinavia, but because it helps illuminate a family model still prevalent in the social science literature and still important in Scandinavian welfare state policies.

Parsons developed a functional analysis in which the needs of the family and the occupational systems were met in a mutual process. The gendered division of labour in this analysis was instrumental (or 'functional') in complying with the needs of both systems. The differentiation of parental roles and the specialization as breadwinner and carer respectively (or as instrumental and expressive functions) follow from the biological differences between women and men in their reproductive capacity, Parsons argued. Sex roles were reinforced and perpetuated by functional differentiation of parental responsibilities, notably of caring and economic provision. The differentiation of sex roles was functional for personality development and for the stabilization of the family, the occupational system and the social system as a totality.

Three elements of Parsons' theory are especially relevant to my perspective: the presumed 'functionality' of the gendered division of labour; the coupling of reproductive capacity to social practices, such as early childhood education and care; and the marginalization of women's economic activity and material provision.

Radical Scandinavian sex role research from the 1960s contested the 'naturalness' of the gendered division of labour, as does feminist scholarship from the 1970s and 1980s, much of which contains an explicit (or at least implicit) critique of Parsons (see e.g. Oakley 1976; Beechey 1978; Benhabib 1987). The feminist critique points to the organization of social reproduction in the nuclear family as contributing to male dominance and women's subordination in modern societies (Barrett 1980; Barrett and McIntosh 1982). Thus, the claim to an overall 'functionality' of this family form is questioned, and the need to 'deconstruct' the concept of the family is underlined in order to allow gender-specific assessments (Thorne 1983; Morgan 1985). The gendered division of labour in social reproduction, and in childcare in particular, may well be regarded as functional for capital, for the welfare state, and for men who have collectively chosen to leave childcare to women, freeing men for more profitable pursuits. It does not therefore follow that this division of labour is also functional for women.

Parsons assumed that there was a strong link between biology and the social practice of motherhood, a view echoed in sociobiology, which proclaims that socially instituted sex roles are rooted in biological differences. Parsons states: 'In our opinion the fundamental explanation of the allocation of the roles between the biological sexes lies in the fact that the bearing and early nursing of children establish a strong presumptive primacy of the relation of the mother to the small child and this in turn establishes a presumption that the man, who is exempted from these biological functions, should specialize in the alternative instrumental direction' (1955, p. 23).

Social motherhood, according to this interpretation, has a strong biological substructure that fatherhood has not. Moreover, childbearing, rearing and caring constitute the basis of the division of labour by gender in society. Although fathers are not presented as incapable of caring, mothers, as a result of biological experiences, emerge as the parent best prepared to care, and as the 'natural' carer of the two (Beechey 1978). The social importance of biology is extended from pregnancy, giving birth and lactation to caring in a wider sense, and to housework and family management and administration. The functional differentiation of parental roles implied that father managed the family's relations to the outside world, mother's place was in the home, with the children. Her loving care and attention were essential to the upbringing of the children (who were to function in a strongly gender-divided society) and for the stabilization of the adult personality. According to Parsons, role-differentiated nuclear families were necessary 'as "factories" which produce human personalities' (Parsons 1955, p. 16).

Child psychology in the early post-war period pictured the loving mother's care for her child as decisive for the child's development of 'basic trust' (Erikson 1965), which in turn was what made possible the development into successful adulthood. 'Maternal deprivation' might represent very serious harm to a child's development and mental health (Bowlby 1951; for a critique see Rutter 1972). Motherly love was perhaps to balance the gloomier aspects of industrialization. The remarkably strong emphasis on aspects of affection in the mother–child relationship contrasts with dominant trends in a society which is not generally pictured as exceptionally 'friendly' towards children[1].

Mothers' care for young children was so much embedded in anticipations of positive affection and unconditional love that the labour aspects of childcare were sometimes obscured. Possibly, regarding mothers' care for offspring as 'labour' meets with stronger cultural objections than does the identification of labour aspects in other forms of caring, because mothers' care for their children is interpreted as an expression of 'natural' or 'instinctual' love, and neither the natural nor love is commonly associated with work. From a different perspective, love, as something freely given, contrasts with labour as enforced.

Analysing motherhood a generation after Parsons published his treatises on the American family, the assumption of an inherent or 'natural' qualification in mothers to care for offspring is more often questioned and examined in greater detail. Feminist scholarship does, however, contain considerable disagreement about the impact of biology on gender in general and on motherhood in particular[2]. The belief in a 'maternal instinct' appears as a recent construct (Rutter 1972; Oakley 1976). Some feminist writers and scholars such as Rich (1976) and Rossi (1977) contend that a propensity for nurture and care is linked with biology.

Feminist analysis more often conceives of motherhood as biological *and* social (e.g. Eisenstein 1979; Harding 1986; Haavind 1987). These different aspects must not be collapsed, but should be kept analytically separate. This position has been forcefully argued by Eisenstein (1979; 1983), who advocates drawing a distinction between the biological and the political aspects of motherhood (see also Ruddick 1980; Hartsock 1983; Harding 1986). Examining the women's part in social reproduction, Eisenstein reserves the term 'biological motherhood' for those aspects of motherhood that, though culturally and socially circumscribed, are determined by the special capacity of women's bodies in reproduction of the species, i.e. becoming pregnant, giving birth, nursing. Other requirements in connection with children's upbringing, such as feeding, fostering, rearing and caring, are not inherent or natural to women. Women's predominance in such activities should rather be conceptualized as 'political motherhood', Eisenstein argues, and, as noted above, as an expression of patriarchal power structures in society. The gendered division of labour in social reproduction, accordingly, is conceived as the outcome of conflicting interests, in which those who are assigned the caring and nurturing tasks lose out.

To me it seems extremely difficult to establish convincingly an unquestionable interdependence between biological motherhood and capability to care for young children, or for caring in general. If a propensity for nurturance and care are linked with biology, then the limits to the impact or influence of biological motherhood on social behaviour obviously need specification. Biological motherhood does not necessarily entail a feeling of love and care for the child. Empirical evidence points to highly differentiated reactions to pregnancy, giving birth and nursing. Ambivalent responses, rejection, even hatred are not uncommon (Rutter 1972; Oakley 1974; Schaffer 1977; Liljeström 1984; Unwin 1985; Haavind 1987).

Motherhood as social practice shows great diversity across cultures and classes (Zelditch 1956; Oakley 1974), which points to a strong non-biological influence. In all cultures the appropriate ways of handling or caring *for* newborn babies presupposes learning (in Scandinavian culture this is increasingly taught, for example by nurses and midwives). Caring *about* children certainly is not directly linked to the biological experience of motherhood, nor is it limited to those who have had the personal experience. The caring about aspects of maternal childcare may even be, it has been hypothesized, a relatively recent phenomenon in European history (see e.g. Ariès 1962; Donzelot 1980; and A. Wilson 1980 for a critique of Ariès). Assuming for a moment that there were an established genetic link between female biological reproductive capacities and experiences and capability for childcare, the incorporation of this aspect of human reproduction into the basis of male patterns of domination is still man-made, a social construct.

A much neglected criticism of Parsons' writing is his marginalization of the economic contribution of women's household management and their production of goods and services for inter- and intra-household consumption. In Scandinavian families of the 1950s and 1960s, the father was usually the main economic provider, but he also carried responsibility for the upbringing and disciplining of the children. Mother bore the main responsibility for early childhood caring and rearing. As a norm, she was not registered in the work-force. However, the majority of married and unmarried mothers contributed essentially to the family's subsistence or level of living, even when they were not in income-generating work (for empirical illustrations from Norway see e.g. Leira and Bergh 1974; Avdem 1984).[3]

In the welfare state context women's economic activities have taken on different forms. The earner aspects of motherhood become more prominent when mothers join the labour market, and the carer aspects, though still important, do not confine women to the home. These are profound changes in the division of labour in society and in the family. As mothers increasingly take on part of the breadwinning responsibility and the state in Scandinavia accepts some responsibility for childcare, family patterns cannot be satisfactorily dealt with by the Parsonian categories developed for the 'isolated nuclear family'. In Parsons' social theory the welfare state is interpreted as 'taking over' functions that formerly belonged to the private sphere or to the family's domain. Yet, in this theoretical scheme, the welfare state does not appear to have any significant influence on the division of labour within the family, which is regarded as functional to the perpetuation of the gendered division of labour in society as a whole. Parsons' paradigm cannot incorporate the employed-mother family.

Scandinavian welfare state policies in the 1950s and 1960s presumed the perpetuation of a gender-differentiated, traditional family. In a modified form, the nuclear family was incorporated as a basic element in the welfare state design. Assuming that childcare and other forms of vitally necessary care for very dependent persons were to remain to a very considerable extent a family concern, and the responsibility of women, welfare state policies apparently took for granted a family in which mother the carer was economically dependent on father the provider. Within Scandinavia this is most clearly evident in Norway, where welfare state policies in the post-World War II period failed to anticipate the emergence of the employed-mother family. Nevertheless, this was a development to which the policies contributed, although modestly, and perhaps not deliberately as seen in the introduction of state-sponsored services for early childhood education and care, and by the expansion of women's job opportunities. Whether the employment of mothers was an intended or unintended consequence of welfare state policies, the concept of the employed mother was not politically institutionalized. In Parsons' thinking, economic provision and child-care were necessary and supplementary activities, as the Scandinavian welfare state also acknowledged. In Sweden and Denmark support of the working mother increased from the 1970s. However, in none of the countries did the welfare state entitlement systems accord equal status to economic provision or 'earning' and caring.

Welfare state, employment and caring

I use the term 'welfare state' as is commonly done to identify those states in which the public sector has acquired extensive responsibilities with regard to the provision of welfare for its citizens, and in which 'welfare' (according to specifications) is formulated and interpreted as individual rights (Marshall 1965). Sometimes the term 'welfare state' connotes certain sectors of the welfare state, such as those dealing with health, education, social security, social welfare, and so on; it may also refer to the state as a totality. Unless otherwise stated, my use of the term refers to the state as such, although I make use of examples from different sectors.

In the welfare state literature different definitions emphasize different aspects of the relationship between the collectivity and the individual. Thus Gough identifies the welfare state by 'the use of state power to secure the reproduction of the labour force and to maintain the non-productive members of the population' (1979, pp. 44–5). Individual entitlements are more pronounced in the definition offered by a Norwegian social scientist: 'The welfare state refers to the system of state and legal measures that guarantees for the individual citizen safety for life, health and welfare' (Slagstad 1981, pp. 453–4, my transl.). Discussing the social divisions of welfare, Titmuss points to the welfare state as an expression of collective self-interest which, in addition, provides for the weaker members of society: 'All collectively provided services are deliberately designed to meet certain socially recognized "needs"; they are manifestations, first, of society's will to survive as an organic whole, and, secondly, of the expressed wish of all the people to assist some people' (1969, p. 39).

In Scandinavia the redistributive aspects of the welfare state are also often underlined, and the welfare state incorporates and is interpreted as an expression of commitment to egalitarian values.

Regardless of perspective, the welfare state is portrayed as a 'caring state'. To provide for the vital needs of persons who for various reasons are incapable of caring for themselves is conceived as a collective concern. Belief in state responsibility to intervene on behalf of very dependent persons is a basic ideological tenet of the welfare state.

Projecting the state as the protector of the poor precedes the post-war welfare state and has been influential in legitimating different forms of the state. Ideologically, an interest in the welfare and happiness of citizens has supported a centralization of state power and authority (Balbo undated). State-sponsored welfare measures have been implemented in order to soften the mass destitution resulting from an uncontrolled market economy and also with the intention of reducing the level of social conflict and unrest (Seip 1977).

However, state-sponsored welfare does not just represent attempts to appease the 'dangerous classes'. A diversity of interests, conflicts of interest and compromises have influenced the making of the individual welfare state. The welfare states of Northern Europe provide evidence of the efforts of the working classes to improve their conditions. To varying degrees values such as solidarity and social equality, benevolence and charity have shaped the formation of the Social Democratic welfare states in Scandinavia. Thus the basic value systems incorporate ideals that, when counterposed, prove contradictory (Siim 1987).

The welfare state introduces distributive systems to supplement or replace the market and the family. Political sociology, following the classification advocated by Wilensky and Lebeaux (1958), commonly distinguishes between 'institutional' and 'residual' (or 'marginal') welfare states, according to which basic principles underlie the main distributive systems. The two models differ on principles of eligibility, the scope and degree of state intervention, what forms of provision in cash or kind the state provides, and for whom. The institutional approach is characterized by the provision of a wide range of services, universally available, as entitlements of the citizens. The residual, or marginal, model favours selectively oriented measures; that is, measures directed towards specially defined target groups. Eligibility is established by needs and/or means testing. Services provided are

generally of a limited range. (On the differences between the two
welfare state models and the philosophies in which they are grounded,
see Wilensky and Lebeaux 1958; Pinker 1971; Allardt 1986.)

According to leading Scandinavian political analysts, the institutional
model takes precedence among the Nordic welfare states (Allardt 1986;
Andersen 1986; Esping-Andersen and Korpi 1987). As an overall
assessment this appears valid when compared to other welfare states in
which more selective, means-tested provisions and restricted eligibility
are favoured approaches. However, in order to show the complexity of
welfare state arrangements the general characterization of welfare states
as either institutional or residual needs the supplement of sector-specific
analyses. Within individual welfare states the development of a multiplicity of policies and provisions has not followed a single course (for
illustrations see e.g. Kamerman and Kahn 1981; Leira 1987a; Moss
1988; Thayer et al. 1988). Thinking about the 'welfare state' that
conceives of it as a monolithic or evenly developed structure needs to be
questioned.

The development of the welfare state, whether as institutional or as
residual, indicates some transfer of responsibility for individual welfare
from the family (and other supportive systems) to the state. In the
welfare state, particularly in the institutional one, the family is commonly portrayed as emptied of its functions (Horkheimer 1936; Parsons
1955). Feminist research from the 1970s often echoes such characteri-
zations, for example, when analysing the welfare state in terms of
transfers from private to public dependency, or of the state's 'taking
over' the tasks of social reproduction (Hernes 1982; Balbo 1982a;
Eisenstein 1983).

The increasing public control of and spending on matters that used to
be left to the family, the church or private charity unquestionably
delineates central features in the history of the welfare state. Nevertheless, institutional analyses that focus too narrowly on the state can easily
underestimate the different family policies pursued by different welfare
states, and the complex and uneven development across various sectors
of welfare state services. Even in Scandinavia, where welfare state
services are generally considered to be well developed, the role of the
state in some fields of social reproduction is remarkably modest.
Providing for the everyday welfare of the very young and the very old is
still to a large extent in private hands. Though not always explicitly
stated, Scandinavian research into caring modifies assumptions implying
that the welfare state has dramatically reduced the family's practical
significance in care provision. Predominantly, but not exclusively,
'family care', 'private' or 'informal care' means caring done by women.

Studies that deal with the production of state-sponsored services only, or with the state–family division of responsibility, readily neglect the importance of services produced informally, for example, by the assistance of kinship, friendship and neighbourly relations or by 'shadow' labour. (For more comprehensive approaches see Stack 1974; Balbo 1982b; Leira 1983.) As Jacobsen (1967) points out, the notion of having attained a welfare state may in itself represent a barrier to its more complete realization.

If we 'deconstruct' the welfare state concept, to allow for sector-specific assessments, the Scandinavian welfare states also give evidence of an internal mixture of institutional and residual features, and of a blending of universalistically and selectively oriented provisions. This is evident if we contrast two of the main distributive systems of the welfare state, the one that aims at providing safeguards against the perils of the market, that is, the income maintenance or social security system, and the other that aims at replacing or supplementing the personal care provided by the family and private charity.

Political sociology projects the welfare state as an economic provider state and as a caring state. Two sets of responsibilities, the provision of care for very dependent persons and the provision of economic security (the social security net) constitute basic activities of modern welfare states. From the Scandinavian evidence I shall argue that the universalist approach is more characteristic of those welfare state provisions that are intended to replace or supplement the market (or employment) than of those that aim at replacing or supplementing the family as provider of personal care. Employment-related benefits are often statutory and commonly conceived of as individual rights. The state-sponsored schemes institutionalized, so far, to provide care for very dependent persons, such as young children, are less firmly established as rights. Services may be universal in principle, but carry a considerably stronger imprint of selectivity and residuality when delivery is examined. The selectivity and rationing of welfare state caring influences the range of services and quality of care available for very dependent persons. It also affects the social positions of carers.

The welfare state relationship to mothers, as earners and carers, I maintain, has to be analysed within a general context which makes explicit the different approaches of the welfare state to employment and caring respectively. Contrasting the employment-related and caring-related entitlements offered by the Scandinavian welfare states, I shall show that welfare state entitlements and benefits are 'packaged', structured according to a general set of premises in which formal employment is more favoured than informal caring. In interplay with the gendered division of labour, this differentiation produces a gendering of citizens' entitlements, available as of right.

I shall spell this out in some detail. As social rights and entitlements are somewhat differently structured within Scandinavia, I take the Norwegian case as my main illustration. The importance of employment status comes out clearly in two central pieces of Norwegian welfare state legislation, Lov om folketrygd (the National Insurance Act) and Lov om arbeidsmiljø og arbeidervern (Act Governing Work Environment and the Protection of Workers). According to the Work Environment Act, a series of benefits concerning work environment or work conditions is reserved for persons in formal employment. This applies, for example, to protection against dangerous work environment, the right to regulated working hours, and to annual paid holidays.

In the eligibility conditions of the National Insurance Scheme, formal employment is in some cases a precondition for access to an entitlement; in other cases it gives a more generous deal. For example, formal employment is a precondition for access to some transitional benefits such as sickness and unemployment benefits. Mothers who wish to take up employment after spending some years at home with their children are not entitled to unemployment benefits if a job is not available. Mothers who are not employed will not get any compensation in cash when ill, even though they may have to spend considerable sums of money to buy substitute childcare. Sick pay and unemployment benefits are defined as income maintenance payments and will be paid only to those who cannot keep up their employment. Time spent on informal caring is irrelevant for access to these benefits.

When it comes to permanent pensions, employment is not a condition for eligibility. All citizens are entitled to state-guaranteed pensions from the National Insurance Scheme, for example, if disabled or on reaching retirement age. However, the National Insurance Act instituted a two-tiered system. The basic (or minimim) pension is universal in orientation, while the supplementary pension is earnings-related and graduated according to the number of years spent in formal economic activity, and to the income earned while formally employed. Up to the early 1990s, caring as such, if done informally or unpaid (like other forms of unwaged activities), gave entitlements only to the minimum pension (for a more detailed exposition of eligibility conditions and entitlements, see P. Knudsen 1988). Formally gender-neutral, the National Insurance Scheme does not in principle distinguish between women and men. The structuring of benefits does, however, interact with the gendered division of labour in society to favour the citizen as wage-worker, which has resulted in men being generally better received and rewarded in the National Insurance Scheme than women (Dahl 1976; 1984; Leira 1976; Sverdrup 1984a; Skrede 1986; Kjeldstad 1988). Class and gender variables interact to produce a significant over-representation of women among those receiving the minimum benefits – an important aspect of the feminization of poverty in contemporary Norwegian society.

When caring is not done as part of a formal work contract it gives access to a minor set of entitlements as compared with employment. Caring-related benefits are somewhat differently structured in the Scandinavian countries. Again I take the Norwegian case as the main example. As entitlements related to caring, the following are important: child benefits, maternity and parental benefits, benefits to single providers, and, to come into effect from 1992, the possibility of earning entitlements to supplementary pension for informal carers.[4] Child benefits, made payable to the mother, may perhaps be considered as a care-related benefit, though the main intention was to give state-guaranteed help with the costs involved in bringing up children. Parental responsibility for a child aged 0–16 years gives access to the allowance. Receiving this benefit does not entail an independent right to social security as employment does. (From 1992 some of the persons receiving child benefits will earn the possibility to obtain entitlements to supplementary pension, not as an employment-related but as a caring-related benefit, (see below)).

Maternity benefits are differentiated according to the employment status of the mother. When giving birth, non-employed mothers receive a state-guaranteed cash transfer; employed mothers are entitled to leave of absence with wage compensation. For employed mothers the maternity benefit represents income maintenance. Considering the differential treatment of employed and non-employed mothers, it is difficult to assess to what extent maternity rights are primarily care-related, or related to the physical restitution of the mothers, or to be regarded as a pro-natalist measure. Some entitlements explicitly aim to accommodate employed mothers and fathers. Mothers' right to leave of absence with pay in connection with giving birth, while retaining job security, is the most important example. Entitlement to parental leave when a child or the minder is ill is another (for an overview of entitlements see R. Knudsen 1990, and also ch. 3).

Norway, but not Denmark and Sweden, offers state-guaranteed economic support to single providers. Thus single providers, of whom close to 90 per cent are women, are entitled to economic support from the National Insurance Scheme if they care for young children, and have only a very modest income from employment (see ch. 5).

The introduction of a 'caring wage', e.g. for parents who care for their young children at home, has been discussed for several years in Norway, not gaining general acceptance so far. A change in the National Insurance Act to come into effect from 1992 extends the possibility of earning entitlements to supplementary pension (within limits) also to persons engaged in unpaid care for children under the age of seven.[5] This entitlement is intended for the person receiving child benefit for the child, that is, most often, the mother. Also to come into effect from 1992 is the possibility to earn the right to supplementary pension for those who provide care for old, sick or handicapped persons not in institutional care (see St. meld. 12, 1988–9; Innst. S. nr 200, 1988–9; *Besl. O. nr 8 (1990–1)*). These alterations of the National Insurance Act acknowledge the importance of informal care to society, and represent a breakthrough for informal carers. The establishment of the entitlements may be interpreted as a 'reward' of traditional family forms and divisions of labour. Alternatively they may be conceived as a compensation for the loss of income inflicted upon unpaid informal carers, i.e. because of shortages in the public provision of care.

In the National Insurance Schemes of Denmark, Norway and Sweden informal care was not incorporated on a par with formal employment. The stronger political institutionalization of employment is also seen in that employment-related benefits are, to a considerable extent, established by law and guaranteed by the state. According to longstanding Scandinavian traditions concerning the division of labour within the public sector, the provision of care for the very young and the very old is a responsibility of local government (Seip 1984), though often economically supported by the state. The level of supply and the quality of services are decided locally. Access to formally organized care is not always established as an entitlement of individuals. For example, as I shall go on to show in later chapters, no child has an undisputed right to attend state-sponsored day care. As the public supply of services for personal care is scarce, the provision of care for very dependent people depends on informal arrangements, which, as noted above, do not furnish the carer with access to the full range of welfare state benefits and entitlements.

The gendering of citizenship

In an influential discussion based on British political history, Marshall (1965) conceptualizes citizenship as consisting of three elements: civil rights, political rights and social rights, which in the course of historical development form an 'equal partnership' (p. 91). 'Citizenship is a status bestowed on those who are full members of a community', Marshall observes, and goes on: 'All who possess the status are equal with respect to the rights and duties with which the status is endowed' (p. 92). Although citizenship is in principle a system of equality, in everyday practice this system tolerates far-reaching social inequality. Welfare state entitlements are commonly formulated as individual rights, which does not imply, however, that individual citizens have equal access to the welfare state benefit system. Citizenship is differentiated. Marshall's main concern is with the impact of expanding citizenship entitlements on social class as a system of inequality, an interest also central to contemporary welfare state analysis (Gough 1979; Offe 1984; Esping-Andersen and Korpi 1987).

Following Marshall, I shall argue that access to 'social rights' (by which Marshall was referring to educational and social welfare services) constitutes a basic element of welfare state citizenship. My discussion deals with the social elements of rights in a more restricted sense, excluding education, and focuses on entitlements and benefits instituted to provide for basic social welfare. The inequalities entailed in the gendering of citizenship is my main concern; I do not consider the influence of citizenship on structural inequalities produced by class and race.

Feminist research reflecting on Marshall's conceptualizations introduces gender as an important, but often neglected, dimension to the discussion of social inequality and welfare state citizenship (Hernes 1987; Pateman 1987b). Women's citizenship developed differently from that of men, feminist scholarship observes, and shows how expansion of citizenship entitlements, even when formally gender-neutral, has different consequences for women and men.

Classical political theory has regarded the concept of 'woman' as opposed to the 'worker', and to 'citizenship', Pateman (1987b) argues. Democratic theory that assumes economic independence as essential to citizenship precludes the concept of women as independent citizens (see also Scott 1988). From the beginning, the welfare state, which expanded on citizens' entitlements, denied women full citizenship. Even modern welfare states like the Scandinavian ones have not granted women full citizen status. The importance accorded to waged work means that paid employment is the basis of citizenship. Hernes (1987, 1988) emphasizes that Scandinavian citizenship was modelled on the worker, or rather, I would say, on the wage-worker. Introducing a woman's perspective shows welfare state citizenship as differentiated; the social division of labour is incorporated in the welfare state design and produces a gendering of citizenship entitlements.

'Deconstructing' the welfare state concept by the differentiation of access to entitlements unveils some of the underlying principles by which welfare state citizenship is constituted. The deconstruction allows for a better understanding of how the welfare state functions, and how it relates to earners and carers, to women and men. In analysing the distribution of welfare state entitlements and benefits, I shall argue that the welfare state in Scandinavia implies a dual concept of citizenship, one associated with citizen the wage-worker, the other with citizen the carer. As considerably more is known about how the welfare state relates to employment, the case may be argued that the more interesting evidence and theoretical challenges now come from bringing caring into the analysis, and by expanding on the systematic comparisons of processes that generate a differentiation of access to welfare state burdens and benefits.

Access to welfare state benefits and entitlement is differentiated according to a set of interrelated premises. I shall discuss three that are of particular importance to mothers as earners and carers, and to the gendering of citizenship. Access is influenced by the definition of the context of the work as either outside or inside formal employment, access is influenced by the welfare state definition of care as a private responsibility, and consequently, since caring is for the most part ascribed to women, by the gendered division of labour.

Formally gender-neutral, Scandinavian welfare state legislation draws a basic distinction between the one category of citizens in whose adult lives labour market participation is the main activity and the basic source of income, and those citizens in whose adult lives formal employment is of less or little importance. The welfare state system of benefits and entitlements incorporated an important premise of industrial capitalism, a differentiation of work forms which gave preference to formal employment over other forms of work. As noted above, a series of welfare state benefits is not universally available, but reserved for those in whose adult life formal employment is a main activity. The more generous and more institutionalized benefits are reserved for the citizen as wage-worker, while a minor set of entitlements is given to those in whose working day waged work is not the main activity (Dahl 1976; Leira 1976; Borchorst and Siim 1987; P. Knudsen 1988).

Welfare state legislation and provisions define the greater part of vitally necessary care, for example, in childcare, as a private concern and as a responsibility of the family. As a 'caring' state the Scandinavian welfare state is supported by and presupposes the operation of private caring systems, such as the family, social networks, informal or 'shadow' labour markets. Most often, but not always, private or informal care means care done by women. Thus the welfare state depends upon women for the provision of basic, necessary care. In childcare apparently, the gender-differentiated family was taken for granted, which meant that mother was the parent to whom the main responsibility for children's upbringing, nurturing and caring was ascribed. Women's responsibility for childcare and other forms of care, and their economic dependence on men, was an assumption of the welfare state design, the structure of caring shows. This is not special to the Scandinavian construction of welfare state citizenship. (For examples from Britain see Wilson 1977; Land 1989; Lister 1990.)

The hierarchy of work forms and the public–private division of responsibility for caring interact to constitute 'employment' and 'caring' as different when access to welfare state entitlements is the issue. What matters is not the hours worked, nor the years committed, nor the social significance of the tasks performed. What matters is the formal work contract, and the wage. Access to the full range of social entitlements, and to the better income when pensioned, is accorded only to those who are attached full-time to the formal labour market in adult years. Caring as such, if carried out informally or unpaid, does not give access to employment-related benefits, nor to more than the minimum level of pensions. Defining care as a private concern, with which women were charged, in practice therefore meant that women, as informal carers, were excluded from a series of welfare state entitlements and benefits. The provision of care is more highly regarded in the welfare state value system and ideology than in the benefit system, where responsibility for care gives access to a limited set of benefits as compared with paid employment. The differentiation of work forms and the welfare state definition of childcare as principally a private concern interacts with the gendered division of labour to produce a gendered division of citizenship.

Mothers who are both earners and carers experience and give evidence of a contradiction inherent in the welfare state structure: welfare state policies acknowledge the need of citizens for material provision as well as for care, yet more comprehensive and generous benefits are accorded to those who participate in wage-work than to those who engage in vitally necessary but unpaid care. The social construction of motherhood is set within this framework, which clearly expresses a preference for formal employment over informal care, and thus for men's traditional activity patterns over women's.

Concepts of care: loving, thinking and doing

Welfare state intervention into early childhood education and care changes the carer aspects of motherhood, but confirms mother as the primary carer parent. Caring for children interlinks the private sphere and the public domain and bridges the gap between welfare state decision-making and the worlds of everyday life. An interface of public authorities and private agents, the provision of care illuminates the modes of operation of the welfare state and also the everyday coping strategies of women and households.

The welfare state design includes two assumptions about care: first that care is to remain predominantly private, and, secondly that it is a public responsibility. Public investment in care introduces a professionalization of what used to be personal relationships and a transfer of private obligations into public sector employment. The expansion of public services for early childhood education and care implies that children's everyday upbringing is more closely integrated with the welfare state economy. With institutional differentiation, care is a public issue and a private concern, an expression of political values as well as personal morals. Institutional differentiation in childcare is accompanied by a multiplicity of carer careers that in mutual influence with mothers provide opportunities for new motherhood models.

In the following I shall look first at some of the conceptualizations of 'care' as social activity, or as 'work' in the theoretical literature. In my opinion, the discussion does not sufficiently account for the complexities of care provision. Using childcare as example, I introduce a model of institutional differentiation which shows the restructuring of the public and the private spheres as important elements in the making of modern motherhood.

As distinct from work with objects and with administrative processes, caring work always involves relating personally to another human being. The Scandinavian languages capture this duality: the term 'omsorg', which can generally be translated as 'care', refers to affection as well as to activity, to love and to labour. The verbal expression (in Norwegian) 'å vise omsorg', that is, 'to care', correspondingly refers to caring for the material needs of another person, and may also mean that the carer feels special concern or devotion for another person. Both connotations of 'omsorg' evoke positive associations.[6] The term 'care' in English carries a similar duality, as shown in 'caring about', which refers to the carer's special affection for or concern for the one in need of care, and 'caring for', which refers to catering for the material (and other) well-being of the one receiving care (Graham 1983).

Sociological studies commonly discuss care in terms of work, for example, in connection with the functionally differentiated nuclear family (cf. above). Marxist-feminist discourses from recent years conceptualize 'care' as embedded in 'domestic labour' or 'social reproduction'. To the structural-functionalist school the gendering of the division of labour did not need explanation; it was according to the nature of things. The domestic labour debate, on the other hand, in the tradition from Engels, called attention to the gendered division of labour as a central problem in political theory as well as in practice.[7]

The early domestic-labour debate underlined the close association of 'production' to 'social reproduction', of mode of production to family form. Challenging the neglect of women's traditional unpaid work in general theories, the gendered division of labour was conceptualized in terms of dominance and subordination. The situation of women, it was argued, cannot be explained by studies of capitalism alone, but by the interconnection of a capitalist mode of production and patriarchal relations of dominance (e.g. Barrett 1980; Hartmann 1981a; 1981b; see also Eisenstein 1979). The relationship between a gendered division of work and a gendered division of dominance was a crucial issue: does women's weaker position within production and in the labour market condition male dominance and women's subordination in modern societies as Hartmann (1981b) argues? Or are gender hierarchies based on the over-representation of women in social reproduction as paid and unpaid carers, as for example Eisenstein (1979) and Connell (1987) contend? Does a gendered division of labour and women's caring by necessity entail gender hierarchy, men's supremacy and women's subordination?[8]

As the discussion unfolded, a gender-neutral interest in the importance of 'social reproduction' to capital accumulation replaced the interest in the gendered division of labour and its impact on women's and men's situations in society. But the question lingered, why did 'social reproduction' and 'domestic labour' remain women's work even when women were full-time wage-workers? Economic analyses did not consider why unpaid housework and care for very dependent people was mainly carried out by women, nor how this division of labour was connected with the structural subordination of women in society (Molyneux 1979).

I agree with the conceptualization of care for very dependent persons as work, but find the use of the terms 'domestic labour' and 'social reproduction' problematic for the following reasons: care is not confined to the domestic arena. Its conceptualization as part of domestic labour apparently accepts a public–private split that care provision in daily life has transcended. In the domestic-labour debate the welfare state intervention into caring and its employment of women was often overlooked. The notions of 'domestic labour' and 'social reproduction' are problematic for another reason, as they work from analogy, drawing on models from paid labour and production which neglect the differences between care and object or commodity production. Moreover, caring for very dependent persons was interwoven into the general domestic-labour debate and in the discussion about this labour's importance to capitalism. The characteristics of caring, as distinct from cleaning the floors, vacuuming or doing the dishes, as different from housework both in kind as 'human work' and in its importance to society gained little attention (Kaluszynska 1980).

Feminist research from the 1970s and 1980s discusses caring in a dual perspective, as experienced in a caring relationship, and as vital to societal life. The dual perspective is forcefully advocated by Balbo (1982a; 1982b), who coins the concept 'servicing' or 'servicing work' as a collective term, as a common denominator for all the other-oriented welfare-producing activities commonly performed by women. To provide for the basic human needs of others, by the use of psychological or practical efforts, is a central element in Balbo's concept.[9]

From a set of descriptions of activities performed by women to satisfy the needs of others (in particular members of their own family), Balbo (1982a) defines 'servicing' as referring to the mediation between human needs and the measures provided to satisfy these needs, and to the creation of supplementary services. 'Servicing' thus encompasses planning, organization, trivial decision-making, physical repetitive labour and psychological and emotional considerations. The activity involved is evoked by the other's needs, be they material or emotional. Even in modern welfare states the gap between individual needs and available resources is permanent, and the responsibility for remedying the situation has devolved on women. Balbo's conceptualization, however, conflates a series of activities whose necessity or usefulness to society may be highly variable. For analytical purposes the term 'servicing' or 'servicing work' is too unspecific.

To capture that essence of caring which is basic in a societal perspective, the situation of the one cared for (or serviced) has to be taken into consideration. The mores and values of society express a rudimentary hierarchy of 'needs' (or demands) according to the necessity of the intervention of others. Persons who are not able to care for themselves represent a stronger moral 'claim' on others to intervene than does a perfectly fit person.

In recent Scandinavian research, conceptualizations of care as work are commonly linked to those situations in which the vital human needs of some persons depend for satisfaction on the involvement of others.

This basic insight underlines the pioneering work of Wærness (1979; 1982), whose classifications develop from the situation of the one in need of care. Wærness distinguishes between 'caring', 'servicing' and 'care-giving work'. 'Servicing' refers to services provided for persons who manage well on their own. The wife who brings the healthy husband his slippers is the favourite example. 'Care-giving work' is defined as 'the caring for those members of society who, according to commonly accepted societal norms, are not able to care for themselves, and in which case an equal, reciprocal give-and-take relationship of providing and receiving cannot be established when it comes to help and support in everyday life' (Wærness 1979, p. 8, transl. mine). This definition carries an immediate, intuitive relevance, and delimits a field of caring of vital necessity to society in which welfare state responsibility and private morality are confronted in continuously changing constellations.

Thus, when care ('omsorg') is conceptualized as 'work', the concept does not refer to the material need to produce for survival, but to the intervention on behalf of the dependent other produced by the normative demand of moral behaviour (Wærness 1979; 1984). Defining 'care' as the special feeling of loving concern which accompanies both 'care-giving work' and 'servicing', care-giving work is constructed as containing a dual normative content: first, an obligation to do something for or on behalf of a person in need of care, and, secondly, that the activity should be permeated by a special feeling of concern or devotion for the one cared for. 'Care originates in a relationship involving (at least) two human beings. The one caring (omsorgsutøveren) shows concern, worry, consideration, love, devotion for the one cared for (omsorgstakeren). The one who needs care is precious to the one who is caring, and when the cared for suffers, the one caring will also *suffer and see to it* that the pain or discomforts are relieved (Wærness's italics (1982, pp. 18–20), transl. mine; see also Noddings 1984 and Ungerson 1990).

Wærness assumes that affection and activity are closely interrelated. 'Caring for' is embedded in 'caring about'. By definition, care-giving work demands not only a willingness to provide for the well-being of another, but also that the activity be performed with a positive, affectionate or loving attitude. This understanding evokes the assumption of an almost endless altruism on the part of the care-giver, an empathy in which there are no boundaries between the cared for and the carer. The definition thus contains problems. Wærness does not discuss what happens when labour outlasts love.

Though agreeing with Wærness that caring for very dependent

persons is work set within the context of a personal relationship, I take issue with the intimate association assumed between devotion and deed. Scandinavian society signals strong expectations or norms implying that a caring relationship ought to be instituted, even if love is missing or lost. Relations of blood and marriage in particular carry strong normative obligations to assist, help and care for a care-needing relative. Caring is not always an affectionate relationship. Moral obligations transcend affective justification. Projecting care as a labour of love in my opinion overdoes the submergence of the carer in the needs of the care recipient. Both parties in a caring relationship, carer and cared for, are entitled to moral autonomy, self-respect and integrity. For both parties the caring relationship may entail that personal identity is positively or negatively confirmed.

The conceptualizations of 'work' commonly found in social science and in everyday life that are moulded by the examples of waged work, and in particular industrial commodity production (the tradition from Marx) or administrative bureaucracy (the tradition from Weber), are not appropriate for understanding the processes of care and caring. Caring differs fundamentally from the production of objects, a difference which does not lie in the hierarchical organization or in the wages, but in the accomplishments required by the different tasks, and in the social experiences that each task entails.[10]

One of the skills required, in fact a premise for a caring relationship to develop, is that potential carers have the capacity to recognize and interpret the situation of the one who is not able to care for her/himself, a mental preparedness, so to speak, to receive the message that care is needed, and, moreover, a willingness to be personally obliged by the social norms which demand that very helpless people be cared for. To this normative anticipation is added a second one: the carer should act so as not to violate the dignity and integrity of the one cared for, which means the minimum level of personal involvement or 'affectionate status' of the carer *vis-à-vis* the recipient of care. The cared for is dependent in material terms, yet in moral/ethical terms autonomous.

To be a carer means that sometimes the needs of the carer come second to the needs of the cared for. Caring requires the integration of menial, mental and emotional skills. To paraphrase Rose (1983), the combined skills of 'hand, brain and heart' grounded in the dependent other's lack of capability to care for her/himself, are the salient feature of the caring process.

Analytically it is essential to draw distinctions between caring for and caring about somebody. The extent to which affections and activity are actually interdependent in caring, cannot be determined a priori.[11] The extent to which affections and activity – labour and love – ought to be interdependent is a different question. It is not evident, I shall argue, that 'better' or more adequate care is provided if one specific set of emotions accompanies or is integrated with the activities involved in caring. Unlimited, emphatic care is not necessarily of higher quality or more adequate than care which is planned and disciplined; it is different. Without underestimating the importance of personal involvement in caring relationships, focusing too narrowly on the carer's affection for the one cared for may come to underplay the considerable collective interests that are also connected with the provision of care. Focusing on caring as an individual responsibility also easily distracts from the conflicts of interest that are often displayed when social reproduction or caring are restructured.

Caring is public and private

The shift from private to public care introduced by the welfare state, an important trend in institutional differentiation, raises questions about shifts in normative standards as well. The model of 'rational' caring behaviour rooted in the basic needs of the cared for, as outlined above, differs in important respects from the model of bureaucratic rationality. Rational organization as witnessed in industrial mass production or in the impartial proceedings of formal bureaucracy does not offer a model compatible with the demands of caring in everyday life.

The public provision of care for people who depend upon others for satisfaction of vital needs points to what Zetterberg (1986) has identified as a dilemma of the Nordic welfare state: the attempt to reconcile humanitarianism and rationality. The efforts reveal contradictions, Zetterberg argues, because rationality as interpreted in the Nordic countries bears the connotations of general rules, objectivity and impartiality. Humanitarianism, which is strongly influenced by Christian values, is mainly concerned with taking care of the individual. Zetterberg interestingly connects the development of the welfare state with the severing of the ties to the Madonna cult of catholicism. Protestant Europe was cut off from the cult of Mary, he argues, and in its welfare development 'secularized and materialized her vision of a helpful hand at every turn of life, available to the fortunate and the unfortunate, the articulate and the inarticulate' (1986, p. 94). Zetterberg, however, does not observe that the responsibility to care for very dependent people defines both the welfare state and womanhood, and overlooks the gendered division of caring still predominant in Scandinavia.

The dilemma that Zetterberg outlines is not, I believe, choosing between rationality and other values, but rather a dilemma or conflict between different forms of moral reasoning (Gilligan 1982). The spread of the caring state raises questions concerning the relationship between the state and the family and of care to bureaucracy. How is the public sector's call for efficiency to be made compatible with standards for high-quality personal care? In what ways can care be transformed from being a private virtue into becoming a public concern? How are professional ethics to replace personal morals as guarantee for competent care? How is the 'rationality of care' (Wærness 1987) to be made compatible with the values of rational bureaucracy? The welfare state dilemma, the contradiction between rationality and humanitarianism in Zetterberg's terms, or between needs-oriented care and the proceedings of a cost-conscious administrative bureaucracy is, I contend, softened by the gendered division of labour, ascribing to women a special capacity for caring in private domestic life and in public sector care.

Institutional differentiation entails a differentiation of the normative codes and appropriate ways of conduct in a caring relationship. Childcare in contexts other than those of family or kin evokes more modest expectations as to the emotional involvement of the carer. Conceptualizing care – even childcare – as work underlines that caring is not 'instinctual' or 'natural', but something requiring skills that have to be acquired or learned. The institutional differentiation introduces a series of different 'carer careers', which activates different sets of norms concerning the content and qualities of the care to be provided. I shall not dwell upon the complexities of the emotional qualities of caring. I suggest, though, that an analysis of institutional differentiation and of carer careers might provide a useful first step in the analysis of caring relationships.

In modern societies in which the state, central and local authorities influence almost every aspect of social life, maintaining the distinction between the public and the 'private' is increasingly difficult, as argued by Stacey (1983), Pateman (1987a), and Sassoon (1987), for example. The 'public' and the 'private' are intermixed. Reality is too complex for the concepts. Empirically, the conceptual difficulties are brought out in the composition of what in Scandinavia is commonly known as 'public day care', which exhibits a mixture of public involvement and private enterprise in ownership, in initial and operating costs and in management.[12] Still, analytically it is important to distinguish between those areas of everyday life, or civil society, for which the state claims some responsibility and control and those that are outside direct state influence. For example, the inclusion under welfare state policies of daily childcare, traditionally conceptualized as an all-private, intra-family affair, calls attention to an important shift in the public–private division of labour and responsibility.

Examining the relationship between the welfare state and working mothers as evidenced in childcare provision, I use the term 'public' to delineate those areas, activities or actors for which the state, central or local, claims some form of control or responsibility (see note 12). Thus I include as 'public' (or, more precisely publicly supported and/or controlled), childcare services that may be private in ownership, situated in private homes, organized as family day care, and so on, if the services receive some public funding, and/or are made a subject of public authorization, supervision or control. Correspondingly, the term 'private' is used for those actors and arrangements that remain outside the intervention of public authorities. However, the 'public–private' dichotomy (as well as the 'formal–informal' distinction) conflates all forms of non-public care. Analytically the concept of the 'private sphere' needs deconstruction, so as to show the institutional differentiation, and to distinguish between family-based care and care provided by inter-household exchanges, social networks, or informal labour markets. Surveys of the institutional differentiation over time show the relative importance of the state in care provision, and as initiator or supporter of new constructions of motherhood (Leira 1985).

Institutional differentiation

State intervention in early childhood care and education reconstitutes the public–private boundaries as conceptualized in the state–family relationship. This expansion of the welfare state in primary socialization is often interpreted as just another example of the public 'take-over' of social reproduction. However, the political history of state-sponsored day care is not adequately dealt with, I argue, if restricted to the state–family relationship exclusively. The analysis has to be situated within a framework which encompasses all the major childcare institutions. Only in this context is it possible to assess the relative importance of welfare state policies as compared to other provisions, and to examine the impact of state intervention as well as the effects of its non-intervention. This general setting also illustrates a diversity of changes in the carer aspects of motherhood (cf. ch. 6).

The interaction of economic and social policies and, in particular, of labour market and family policies has generated an institutional division of labour in childcare provision. This institutional differentiation is produced by processes effecting both supply of and demand for extra-familial childcare. Two sets of processes are of special importance in the 'dynamics' of institutional differentiation in this field. On the supply side there is the series of processes that I have summarily described as the 'collectivization of childcare' (see ch. 4), referring to the transformation of childcare from being mainly a private, family affair to gradually becoming a matter of collective consumption and state control. The second set of processes that influences institutional differentiation is generated by the demand of the employed mothers, whose children are not accommodated by the public services. The 'informal economy' of childcare thus differs from the informal economies generated within other sectors of the economy (cf. chs. 5 and 6).

The interactions between the family, the state and informal service systems in childcare provision are shown in figure 2.1. In everyday practice, institutional exchange is still for the most part mediated by women, who are the ones primarily responsible for care provision, as mothers in families, as childminders in the informal economy, as professional childcarers in the formal economy.

Family-based childcare includes care by immediate kin, parents or siblings, but not care provided by domestic servants or by relatives not living in the household. The formal sector of the childcare economy refers to that part for which some public control is instituted (disregarding the public–private split in ownership and management). The informal sector comprises private childcare arrangements provided by someone not a family member, whether paid or unpaid.

The formal childcare sector shows the outcome of national policy-making, and is shaped by decisions and economic priorities made by local authorities (see ch. 4 for an examination of the Norwegian political history of childcare). The informal sector is more closely linked with developments in local labour markets influencing mothers' economic activity. The character of the interactions between institutions indicated by the double arrows therefore differs. Between the family and the formal sector exchanges are of a 'cash for care' kind, as also are the exchanges between the family and 'shadow' labour markets. Exchanges between family and social networks may include cash, but are sometimes integrated with complex and comprehensive exchanges between households (for illustrations see Leira 1983, chs. 5 and 6).

The double arrows between the formal and informal institutions indicate the mutual influence of the two sectors. Public involvement in childcare constitutes the 'arena' of the private informal sector, in that the range and scope of public provisions greatly influence the development of an informal economy, which in turn prevents the formal system of supply from collapsing.

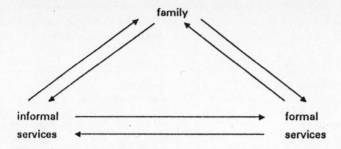

Figure 2.1 The childcare economy

The interactions shown in figure 2.1 between the family and other institutions providing early childhood care and education indicate a transfer of responsibility and labour directed mainly from the family to other institutions. Accommodation in extrafamilial care supplements the family, and offers part-time substitution or replacement for family-based care. Overall responsibility for children's upbringing is not relinquished, but remains with the parents, who are charged with provision, control and co-ordination. As far as Scandinavian research can tell, this responsibility is most often allocated to mothers (Wadel et al. 1983; Borchorst and Siim 1987; Haavind 1987; Kugelberg 1987). In quantitative terms, mothers' care becomes less important, which does not necessarily imply that the quality of care is lowered.

Everyday childcare and other kinds of care encompass a great variety of organizational forms. The institutional differentiation reflects the impact of welfare state policies as well as the importance of individual agency in generating structural change. The distinctions often made between formal and informal, paid and unpaid, private and public care-giving are too simple to show the diversity of arrangements. Moreover, they are inadequate when it comes to tracing the emergence of new patterns or processes generating change. More detailed information is required in order to analyse the transformations in the childcare structure. From observations of everyday childcare arrangements I have developed a more specified typology, derived from the institutional setting of childcare, to which is added a consideration of the types of contract or norms of reciprocity that are used to regulate the exchange (Gouldner 1960; Sahlins 1969; see also Leira 1983). The institutional differentiation of childcare provision (and other forms of care-giving work) is shown in table 2.1.

The table presents the basic elements of the childcare structure. Everyday life shows a more diversified picture. According to my

Table 2.1 *Institutional differentiation of childcare and corresponding carer careers*

| Institutions providing childcare | Carer careers | |
	paid	unpaid
Family and household	au pair girls, nannies, servants	mothers
Social networks		relatives, friends, neighbours
Informal labour markets	grandmothers, friends, childminders	
Formal labour markets*, private and public sector	professional childcare	volunteers

*In Scandinavia childcare is provided by a number of parties, private and public (see note 12). The establishment of day-care services by private bodies, such as parent co-operatives or voluntary associations usually presupposes approval by central or local authorities.

typology the basic institutions in the production of childcare and of care generally are:

family and household,

social networks and self-help organizations, based for example on kinship, friendship and neighbourly relations, which shade into

informal labour markets, an 'informal economy', which include paid services and unpaid exchanges,

formal labour markets, which in Scandinavian childcare predominantly encompass services provided, and/or subsidized or controlled by public authorities.

The interactions between all these institutions have to be examined if we are to arrive at an informed picture of the current patterns of organization and distribution within social reproduction in general and within childcare in particular. Charting the diversity of institutional arrangements is necessary if we are not to conceal or marginalize the importance of provisions generated outside the formal schemes. The institutional differentiation (examined in greater detail in ch. 6) shows that childcare is carried out at home, unpaid, by parents, siblings and domestic servants. Childcare is also carried out by professionals,

Table 2.2 *Carer careers*

| | Childcare arrangement | |
	Contractual	Non-contractual
Paid	private and public employment contracts, 'cash for care'	non-contractual, 'shadow' work
Unpaid	marriage contract	non contractual exchange; reciprocity, altruism

working for pay in crèches, day nurseries and nursery schools. In addition, a wide range of informal arrangements have been established, by mobilization of social support networks, reciprocity systems, and also via 'shadow' labour markets. (For a discussion of different spheres of work, see Leira and Nørve 1977; Pahl and Wallace 1982.) In everyday practices the distinction between social networks and 'shadow' labour is often blurred. Network relations are 'commercialized', for example, when relatives, friends and neighbours are paid for their childminding.

The institutional differentiation of childcare is accompanied by a diversification of carer careers. I use the term 'carer career' for those carers whose working lives include sequences where caring, in this case care for children, represents major time commitments. A career may encompass paid and/or unpaid care, and may or may not be combined with other forms of employment.

Table 2.1 can be reorganized to identify the set-up of the main forms of carer careers, as shown in Table 2.2.

Childcare provided by the family or household and by social network relationships may be paid or unpaid. There are contractual elements in parental childcare and in other forms of domestic care. Childcare that is network-based may be regulated by norms of reciprocity or by formal contract. Childcare organized by informal labour markets is irregular paid work, but may be contract-based, whereas state-sponsored care is always contractual and waged.

Family-based and informal childcare are private in the sense that they escape public supervision, subsidies and control. To a varying extent private forms are influenced by interfamily exchanges and also exposed to and subject to local, social control. In this perspective childcare relationships form part of a 'lokal offentlighet', that is, of local public life (Habermas 1980; Dahlström and Liljeström 1981).

In a structural perspective childcare provision transcends the public–

private distinction, as do also the everyday childcare histories of parents and children, which consist of joining together components of family-based care, formal and/or informal services. In everyday life the provision of care interlinks the public and the private, the formal and the informal. In the mediation between individual needs and available resources the distinction between the individual private arena and the public is blurred. The 'production' of everyday care also shows an ongoing renegotiation of boundaries between the state, central and local, and the family, particularly the mothers. The social division of labour is in a process of change, whereas the gendered divisions are upheld. Exploring the dynamics of women's coping strategies within the context of everyday life is essential, I argue, if the analysis is to capture the reconstruction of motherhood and its importance not only to mothers and childminders, as earners and carers, but also to the functioning of the welfare state. The deconstruction of the concepts of 'public' and 'private', 'formal' and 'informal' provides a starting point from which to examine the institutional differentiation as well as the mutual influence of welfare state policies and working mothers' every-day practices in introducing structural change.

3 Welfare states and working mothers: the Scandinavian experience

The state and childcare

What is the relationship between the Scandinavian welfare states and working mothers? In welfare state literature dealing with Scandinavia it is often assumed that the welfare states in the region are developed according to a common 'model' (Allardt 1986; Andersen 1986; Erikson et al. 1987). The model is usually identified with an institutional approach, and with a Social Democratic tradition in government. The Social Democratic Labour parties have remained in power in Norway and Sweden throughout the greater part of the post World War II period, and predominated also in Denmark up to the 1980s. Thus, according to Esping-Andersen and Korpi (1987), a central characteristic of the Scandinavian model is that legislation is universalist and solidaristic, and that social policy is more comprehensive and institutional than in most other welfare states.

Empirically, however, 'reproduction policies' or, more specifically, policies concerning the provision of care for very dependent people, challenge the idea of the Scandinavian welfare states as uniformly institutional. As I have argued above (ch. 2), the economic maintenance systems of the Scandinavian welfare states (the state-guaranteed economic transfers established to replace market-based income) have a stronger institutional imprint, while the care providing systems (referring to the state-sponsored services that supplement or replace the family and private charity in caring for very dependent persons) are more residual or marginal. Still, the policies of caring might demonstrate a common Scandinavian design.

In this chapter I examine welfare state approaches to mothers who combine earning and caring commitments in Denmark, Norway and Sweden, and discuss the notion of a Scandinavian model. Although the similarities are clearly discernible, I take issue with the assumption that the Scandinavian policies are developed from one common 'blueprint'.

The Scandinavian countries in the 1970s and 1980s saw a change in family form among the families with young children, a shift from the functionally differentiated nuclear family towards the employed-mother family. As motherhood changed and commonly incorporated wage-work among the everyday practices, and the use of domestic servants rapidly declined, the problems created by the incompatibility of labour market and family organization was felt by an increasing number of families. Looking at the relationship between the welfare state and working mothers I pay special attention to two processes: the 'modern-ization of motherhood' introduced by the mothers who joined the formal labour market, and the 'collectivization of childcare' represented by the development of state-sponsored schemes. By examining the mutual influence of these processes I shall outline how the relationship between the welfare state and mothers is being reconstructed. Two sets of questions are of special interest to my analysis: What are the similarities and dissimilarities of the overall approach of the Scandi-navian welfare states' policies concerning mothers who are both earners and carers? And, which models of motherhood do the different welfare state policies support or promote?

Childcare policies are central to the welfare state definition of motherhood. Connell (1987) argues that childcare is essential in main-taining the dominance of men over women, while Eisenstein (1983) and Brown (1981) likewise contend that 'political motherhood' (the respon-sibility accorded to women for the primary socialization, care and upbringing of children) is a strong element in the subordination of women. Therefore, I take the policies concerning employed mothers' (and parents') childcare entitlements as my main case in dealing with Scandinavian motherhood policies.

As noted above (ch. 1) my intention has not been a strictly compara-tive analysis. I have aimed more at a better understanding of the Scandinavian approach to motherhood by contrasting the political institutionalization of the concept of the employed mother in Denmark, Norway and Sweden. Policies concerning biological motherhood (e.g. fertilization, abortion, giving birth, nursing) are not dealt with. I present a fairly detailed examination of state-sponsored childcare in the three countries, focusing on the accommodation of the demands of employed-mother families. Policies addressing mothers as economic providers are considered in connection with my discussion of childcare provision.

Generally, the equal status policies of the Scandinavian welfare states emphasize women's right to economic independence. Basically, Den-mark, Norway and Sweden address employed parents' childcare com-mitments in two ways: by entitlements to leave of absence and by sponsoring childcare services. The leaves of absence give priority to the carer aspects of parenthood when these conflict with the employment, while state-funded day care encourages expansion of the earner aspects. In the first instance, the employed parents' care for offspring, in the second it sut others. Each of the three countries offers employed opportunities to care for their very young children, while reta.... security, and with wage compensation. All three countries also provide state-sponsored childcare. Denmark and Sweden offer the children of working mothers priority of access. Norway's policies concerning single providers offer an interesting alternative to the general support of the economic-provider aspects of motherhood of the neighbouring countries. For single providers, Norwegian policies subsidize the carer aspects of parenthood. Single providers, of whom the great majority are women, are entitled to economic support from the National Insurance Scheme if they care for young children and have only a modest income from employment.

The sections following this introduction overview the main entitlements of Scandinavian employed mothers and fathers with respect to care for children from birth to the beginning of elementary school. Considering in context the entitlements and services each country offers employed mothers (and fathers), I call attention to similarities as well as differences. After a brief overview of the main entitlements to leave of absence, maternity rights, paternity and parental leave, I shall turn to a more detailed examination of policies and provisions concerning the education and care of pre-school children. I do not discuss the educational contents or merits of different forms of childcare. In the last sections I discuss policy approaches to employed mothers in Denmark, Norway and Sweden and return to the images or models of motherhood projected and promoted by welfare state policies.[1]

Leaves of absence

Employed parents' entitlements to leave of absence for family reasons vary between the Scandinavian countries. Maternity, paternity and parental leaves are differently set up. For the early months of a newborn baby's life the policies of all three countries express a preference for private, parental to collective care. In practice, predominantly this means maternal care. Central authorities accept the subsidizing of these reproduction costs to a varying degree. In all the countries efforts have been made to expand the entitlements to leave of absence in connection with childbirth, and to retain job security. In addition to securing mothers' restitution, a prolonged leave of absence reduces demand for public day care for very young children and may offer parents and children a better start together. Fathers are encouraged to use their rights to paternity leave and to participate in the leave of absence, but in none of the countries have they joined in large numbers. Sweden reports of fathers gradually increasing their use of the entitlements. However, if taken out solely by one parent, the mother, a prolonged leave of absence may emphasize rather than reduce gender inequality in the labour market. (For an assessment of the impact on gender equality of Sweden's parental leave, see Åström 1990.)

For children under 3 years old the state in Denmark and Sweden takes on a considerably greater share of reproduction costs than in Norway. The Swedish welfare state covers a larger part of these costs by means of paid, parental leave. Denmark, on the other hand, has invested more in collective care for the very young (cf. table 3.2). Norway's plans for future development are more like the Swedish than the Danish approach.

In 1989 the main regulations that applied to employed parents were as follows. In Sweden the entitlement to parental leave of absence with income compensation covered 450 weekdays. The mother may make use of sixty of these days before parturition. Alternatively, the leave may be split between the parents, if they so wish, and in different ways. It may be used to reduce working hours, but should be spent before the child is 8 years old. Income compensation corresponding to 90 per cent of the wage, up to a maximum level, was offered for 360 days, for the remaining period at reduced rate. In Norway employed mothers in 1989 were entitled to leave of absence for twenty-four weeks with 100 per cent wage compensation, or thirty weeks at 80 per cent compensation (within maximum limits). Twelve of the weeks may be used before parturition. Of the leave to be spent after parturition, six weeks are reserved for the mother, the remaining weeks the parents may share as they wish. Employed Danish mothers were entitled to leave for four weeks before giving birth, and for fourteen weeks after parturition, with income compensation corresponding to 90 per cent of the wage, within maximum limits. Thereafter the parents may split ten weeks of parental leave, also with wage compensation (see R. Knudsen (1990) for details). In addition, fathers in the three countries are entitled to two weeks of paternity leave at the birth of a child, either with wage compensation, as in Denmark and Sweden, or without, as in Norway (R. Knudsen 1990, pp. 27–30).

In the event of a young child becoming sick, Sweden and Norway opt for parental care in the family, and offer parental leave with job security and wage compensation. In 1989 Sweden offered sixty days per child per

year for children aged under 12 years. In cases of severe illness the leave
might be prolonged to ninety days. For children aged 0–10 years
Norway offers ten days per parent per year and twenty days for single
providers (R. Knudsen 1990, p. 32). In the case of a child being severely
ill, parents are entitled to a prolonged leave of absence. Denmark, on
the other hand, offers no statutory parental leave to care for sick
children.[2] Local authorities may, however, provide a paid childminder
to replace the employed parent. (This is also the case in Norway.) In the
provision for sick children and also in the provision of centre-based care
for the under threes, Danish policies appear to give priority to the
wage-worker or earner commitments of parents when they conflict with
caring obligations, while Norway and particularly Sweden in their
systems of paid parental leave offer considerably larger concessions to
the carer aspects of parental obligations.

The Scandinavian countries are not alone in this endeavour to
mediate between work and family obligations, but Sweden in particular
is advanced compared to the other countries of Western Europe. All EC
countries offer maternity leave, and some countries have instituted
parental leave. Only one member state, Denmark, has statutory paid
paternity leave. Six of the member states provide some leave to care for
sick children (Moss 1990). As regards statutory entitlements to paid
maternity leave, paternity and parental leave, Scandinavian employed
mothers fare well when compared with their British sisters (Moss 1990,
table 2, p. 8, and pp. 34–5).

Parents' entitlements to leave of absence to care for a young or sick
child offer interesting experiments with change in the relationship
between the state and the family in Scandinavia, represented in the
plurality of cases by the mothers. By comparison, however, developing
state-sponsored programmes for early childhood education and care
represent far more comprehensive intervention in the private sphere of
the family. Welfare state sponsorship of collective childcare projects
new visions of childhood that explicitly or implicitly entail an expansion
of mothers' opportunity situation. In the following I shall turn to a more
detailed examination of policies and provisions concerning the education and care of pre-school children. The discussion of the 'Scandinavian
model' is in the main based upon my investigation of day-care policies in
Denmark, Norway and Sweden (Leira 1987a; 1990).

Collective childcare in Scandinavia: similar features

The notion of a 'Scandinavian model' in reproduction policies implies
that the policies of Denmark, Norway and Sweden contain basically

similar features. Following Esping-Andersen and Korpi (1987), the notion also implies that social policies are comprehensive, universal in orientation and institutionalized in legislation. However, as I shall show, depending on the variables studied, the Norwegian, Swedish and Danish policies concerning early childhood education and care display a mixture of similarities and dissimilarities in approach. According to my analysis the similarities which add to the image of a Scandinavian model in reproduction policies are primarily seen in some common assumptions or a common 'philosophy' underlying state intervention in early sociali-zation and childcare and in the overall structuring of public day-care provision. Yet, I must emphasize that my study also shows pronounced dissimilarities in national 'provision profile', as can be seen for example in the proportion of pre-school children attending public day care, and in the public share of reproduction costs. Moreover, I find dissimilarities in the objectives for which public day care is provided, Denmark and Sweden being more concerned than Norway with integration of labour market and reproduction policies.

In the following I consider several aspects of day-care policies and provisions, the aims and means, the relation of supply to demand, and I pay special attention to the employed mothers' demand for childcare. Dealing first with the similar features identified in my study, I discuss the aims of national policies, the conceptualization of day-care content, the structuring of provision as seen in the relationship between central and local government, and between public and private interests. I also look at the problems with distributive justice reported from the three countries.

Investigating differences, I focus on the ones that to me are the most striking, as manifested in the level of provision and the distribution of reproduction costs between the state and the family. I also discuss policy approaches to different models of motherhood, and to employed mothers in particular.

Over the last twenty to thirty years, day care for pre-school children has become increasingly important in national policies in the Scandinavian countries. Although the idea of collective day care supported by the public purse originated earlier, public provision was not developed for 'mass consumption' until after World War II. In the early post-war period the relationship of production to social reproduction was managed by a pronounced gendered division of labour penetrating all spheres of life. Among the child-rearing families, the economic provider and the carer aspects of parenthood were sharply gender divided: father was the main breadwinner, mother was the primary carer-parent and home-maker. The majority of children of pre-school age were cared for at home by members of the family or household.

The transformation of family patterns witnessed in the following decades was induced by two processes in particular. The introduction of collective childcare contributed to a 'deprivatization' of family life, as did the increasing economic activity of the mothers. Entering the labour market to work for pay, the mothers' time for childcare was reduced, while their economic-provider role was expanded. The gender differentiation of parenting took on new forms. These processes, which emerged earlier in Denmark and Sweden than in Norway, are seen throughout Scandinavia, and represent dominant trends in the changes in the family patterns and practices.[3]

Day-care policies or, more accurately, policies concerning early childhood education and care, illustrate processes that Marshall (1965) described as a general trend in modern welfare states, namely that basic human needs are transformed into individual entitlements. State expansion into the early childhood years develops earlier and is more comprehensive in Denmark and Sweden than in Norway. The ambition of pre-school policies is, however, similar: high-quality services, state-sponsored and developed by professionals under public auspices, are to be made available for all children whose parents want them, irrespective of social, economic or ethnic background. Access to state-sponsored childcare is thus presented as an entitlement of children, as their democratic social right.

The post-World War II period has seen a distinctive shift in orientation of Scandinavian policies for early childhood education and care. Using the concepts of R. M. Titmuss (1968), national policies for the pre-school years are reoriented from being predominantly selective to being predominantly universal in aim. Public policies that previously were restricted to preventive measures, selectively oriented to children at risk, ill-treated or abused children, have been expanded to encompass a wider range of programmes, aimed at the pre-school population at large. Titmuss's distinction is important not only for characterizing the orientation and approach of different social policy measures, but also for contrasting policy aims with the practical results. Early childhood education and care show the Scandinavian policies as universal in principle, but as selective when everyday practice is the issue.

State involvement in the early childhood years is for the most part a post-war phenomenon in Scandinavia. Not until the 1960s and 1970s were policies instituted to provide large-scale investments in day care. In the 1970s, government-appointed commissions in Denmark, Norway and Sweden prepared the ground for increased public investment in the education and care of pre-school children. The Norwegian commission recommended that day-care provision, like the provision of elementary schools, be made mandatory for the local authorities (cf. ch. 4). This recommendation did not achieve sufficient political support at the time. The issue has been repeatedly discussed in Norway and Sweden, but making day-care provision mandatory has not so far been accepted as part of national policies, possibly because of strong opposition from the local authorities that are charged with provision.

The introduction of welfare state policies for the care of offspring signals a redefinition of the relationship between the state and the family. Childcare is more closely integrated into the public service system. In a relatively short space of time, state-sponsored, collective childcare, which was once widely opposed, is now embraced, accepted as well as expected by a majority of families with young children. In recent decades the reluctance of politicians and parents to accept the idea of children being minded outside the home has gradually been replaced by a favourable reception of the high-quality childcare schemes subsidized by the government. The experience of professional day care is commonly perceived as socially and educationally advantageous for young children, and as a norm for 'good upbringing'.

Universalist aims

A basic convergence in the 'day-care philosophies' of Denmark, Norway and Sweden is easily observed, for example, in the ways in which day-care services are conceived and integrated in national welfare policies. The central and local government intervention in early childcare and socialization was rooted ideologically in the strong egalitarian traditions of the Nordic welfare states. State-sponsored day care was projected as a benefit for all children, and as an experience that could offer children a chance for more equal opportunities, despite differences in social background. The principle of universally oriented welfare state benefits and services is closely linked with the idea of a common 'Scandinavian model' of the welfare state. The principle of universal provision does, however, contrast with the results obtained. No child in Denmark, Norway and Sweden has an unconditional entitlement as regards access to state-sponsored day care. (Alone among the Nordic countries Finland has instituted the right to state-funded care either in the home or in a day-care centre as an individual entitlement of children under 3 years, to be extended to all children under school age by 1995 (Leira 1990).) In all the Scandinavian countries demand has consistently exceeded supply. However, despite the discrepancy between political intentions and everyday practices, the national ambition of providing early childhood education and care for all children represents an important aspect of Scandinavian policies.

An expression of a common 'philosophy' underlying public day-care provision may also be seen in the conceptualization of 'day-care content', in that all three countries have favoured the development, by professionals, of a public day-care system in which both caring and educational aspects are integrated and attributed equal importance. Modern Nordic day care thus differs from that of other countries of Western Europe, where day care and pre-school education form separate systems (Moss 1988; Thayer et al. 1988). The integration of education and care into one day-care system was a planned alternative to the class-divided childcare experienced in the pre-war years. The aim of welfare state day care was to offer all children equity of access, and parents' means were not to decide the quality of accommodation.

Central and local government

The structures of the different national day-care systems have some prominent common features. Central government defines the national aims for day-care provision. Provision is regulated by law. In Denmark and Sweden it is incorporated under general laws on social services, while Norway has separate legislation.[4] Questions concerning day care come under the province of one of the Ministries within the government administration, the Ministry of Social Affairs in Denmark and Sweden, in Norway the Ministry of Government Administration and Consumer Affairs (renamed the Ministry of Children and the Family in 1989). The planning and actual provision of day care is primarily a local responsibility in all three countries. Local authorities, of which there are more than 200 in both Denmark and Sweden and more than 400 in Norway, are charged with the responsibility for planning, provision and distribution of day care.

The concern with local autonomy is another common characteristic of the day-care systems in Scandinavia. In the 1980s the tendency has been towards an increasing decentralization of decision-making in most questions related to the form and content of day care, and also the level of supply to demand. The wish of central government for continued decentralization of decisions concerning the early childhood years is substantiated in Denmark in the changes introduced with respect to government grants. Up to 1987 there were government grants earmarked for day care. From then on, Denmark incorporated these grants into the general block grant, which leaves greater autonomy to local authorities (Leira 1987a). In Norway, similar changes have been postponed for the time being, thus Norway and Sweden retain the specific state grants to early childhood education and care. The Norwegian Day Care Act was changed in 1989 leaving more decisions concerning day-care standards and quality control to local authorities.

Central government in the three countries has aimed at increasing the supply of day care by recommending that local authorities invest more in this field, that they try out lower-cost services, and that they reduce area norms and the staff/child ratio. These efforts have not eliminated the gap between demand and supply. Extending maternity and/or parental leaves following the birth of a child and lowering the age for school entrance represent bolder and more efficient approaches, and are also much discussed.

Public–private mixes

Each of the Scandinavian countries has developed a system of state-sponsored services for early childhood education and care. Although day care is regarded as a public responsibility and public intervention and investment in this field is anticipated, the state-sponsored day-care system is not 'all public' in any of the countries, nor is the private 'all private'. I use the term 'public day care' to refer to those forms of day care for which public approval is demanded and public subsidies given, even though ownership and operation may be in private hands.

The mixture of public and private affairs differs between the countries. Denmark and Norway have welcomed the initiatives of voluntary organizations and other private bodies in day-care provision. Approximately 40 per cent of all day-care centres are established by housewives' associations, residential and religious associations, by parent co-operatives and by employers. Private initiatives have up to now played a comparatively smaller role in Sweden. So far, large-scale 'private for profit' schemes have not been accepted into the general day-care programmes. Leaving day care to parents alone or to a 'free market' has not been the national policy in any of the countries. If this were to be changed, the use of state subsidies for day care could not be taken for granted.

Private initiatives in day care are not, as observed above, 'all private'. Provided that a certain number of children are accommodated, all day-care structures, whether initiated by public or private bodies, have to be approved by public authorities. In Norway and Sweden the facilities, when approved, are entitled to specific state subsidies.

Another aspect of the variation in national public–private mixes in day care is illustrated in the distribution of running costs, as shown in

Table 3.1 *The division of day-care running costs in Denmark, Norway and Sweden in 1987*
(per cent)

Contributors	Denmark	Norway	Sweden
State	0.0	31.9	41.5
Municipalities	81.7	49.5	46.0
Consumers	18.3	16.3	10.8
Others	0.0	2.3	1.7

Source: Social tryghed i de nordiske lande, Copenhagen 1989, excerpt from table 5.3.5.1,
p. 97.

table 3.1. Three parties, the state, the local authorities and the parents
(the consumers), share the running costs. The distributive patterns are
relatively similar. The state and local authorities constitute the largest
contributors, covering approximately 80 per cent of the costs in Denmark and Norway and close to 90 per cent in Sweden. In Denmark and
Norway parents contribute more to the running costs, 18 per cent and 16
per cent respectively, while in Sweden the parents' share is only 11 per
cent.

Distributive justice

Emphasis on local decision-making has resulted in great variation with
respect to form and content of services. This local 'colouring' was
intended. Local autonomy, however, also produced considerable
regional differences in the proportion of pre-school children admitted to
public day care. Not surprisingly, decentralized decision-making proved
inadequate as a means of fulfilling the national aims for day-care
provision. The division of labour within the public sector, between
central and local government, which makes the catering for very
dependent, care-needing people a responsibility of local government,
has strong traditions in the Scandinavian countries. Leaving care
provision to the discretion of local authorities means that in a social
rights perspective the entitlement to personal care is less well institutionalized than are the benefits guaranteed by the state (cf. ch. 2).

Surveys from the three countries report inequities in access to day
care, referring to the distribution of available places between children of
different socio-economic backgrounds. The distribution appears to
favour children from better-off families more than those coming from
families with comparatively fewer socio-economic resources. From
Sweden, Näsman, Nordström and Hammarström (1983) report

an over-representation of children from middle-class families as compared to working-class children. Children from families with more socio-economic resources are over-represented in state-sponsored Danish day care as compared to children from families with fewer resources (Grønhøj 1981; Christoffersen, Bertelsen and Vestergaard 1987). Norwegian studies point to an over-representation of children from middle-class backgrounds (Hansen and Andersen 1984), and of children whose mothers are well educated (Gulbrandsen and Tønnessen 1988).

These distribution patterns are not easily explained, as consideration of needs is part of the assignment procedures in all the three countries. However, in Denmark and Sweden employed mothers working full-time are given priority of access, which might to some extent explain the distribution in these countries. In Norway, on the other hand, where other criteria are often given priority, the majority of employed-mother families in the 1980s did not have access to public day care. In all three countries the differences in 'consumption patterns' are partly related to the regional differences in level of supply. Hours of opening, travelling distance and cost of places may also prevent some families from using the services offered locally.

Families that command more resources obviously may be more efficient in dealing with assignment systems. The form and content of collective day-care services may appeal more to the educational values and norms for socialization of some families than others. Well-educated, middle-class parents do perhaps appreciate state-sponsored day care more than do families with working-class background, and may be over-represented also among those who apply for such services. If this be the case, public day-care services are not, in socio-cultural terms, equally accessible to all families, and the values and attitudes transmitted by the public day-care system obviously need discussion.

Knowing that the experience of state-sponsored day care is commonly regarded as advantageous to young children, and keeping in mind the egalitarian traditions of the Scandinavian welfare states, it is not surprising that the distributive effects of public day care have been debated in recent years. The discussion touches on different aspects of distributive justice associated, for example, with the needs of children, the economic situation of families and, lately, also with gender equity.

As high-quality day care is a scarce commodity, offering places to children 'most in need' may seem the appropriate way to act; deciding which needs are the most demanding, however, poses problems.[5] Moreover, day care is usually planned for 'ordinary' children, and does not possess the necessary resources for treatment of children with severe handicaps or disorders. Accordingly the counterargument is that unless a child can benefit from day-care attendance, priority of access should not be granted. Employed mothers arguably have more need for extrafamilial day care than home-making mothers. Employed mothers also contribute to the state's income through taxes. Access to day care facilitates mothers' employment, and may promote greater equality between mothers and fathers of young children. Supporting the dual-earner families, however, increases the inequity between families with single and dual incomes. Offering state-sponsored day care to mothers who are not economically active may equalize the situation of the children attending the services while the economic differences between families remain. Pointing to the socially 'skewed' distribution and underlining that childcare arrangements should be a 'real choice' for parents, political parties in Sweden and Norway have argued that the state subsidies should be equally distributed directly to all families with pre-school children. Presumably, this alternative offers parents greater freedom of choice with respect to care by mothers or others. It does not, however, guarantee access to high-quality state-funded day care for those parents who wish for this kind of service. If implemented, this proposal would signal a profound reorientation of welfare state policies for the early childhood years.

Public investments in early childhood education and care have not represented basic redistributive measures in Scandinavian welfare state policies. Yet, if state-subsidized services favour families that are well off, this represents a challenge to the egalitarian traditions and under-mines the legitimacy of state-sponsored childcare. However, as long as a shortage of places prevails and access is decidedly local, 'skewed' distributions will remain. The national surveys of distribution show the aggregate results of local assignment processes. In regions where demand exceeds supply, children who may all belong to high-priority categories will compete for the places available. What is locally con-sidered as the 'best' or most justifiable distribution does not necessarily produce a similar result nationally, when the results of all local decisions are added. The importance attributed to local autonomy in decisions concerning day care contrasts with the principle of equality of access and contributes to the national consumption patterns, which raise questions about distributive justice.

To a large extent the problems with 'distributive justice' in day care stem from a general shortage of places, and from local autonomy being established as a dominant principle of day-care provision and distribu-tion. Within this framework, an expansion of services is necessary if equitable access is to be ensured. A state-supervised or centrally organized assignment system might achieve more equitable access for children from different socio-economic backgrounds. This option is not being considered seriously. Class arguments will not outweigh regional concerns. The principle of local autonomy, which is very pronounced in Scandinavia, will not be set aside.

Scandinavian differences

Despite the many common features in day-care policies and philosophies and the similarities in the structuring of provision, striking differences between the countries are also seen, notably as to the proportion of pre-school children admitted. In Denmark and Sweden, where public day care accommodates a larger proportion of the children, the state takes on a greater part of the reproduction costs, while in Norway, because such a large proportion is cared for outside the public programmes, the costs of childcare are principally a matter for private consumption. Table 3.2 overviews the proportion of pre-school children in approved day care by age in the Scandinavian countries in 1989.[6]

In all three countries the proportion of children admitted to the public day-care systems has been on the increase, owing mainly to an expansion of places and, to a lesser extent, to a decline in the number of pre-school children.

Most pronounced is the difference shown in level of provision for the children aged 0–2 years. More than 47 per cent of the Danish children and close to 30 per cent of the Swedish children in this age bracket were accommodated in state-sponsored day care in 1989. For this age group the two countries have a better supply of approved day care than other countries in Western Europe (Pichault 1984; Leira 1990; Moss 1990). Even so, it is interesting to observe that the childcare needs of the families of children under 3 most often are *not* met by the formally approved day-care systems. In 1989, 52 per cent of the Danish children under 3 years, 70 per cent of the Swedish children and 90 per cent of the Norwegian children of this age were not admitted to public day care. In the Scandinavian context, the Norwegian level of provision for the children aged 0–2 years is far behind the Swedish and Danish, a gap which is not compensated for by more generous maternity and parental leaves.

Compared to the rest of Western Europe, the Nordic countries, except Norway, invest more in public day care for the very young. Overviews from the late 1980s of state-sponsored childcare in the Nordic countries (Leira 1990) and the EC countries (Moss 1990) show that Denmark, Sweden, Finland and Iceland provided for more than 20 per cent of the under threes, as did France and Belgium. Italy, Portugal and Norway

Table 3.2 *Pre-school children in state-sponsored day care, by age and form of care, 1989.*
(per cent)

| | Age of child | | | | | |
| | Denmark | | Norway | | Sweden | |
Form of childcare	0–2	3–6	0–2	3–6	0–2	3–6
Day care in centres	19.0	58.0	9.0	54.0	18.0	61.0
Family day care	28.3	8.1	1.0	0.6	11.4	20.1
Total	47.3	66.1	10.0	54.6	29.4	81.1

Source: NORD 1991: 1, tables 218–19, pp. 320–2.

provided for 5–10 per cent of this age group, while Germany, the
Netherlands, Luxembourg, Ireland, the United Kingdom and Greece
offered access to only 2–4 per cent of the children aged 0–2 years old.

Why these differences in provision patterns? In an analysis of
motherhood policies in England and France at the turn of the century,
Jensen (1986) underlines that these two states identified a common set of
problems (to do with falling birth-rate and infant mortality) that were
differently diagnosed, and for which different sets of policies were
instituted. In the three Nordic countries whose policies are considered
here, the question is why a relatively similar set of policies produce quite
dissimilar results. I shall point out only two main differences in approach
between Norwegian policies on the one hand, and Swedish and Danish on
the other: the one concerns the state's relationship to motherhood, the
other the relationship to labour markets, formal and informal.

Markets in childcare

Table 3.2 shows that state-sponsored childcare is differently composed in
each of the Scandinavian countries. Norway opts almost exclusively for
centre-based care, and, as I shall go on to show in chapter 4, Norwegian
childcare policies reflect a distinct lack of interest as regards private
childminding arrangements and the childcare concerns of the working
mother. In Denmark and Sweden centre-based care is supplemented with
day care in private homes; this is incorporated into the state-sponsored
services as 'family day care'.

'Family day care' (a euphemism referring to childcare provided in
private homes, by childminders, approved, subsidized and/or employed

by public authorities) is far more important in Danish and Swedish day-care supply than in the Norwegian supply. In 1987, of all state-sponsored day care, family day care represented close to 30 per cent in Denmark, and close to 40 per cent in Sweden, but made up less than 3 per cent in Norway (see Leira 1988). This difference in the forms of service offered is not easily explained. In Denmark and Sweden, staff for family day care is perhaps more available, professional opposition to such services is perhaps less strongly voiced, and the willingness of local authorities to meet demand by integrating private childminding into the formal supply system is possibly greater than in Norway. Whatever the most plausible explanation, by expanding family day care Denmark and Sweden authorize, subsidize and control a larger share of the childminding markets than Norway does. In Norway, on the other hand, private childminding has only marginally been incorporated in the state-sponsored services. For the main part, childminding has remained private and informal, arrangements for which the state has accepted no responsibility. However, in Denmark and Sweden, too, though to a lesser extent, informal childminding services, unauthorized and uncontrolled, represent an element in childcare supply.[7]

According to a 1985 Norwegian survey of the childcare arrangements used by dual-earner and dual-student families, 37 per cent of the families reported the use of public services, almost half of the respondents, 48 per cent, made arrangements privately, through kinship, friendship and shadow labour, while 13 per cent managed without family external help at all (Bogen 1987; see also table 6.2). Danish services for early childhood education and care are more comprehensive than the Norwegian services, yet even Danish studies indicate an informal childcare market. In a nationwide survey carried out in Denmark in 1985, employed mothers reported using the following childcare arrangements: 60 per cent of the children aged 0–6 years attended public day-care services (day-care centres or family day care), 23 per cent were accommodated by informal, private arrangements and 17 per cent were cared for by the parents (Christoffersen 1986). Data from Sweden show that 51 per cent of the children aged 0–6 years were accommodated in public day care, private arrangements were used for 11 per cent and 39 per cent were managed by the parents (SCB: Barnomsorgsundersökningen 1986).

Markets for mothers

State intervention in early childhood care and education differs throughout Western Europe. Moreover, there are some pronounced differences in the objectives and aims stated by national governments when it comes to why public day care is provided and for whom. Some countries state the objectives of public day-care provision first and foremost as contributing to the socialization process, as a measure of improving, supplementing or controlling the upbringing of the family. In other countries equal or more importance is attributed to reproduction policies as a support of production, when public day care is intended as a means to recruiting labour and/or to supporting the family economy (Moss 1988; Thayer et al. 1988). Both aspects are present in the development of public day-care systems in Scandinavia, but the importance of the one to the other varies. In Sweden and Denmark, reproduction policies as exemplified by day-care provision have been more oriented towards the demands of production for labour, and towards the demand of the employed parents for day-care services (Kyle 1979; Borchorst and Siim 1987; Kugelberg 1987). In the policies of Norway, socialization aspects have been more prominent (Leira 1987a).

Demand for extrafamilial childcare has risen in all the Scandinavian countries during recent decades. The single most important driving force in increasing the demand is the emergence of the employed-mother family. By the early 1980s the majority of Scandinavian mothers of pre-school children were in paid employment. Thirty years back the employment of mothers was unusual and unexpected, in particular when the children were still very young. In the course of one generation the norm was changed. The 'modernization of motherhood' represented by the mothers who joined the formal labour market was registered first in Denmark and Sweden, where participation rates of mothers with pre-school children are still higher than in Norway. The different employment rates of mothers in the three countries are often attributed to Norway's later industrialization and urbanization, Anttalainen (1984) observes, and also to the fact that Norwegian mothers, from a Scandinavian perspective, are latecomers to the labour market. Close to 80 per cent of the Danish and Swedish mothers and 70 per cent of the Norwegian mothers of pre-school children were in employment in 1990 (Leira 1990). Among the mothers of children under 3 years, employment rates are almost as high, and increasing. Even though a substantial proportion of these mothers of young children work less than full-time (which is the case in all three countries), the labour market participation of Scandinavian mothers is still much higher than is commonly found in the countries of Western Europe (Moss 1990).

All over Scandinavia mothers' participation in the labour market necessitated new approaches to everyday childcare. A connection is generally assumed to exist between the mass entry of mothers into the labour market, and the state intervention in provision of early childhood education and care. However, within Scandinavia the welfare state's contribution to the change in family forms varied. National policies in Denmark and Sweden appear as having actively supported the economic activity of mothers, providing public day-care services to this end.

In Norway the economic activity of mothers increased rapidly from the late 1960s with negligible assistance from public day care. Public provision simply came too late to be of special importance in furthering the employment of mothers (Leira 1985). By the mid-80s, the great majority of the employed mothers' children still did not have access to public day-care services. In 1989, when more than 70 per cent of the mothers of pre-school children were in the work-force, only 34 per cent of all pre-school children and only 10 per cent of the under threes attended public day care. The increase in mothers' labour market participation certainly contributed to the increased demand for state-sponsored day care. However, in Norway the conflict created by the structural incompatibility of formal employment and childcare commitments remained largely a private concern, and implicitly a problem defined as a matter mothers were to manage.

Norwegian mothers did not wait for state assistance. Mothers favoured the expansion of the earner aspects of motherhood, and developed the employed-mother family as the predominant family form, primarily through co-operation with other women. A lateral self-organization of women in private child-minding has up to the mid-1980s meant more for the employed mothers' provision of everyday childcare than the intervention of the state.

Everyday childcare illustrates a point made by Hernes (1984), who notes that in situations of cross-pressure women have the possibility of forming alliances with several partners, the most important being the state, men or other women. The institutional differentiation in childcare shows the variety of 'alliances' made, with the state taking a more important role in Sweden and Denmark than in Norway. Borchorst and Siim (1987) have argued that a partnership was established between the welfare states in Denmark and Sweden and the mothers, in which the state acknowledged and supported the model of a dual motherhood that included women's active participation in production and in social reproduction. Although this interpretation may evoke too rosy a connotation in the view of recent Danish studies of day care (Christoffersen 1986), obviously economic and family policies were synchronized in Denmark and Sweden to an extent not seen in Norway, where the welfare state did *not* actively develop policies to support the employment of mothers.

My analysis of the political history of modern childcare in Norway does not support the view of state intervention as a partnership (see chs. 4 and 5). Labour market policies presumed the development of the employed-mother family (as single- or dual-earner). Increasingly, mothers of young children were recruited to labour market participation. However, the duality of mothers' lives as carers and economic providers was not acknowledged in any successful effort to co-ordinate labour market and childcare policies. In retrospect the policies of all three countries are slightly outdated. Danish and Swedish policies concerning early child-hood education and care, as formulated in the 1970s, even the Norwegian policies, were influenced by the image of the emancipated woman of the 1960s, who was to be integrated in the labour market on equal terms with men. All other things not being equal, the shortcomings of this approach have become apparent. Women are still responsible for the greater part of childcare and primary socialization, and the gender barriers within the labour market remain remarkably strong.

In none of the countries have 'reproduction policies' been developed to meet the needs of the employed mother. The demands of production for labour have been satisfied to an extent that the demands of social reproduction have not. State intervention in early childhood has not made private childminding superfluous. In none of the three countries did reproduction policies seriously infringe upon the traditional role of the father. In all the countries up to now, 'political motherhood', that is, mothers' responsibility for care of offspring, has prevailed as an impor-tant structural element in childcare.

Motherhood: Scandinavian models

Comparing the state's approach to mothers in the UK and Sweden, Ruggie (1984) assumes that the stronger political institutionalization of working-class interests in Sweden made the state more responsive to demands for working-class reforms, which presumably explains the better provision of state-sponsored day-care services in the Swedish Social Democratic welfare state than in the liberal UK. However, the considerable differences between the Scandinavian Social Democratic welfare states in their policies of social reproduction this analysis does not account for. Norway has a social democratic tradition in many ways similar to, and arguably as strong as, that of Sweden. As regards provisions for early childhood education and care, Norway is more like the UK than Sweden, particularly when it comes to provision for under threes (cf. Leira 1987a; Cohen 1988; Moss 1988). What then, about a Scandinavian model?

The provision of high-quality day care is commonly regarded as a national concern and as a part of the welfare state service system in all three Scandinavian countries. In principle, national policies aim at making state-sponsored day care available to all children. The modes of state intervention and the structure of day-care provision are basically similar. However, the ambitious aims of national policies for early childhood education and care have not been fulfilled in any of the countries. The universalist ambition and its solidaristic promise called for more comprehensive intervention by the state (central and/or local) than what has so far been instituted. The persisting shortage of services and the socially 'skewed' distribution underline that access to state-sponsored childcare is not established as an entitlement of employed-mother families. Yet, as my examination shows some essential differences between the countries, I question the assumption commonly made that Scandinavian 'reproduction policies' are developed in accordance with one common model. As demonstrated above, Denmark and Sweden compare favourably with Norway when it comes to supply meeting demand for public day care.

What makes Norway different? The different outcomes as witnessed by Denmark and Sweden on the one hand and Norway on the other are, of course, generated by the interplay of several processes. My study does not offer the complete answer to this complex question. I shall give some hypotheses and indicate issues of interest to further research. One set of hypotheses concerns the relationship between central and local government. As pointed out, the level of national provision is decided by the sum of decisions made by individual local authorities. The sheer number of local authorities in Norway has not facilitated the rapid follow-up of national aims. The structure, size, demography, local economy and political party structure of local authorities may influence decisions on day care. An examination across countries might show relative similarities in provision levels when comparing similar types of local authorities, for example in the metropolitan areas of Copenhagen, Oslo and Stockholm, or in the sparsely populated rural districts. Such an undertaking has been beyond the scope of my study.

Another possibility is that the data-sets merely indicate a time-lag. In Denmark and Sweden industrialization and urbanization developed earlier, and so also did large-scale state-sponsoring of childcare. In some years' time, it may be hypothesized, Norway will catch up with the early starters.

The Norwegian economy may have been harder hit by the German occupation of 1940–5 than the Danish, which may have influenced day-care provision. Sweden was not occupied. Supply of day care for pre-school children was certainly not a top priority in the early post-war years in Norway; the reconstruction from war-time damage demanded that more pressing needs were met first (cf. chs. 4 and 5). Moreover, demand for public day care was perhaps manifested later in Norway than in the neighbouring countries. Obviously, answering such questions concerning national differences necessitates more detailed historical investigation and comparison of traditions and policies in the three countries than I have ventured to undertake.

The demand for women's labour may have been stronger in Denmark and Sweden than in Norway, Borchorst (1987) assumes. Though interesting, the hypothesis is not easily assessed. From when the war ended and throughout the 1950s and 1960s there was a shortage of labour in Norway, yet few efforts were made to mobilize women to labour market participation (Tornes 1986; see also ch. 5).

Differences as regards the conceptualization of collective childcare and motherhood also need consideration. Although the Social Democratic traditions have been strong in all the three countries, having made a profound impact on the welfare state development, family policies also reflect the influence of different family and motherhood values (see Siim 1984). For example, the policies concerning early childhood education and care that I have examined appear to aim at different family forms and, moreover, to be grounded in different images of the mother–child relationship and of the relationship of the welfare state to mothers. Preference for the gender-differentiated nuclear family was more pronounced in Norway, where this family form has attracted stronger political and popular support than in the neighbouring countries (see also ch. 5). The Christian People's Party, one of the Norwegian political parties represented in the Storting (Parliament), has for example strongly advocated traditional family values.

In Sweden and Denmark policies for early childhood education and care were closely integrated with economic policies. The combination of motherhood and employment was supported by large-scale public investments in childcare (Kyle 1979; Näsman; Nordström and Hammarström 1983; Borchorst and Siim 1987). State funding of childcare was among the measures adopted to meet the economy's demand for labour. The demands of production were, so to speak, incorporated in reproduction policies, as one important objective of public day-care provision. 'Good' day care was regarded not only as good for children, it was also good for the economy, which needed mothers' labour. In Sweden it was even suggested that day-care policies ought to come under the province of labour market authorities, so that economic and family policies could be more co-ordinated and accommodate the demand for labour by facilitating mothers' employment (Kugelberg 1987). The model of the mother as homemaker and carer diminished in importance, while the model of the mother as economic provider was the one favoured by national day-care policies. These two countries, in which reproduction policies were closely co-ordinated with labour market policies, were more successful with regard to meeting the demands of new family forms, and also with regard to approaching national aims for provision of childcare.

As I have shown (Leira 1985; 1987; cf. chs. 4 and 5), Norwegian policies concerning pre-school children did not aim at facilitating mothers' employment or accommodate the economy's demand for labour. Childcare policies were more exclusively oriented towards the socialization of the child. Making state-sponsored day care universally available was a long-term objective. Norwegian childcare policies from 1945–90 did not conceptualize married women and mothers as 'labour'. The concept of the employed mother was not politically institutionalized. As the everyday construction of Norwegian motherhood changed to include employment, the lack of co-ordination of labour market and family policies created problems for an increasing number of families with young children. Welfare state policies were remarkably out of step with actual family practices.

Examining the idea of a 'Scandinavian model' in reproduction policies, and focusing on the provisions instituted to meet the employed-mother families' demand for childcare, I have drawn attention to the different approaches of the policies of Denmark, Norway and Sweden. In the policies concerning early childhood education and care my study shows Danish and Swedish policies as comparatively similar, while Norway's policies have a different 'profile'. Theoretical and empirical generalizations about the Scandinavian model of reproduction policies need qualification when confronted with the Norwegian case. However, what makes Norway different my study does not answer. Rather, my analysis leads on to more questions, beyond the scope of what I have been able to undertake in this project. More detailed studies of the relationship of central to local government might give more information on why political profiles differ, as might historical examinations of the development of national policies concerning the family, mothers' employment and childcare in the three countries.

Situating the Norwegian case within a Scandinavian context, I have in this chapter called attention to similarities as well as differences in the welfare state approach to working mothers in the three countries. In chapters 4 and 5 I shall turn to a more detailed examination of the political history of motherhood and the social construction of the working mother in the Norwegian welfare state.

4   The collectivization of childcare

Welfare state and early childhood care

Up to the end of World War II state policies for early childhood education and care were virtually nonexistent in Norway. Only in cases of severe neglect or abuse, or if a child had been abandoned, orphaned or was temporarily lacking an economic provider, was it mandatory for public authorities to intervene (Seip 1987). Otherwise the state did not interfere with the everyday arrangements for the youngest children. Rearing and caring was left to the family.

In chapter 4 I examine the political history of early childhood education and care in Norway in the period 1945–85, dealing first with the deliberations preceding legislation in 1975, and then with the development of services in the next decade.

My analysis focuses on the reconstitution of the state–family relationship as evidenced in the introduction of national policies for the early childhood years. Childcare and upbringing being primarily the mothers' responsibility, state-sponsored programmes for pre-school children signalled a change in the relationship between the state and mothers. Special attention is given to the part played by the state as initiator or instrument of change as regards the carer aspects of motherhood. Whether explicitly stated or not, childcare policies always contain certain assumptions about the family and about the parent–child relationship.[1] Which models of motherhood did the Norwegian policies promote?

The chapter centres on two issues of particular importance to my analysis of motherhood change: how was state responsibility for 'generational reproduction' defined? And, what measures were applied to reach the stated aims? Did the welfare state plan for massive changes in the carer aspects of motherhood by defining state responsibility for children as universal in principle, providing services for all? Or was the intention to produce marginal changes only, by defining childcare policies as residual, aiming at just a few? What were the modes and scope of state intervention? More specifically I deal with the questions of which forms of day care were to be included under state jurisdiction, and which children were to be the target groups.

Focusing in this chapter on changes in the carer aspects of motherhood introduced by welfare state childcare policies, I discuss political initiatives explicitly aimed at diversifying the supply side of day care. Processes influencing demand are dealt with in chapter 5, in which I examine changes in the earner aspects of motherhood and relate the institutional differentiation in childcare to changes in labour market and family structure in the period.

I use the term 'childcare' with the connotation of everyday, ordinary care for children, whether it is carried out by parents, childminders or day-care staff. The terms 'day-care policies', 'childcare policies' and 'policies concerning early childhood education and care' are used interchangeably, to designate policies concerning extrafamilial care of children that are intended to supplement the care, upbringing and primary socialization in the home during parts of the day. Forms of childcare aimed at child protection or established for children for whom local authorities have taken over parental responsibility are not included in the discussion. The examination does not consider didactics or schools of educational thought, nor the effects of state-sponsored childcare on childhood and children, though these aspects certainly merit attention, nor do I deal with all aspects and implications of state-sponsored childcare dealt with in the development of state policies.

The remainder of the chapter takes the following form. The first section gives a short introduction to collective day care prior to 1946. Based on the modes of intervention adopted by the state, the subsequent section identifies the three main phases in the history of state-sponsored day care in the period 1945–75, starting with supervision, later adding subsidies and finally separate legislation; and the narrative is subdivided accordingly. Thereafter I discuss the experiences with public day-care provision in the years following legislation, contrasting the universalist principles of national policies with the mediocre results obtained. The outcome, I argue, demonstrates a striking degree of non-interventionism as regards the working mothers' problems with combining jobs and children. Faced with the competing and partly contradictory interests of the main target groups, the providers and the consumers, the policies adopted represented a compromise that was not sufficient to meet demand. Moreover, welfare state approach to childcare was moulded in a series of compromises entailing considerable concessions to those political parties to the centre and the right (usually

termed the bourgeois parties in Scandinavia) who opposed state intervention in early childhood education and care. National policies give no
evidence of bold attempts to come to grips with the demands of the
largest category of potential consumers, the working mothers, in whose
lives caring and earning responsibilities were combined.

Collective childcare prior to 1946

In 1946 when the first steps of state intervention in early childhood care
and education had been taken, centre-based childcare or day-care
institutions were rare in Norway, and typically an urban phenomenon in
a mainly rural country. However, the tradition of collective childcare
dates back to 1837, when the first children's asylum was established by a
benevolent association called 'Nødlidendes Venner' (Friends of the
Poor). The early asylums were inspired by the day-care institutions
created earlier, by Robert Owen, in England (Grude 1972). Some local
authorities supported these day-care institutions economically. It was
not until 1920 that the first public day-care institution for pre-school
children was opened in Oslo (Søsveen 1974).

The early day-care provisions were strongly class divided. Children's
asylums and crèches accommodated the children of working-class
mothers whose waged work was essential for the family's subsistence.
According to the records, the aims of these institutions were threefold,
to support the economic provider aspects of motherhood, to protect the
children from the dangers of the streets, and to improve future labour.
Hours of attendance largely covered the mothers' working hours, and
the fees paid were minimal, intended to help with expenses for the
children's food only (Grude 1972).

The Fröbel kindergartens had a distinctly middle- or upper-class
character by comparison. The fees charged rendered them inaccessible
to poorer people and hours of attendance were part-time. These
institutions aimed at children's harmonious development, and were in
no way intended to serve the needs of mothers working full time in
industry or as domestic servants, which were the main urban job
categories for women in the late nineteenth and early twentieth
centuries.

The development of day-care services for young children substan-
tiates a pattern commonly seen in the history of social or welfare
services provision in Norway and elsewhere. Voluntary or charitable
associations took the lead, introducing new initiatives and 'model
services' that were later supported, supervised and controlled – eventually entirely taken over – by public authorities. 'Typical' also was the

involvement of women in the early charitable associations. The early political history presents day-care provision as an activity arena that attracted women from the upper classes, offering them a rudimentary political experience, and an outlet for organizational initiative. Moreover, the childcare institutions offered jobs for women, and a basis for professional training.[2] (For an overview of the historical background to modern day care in Britain, see Cohen 1988.)

In 1946, when questions concerning state intervention into the early childhood years were placed on the political agenda by the Labour government, this was in many respects a return to the issues which were raised in the late 1930s but were left unresolved during the war. Much discussed in Norway were the writings of two Swedes, the prominent Social Democrats Alva and Gunnar Myrdal (1934), which voiced concern about the fall in the Swedish birthrate and called for stronger political commitment to the population question. Alva Myrdal (1935) also strongly advocated state-sponsored collective childcare, particularly for children in the cities. Population concerns were less pronounced in Norway, but the influence of the Myrdals is felt in Norwegian contemporary debate. In Oslo a well-known paediatrician, head of the city's health services for schools and chairman of the city's childcare services, in a public lecture in 1937 raised the question of what was to be done with the children (L. Stoltenberg 1937). The lecturer directed attention to the population problem, and to the poor quality of life of many city children living in overcrowded apartments, with dangerous outdoor areas, and health and hygienic standards considered detrimental to children's health, and so on. Following the debate raised by this lecture, the Oslo branch of 'Hjemmenes Vel' (an association formed to promote the common interests of housewives) and the pre-school teachers' association organized a committee for childcare provision. Joined in 1941 by the Oslo branch of the Norwegian Housewives' Association and renamed as 'Komitéen for husmødrenes barnehager' (the Committee for the Housewives' Kindergartens), this committee became a driving force in the provision of day care in the capital. Activities were kept up but at a reduced rate during the war. In the early post-war period the Association intensified its work, and this has been continued up to the present day (Aa. Stoltenberg 1962; Lien 1987).

Norway had no experience of war-time nurseries like the ones established in the US and the UK. The economy did not call for the mobilization of the Norwegian labour 'reserves'. When the war ended, existing institutions remained but were worn-down, and the quality of the services was decidedly mixed.

The state and childcare: supervision, subsidies, separate legislation

From 1945 when the Labour Party gained a majority in the first general elections held after the war, a series of state initiatives and reforms were instituted, aiming not only at the considerable task of reconstruction from war-time damage, but at establishing a 'welfare state'. Expansion of state-sponsored services to children and their families was a part of this ambitious undertaking. A need to support and assist families with young children was acknowledged from early on, and some state responsibility for the early childhood years was accepted in principle, across political parties. Child benefits were introduced in 1946 and legislation was passed in 1947 concerning the supervision and control of existing day-care facilities. Restricted, selective intervention was supported in early childhood education and care, but the development of comprehensive state-sponsored schemes met with opposition.

As the welfare state expanded, responsibility for the early childhood years was reconceptualized so as to lend greater importance to state involvement. Children and childhood were increasingly drawn under the state's sphere of influence. Welfare state 'reproduction politics' was to introduce collective childcare for mass consumption, supplementing parental upbringing in the home by professional socialization practices, transforming childcare to waged work and altering the contents of childhood, motherhood and family life in the process. As state-sponsored provisions developed slowly, these were to become the dominant trends in the long-term perspective. Thirty years of deliberation preceded day-care legislation.

Opposition to state intervention was voiced from monetary as well as from moral concerns. Through day-care policies the welfare state intervened directly in the ideology and economy of generational reproduction, and in both cases was contested. Obviously money mattered. To provide high-quality services for all pre-school children was cost-demanding. Among the local authorities charged with the main responsibility for provision, enthusiasm for day care was mixed, indeed. Ambivalence to state intervention in the early childhood years was grounded, moreover, in a concern that state expansion might undermine the family. In Norway, responsibility for pre-school children was traditionally moored in the private sphere, with the family, primarily with the mothers. State intervention in this field represented a break with traditional lifestyles. State-sponsored, professional upbringing challenged parental authority. Opposition to welfare state childcare policies carried more than a tinge of 'motherhood morals', of ambivalence over or outright resistance to the redefinition of motherhood that a pledge to universal provision of state-sponsored childcare contained. The development of the Norwegian welfare state in the early post-war decades is closely associated with the Labour Party, which was the largest party in the national assembly throughout the period under consideration. From 1945 to 1965 Labour remained in power (with an interval for a non-socialist coalition government lasting only one month) and held absolute majority until 1961. In Parliament in this period they could do as they wished (Bull 1979). Labour was the first of the political parties to support centre-based day care for pre-school children, which was entered in the party programme from 1949. Not until the 1960s did most of the other parties follow suit (Sande 1984, p. 109).

Policies for early childhood education and care were discussed in the early post-war years (cf. below pp. 70–3). Restricted, selective intervention was commonly supported, but the development of comprehensive state-sponsored programmes for pre-school children, advocated by one government-appointed committee working with educational reform (Samordningsnemnda for skoleverket), met with opposition. The Labour Party itself was divided over the aims and means of state intervention, and over the division of labour and responsibility between the state and the family. Was the state to prepare a general set of policies aimed at the pre-school population at large, making state-sponsored services universally available? Or was state involvement to sponsor restricted programmes only, aimed selectively at specifically defined target groups? Not until 1975 was the controversy over the aims of policies for early childhood education and care settled, when the universalist approach gained cross-political support in Parliament. Controversy remained, however, over the implementation of the universalist principle, and over the modes and scope of state (local and central) intervention.

Next, I shall trace the development of the state's approach to early childhood care and education, examining in particular the orientation of policies as either universal or selective, to use the terminology of R. M. Titmuss (1968), as evidenced in questions concerning modes of intervention, by which measures and for whom. The orientation of childcare policies as either universal or selective had important consequences for motherhood change, as noted above. Opting for universally oriented childcare programmes meant a general, if indirect, state support for new models of motherhood. Selectively oriented intervention, on the other hand, represented no great challenge to the gender-differentiated family in which mother was the home-based carer.

The narrative is divided into three subsections, each dealing with a period when new elements were introduced into state policies for everyday childcare. The first period, which runs from about 1945 to about 1960, I have termed the period of supervision, as the state defines as its primary responsibility the supervision, inspection, control and approving of existing day-care establishments for young children. In addition, the state subsidizes rehabilitation of such structures and supports the professionalization of pre-school teachers.

From about 1960 to 1975 follows a period of subvention. State responsibility is extended to cover part of the running costs. Gradually day-care services are accepted as 'goods' for collective consumption, to be provided by the public purse. Concretely this is expressed in the state budget, in which a special code for day-care grants is entered. Subsidies are linked with a closer state supervision and quality control. In this period the National Housing Bank starts providing loans at reduced interest for day-care provision.

In 1975 the state codifies the responsibility for day care in a separate law, Lov om barnehager (Act governing day care), which restricts the state's field of interest to including day-care services run by professional pre-school teachers only. The law also defines a division of labour within the public sector. For professional services the state maintains control of standards and expands supervision and subvention. Local authorities are charged with the superordinate responsibility for the planning, provision and running of day-care services. Planning of services to meet local demand is made mandatory for the local authorities. To provide services according to plans is discretionary, however.

A period of supervision, ca. 1945–60

From early on in the post-World War II period it was commonly agreed in Norway that some form of state involvement was needed to assist families with young children and/or to improve the quality of future labour. In the early reports on day-care provision (e.g. Samordnings-nemnda for skoleverket of 1947, Barnevernskomitéen of 1947), state intervention was not discussed as a matter of principle, involving in a general way a reconstitution of the sphere of influence of state and family respectively. Rather, the issue was approached in practical or pragmatic terms, the discussion evolving around questions about the appropriate modes of intervention, and what measures to apply. The lawmakers favoured a dual approach, providing cash transfers as a means of subsidizing the costs that occur in child-rearing and fostering, and provision of services to supplement family-based care.[3] In this chapter I deal with services provision only.

When the war ended, a need for some control over childcare provisions was recognized. Parliament voiced concern about the quality of existing provision, and legislation was forwarded to meet an immediate need to improve existing structures and to ensure the standards of facilities to be provided. In 1947 an amendment of earlier legislation rendered it mandatory for the state to inspect, supervise and approve the standards of structures in which children were accommodated, i.e. orphanages, foster homes, and also day-care facilities for pre-school children (Lov av 7.mars 1947. Om tillegg til lov om pleiebarn). The authority for approval was placed with the Ministry of Social Affairs, which had also established an inspectorate in 1946. State policies did not include any direct involvement in the provision of facilities. Supervision and control was restricted to centre-based care. Private childminding was not included under the state's responsibility.

However, the government envisaged a need for a more comprehensive state involvement in the care of children. Two government committees, both appointed by the Labour majority in 1947, were to look into childcare (or day-care) provision for pre-school children and to elucidate the role for state intervention in this field. A general political acceptance of state intervention in early childhood education and care was thus expressed both in the appointment by the Ministry of Education of the committee that dealt with childcare within the context of broad reforms of the educational system (Samordningsnemnda for skoleverket), and also in the appointment by the Ministry of Social Affairs of the committee which was to prepare a revision of legislation concerning child protection (Barnevernskomitéen).

The two committees agreed that the state was to play a part in the provision of services, but differed strongly on the form of intervention, that is, whether state-sponsored day care was to be provided on a universalist or a selective basis. The two committee reports present opposite approaches to state-sponsored day-care provision. One is universalist in orientation and underlines the educational importance of early childhood care and education/socialization. The other is selective in orientation and conceives of public day care as a device for social policy and a service for the few.

The committee appointed by the Ministry of Education envisaged an integration of pre-school services into a comprehensive educational system. Like elementary schools, pre-school services were to be made available to all children under school age, at no cost to the parents. In this perspective the committee logically concluded that pre-school services were to come under the province of the Ministry of Education and Ecclesiastical Affairs (Samordningsnemnda for skoleverket. *Tilråding*

XV, 1951, p. 6). The committee charged with revision of legislation related to the protection of children acknowledged the educational benefits offered by high-quality day-care services. However, considering that very few day-care institutions were actually in operation, and that the number of places was not likely to increase rapidly, the committee assumed that it was more realistic to conceive of such services as a social policy measure directed toward those in need of special assistance. The committee accordingly recommended that responsibility for day-care issues was to remain with the Ministry of Social Affairs (Innstilling fra Barnevernkomitéen I, 1951, p. 54).

The proposals of this last committee were the ones followed up in later legislation. When Lov om barnevern (Act governing child protection) was passed in 1953, the authority to approve day-care institutions remained with the Ministry of Social Affairs. Child protection, according to the Act, was the responsibility of the local authorities. Hence the local authorities were also charged with the provision of day-care facilities. To make the provision of day care mandatory for the local authorities was not at issue. The law, however, contained a general call upon local authorities to consider the possibility of providing day care for pre-school children, formulated as follows in no. 45: 'Considering the demand, local authorities ought to establish or support the establishment of day-care institutions [for pre-school children]'. This law did not introduce substantial changes in state involvement in early childhood education and care. Supervision, inspection, control of standards, approval of premises were the basic measures adopted. Improving the quality of services in the institutions providing day care for pre-school children became important when, from 1946, the state supported the education of professional pre-school teachers (Grude 1972).

In the early post-war years the state, on a temporary basis, subsidized the rehabilitation of day-care institutions and the construction of new ones from a special fund (Grude 1972; Lea 1982). After some years, when the money in this fund was all spent, special grants for rehabilitation were still given from time to time. No regular nationwide system of subsidizing day-care operating costs was established. In 1954 the Ministry issued regulations governing the operation of day-care centres, but in the following years the state contributed minimally to the provision of structures (St. meld. 89, 1961–2, p. 12).[4]

In 1958, questions concerning day-care centres or early childhood education and care were transferred from the Ministry of Social Affairs to a newly established Ministry of Family and Consumer Affairs (which was later renamed the Ministry of Government Administration and Consumer Affairs, while still retaining responsibility for family and childcare policies).[5]

The comprehensive reforms concerning early childhood education and care recommended by the 1947 committee on educational reforms, and advocating the provision of gratis childcare for all children, were pigeonholed. From 1949, Labour, as noted above, voiced an interest in the provision of day-care services, but this was not translated into actual policy-making. Outside the larger cities the demand for collective childcare was minimal, as mothers generally were domesticated and the gender-differentiated nuclear family predominated.

Quality control, supervision and approval of existing structures are the concerns that emerge as the central ones in the early political history of day care. State initiative in the provision of services was very modest. Local authorities commonly did not venture into this field. Day-care services were conceived as measures of social policy, aimed preventively at children and families with special needs. Large-scale intervention was not considered, though the principle of universal provision had been aired.

Considering the development of day-care policies in this period the situation after five years of war-time occupation must be taken into account. The reconstruction economy of the early post-war years set the priorities of investment. When the Labour Party made a mention of day-care provision in the working programmes of the late 1940s and early 1950s, it was with the aim of relieving the home-based mothers of the drudgery and difficult conditions that many of them had to cope with. Obviously, this was not to be a top priority in a situation in which basic necessities such as health services and housing were lacking and strongly in demand. A cost-demanding reform such as day care had to wait.[6] Interestingly, in an economic perspective public investment in day care was presented, quite differently, as profitable, in that it could help mobilize the labour reserves among women and reduce the shortage of labour (see ch. 5 for a more detailed discussion). However, this line of thinking was not followed up in practical policy-making.

State subsidies for early childhood education and care, ca. 1960–75

The Labour government initiated a new phase in the development of state policies for the early childhood years in 1959 when appointing an expert committee of four women and three men to elucidate several aspects of centre-based day-care provision. This committee is often referred to as Lysethkomitéen, the Lyseth committee, named after the chairperson.[7] The committee was instructed to prepare an overview of the status quo in day-care provision for pre-school children nation-wide, and to assess the future need for various types of institutions as well as the practical and economic possibilities of meeting the demands. As for day-care provision, the committee was to outline standards of quality, area norms, staff/child ratio, hours of attendance, organization of work, etc. Moreover, the committee was to consider the possibility of securing economic support from private resources, and to evaluate whether day-care provisions could be financed by firms, associations and consumers' fees. They were not explicitly asked to assess the need for state subsidies for day-care provision, but they did this anyway. According to the mandate the committee was to base its work upon the principles of the Lov om barnevern (Child Protection Act), which charged the local authorities with the responsibility for day-care provision. The local child-welfare committees (barnevernsnemndene) were central in questions concerning day care, the Ministry stated (Lysethkomitéens innstilling, pp. 5–6).

When the committee first set to work, centre-based day-care services were only moderate in scope. According to a national survey of activities from 1960, quoted by the committee, a total of 259 institutions accommodated 7,565 children, representing less than 2 per cent of the pre-school population, which in Norway encompasses children aged 0–6 years. Supply was not sufficient to meet the demand, as was amply demonstrated by the waiting-lists for children who had registered for admission. Day-care centres were typically urban institutions. Oslo offered more than half the places available.

The committee report from 1962 gave a detailed and vivid picture of the situation of day-care provision in the early 1960s in Norway, presenting evidence from other countries as well, and providing comprehensive material concerning quality standards. Based on estimates concerning the proportion of employed mothers, the number of children from single-parent families and the number of children with handicaps, the committee recommended that day-care facilities be developed for 25 per cent of the population aged 3–6 years (Lysethkomitéens innstilling, p. 32).

In the main, ownership of existing institutions was private. Only one in six had public owners (Lysethkomitéens innstilling, pp. 12–13). A series of small-scale and some larger entrepreneurs offered day care. 'Self-help' organizations, such as housewives' associations, parent co-operatives and residents' associations, provided 106 of the institutions. Voluntary and charitable associations owned 77, whereas central and local authorities together had the ownership of 41 institutions. Grants from central and local government, owners' contributions and parental fees covered running costs. In 1960 there was no nation-wide regular system of state subsidies encompassing all forms of approved day care (Lysethkomitéens innstilling, p. 57).

The committee considered essential an increase in public subsidies to day-care provision. For central and local authorities to control and supervise existing structures was not sufficient. Economic support was needed to shoulder both establishing and running costs. As for establishment costs, the committee assumed that the state and local authorities each ought to contribute one-third (Lysethkomitéens innstilling, pp. 60–1) and that later they should combine to defray three-quarters of running costs (Lysethkomitéens innstilling, p. 59). The remainder was to be borne by the owners and by parental fees.

In principle, state subsidies for childcare could take different forms: for example, as cash transfers to parents, who were then free to organize care as they wished, or by subsidizing the production of services. The committee report does not discuss this issue. Apparently, subsidizing of day-care provision was regarded as necessary if centre-based day care was to be an option for parents at all. In later years the form that subsidies should take has been repeatedly debated, the parties to the left generally being more in favour of the production of services and the parties in the centre and to the right more in favour of cash transfers to parents (Bay 1988).[8]

Later, in 1962, the Ministry of Family and Consumer Affairs presented a report on day-care institutions to the Storting (Parliament) that acknowledged the considerable gap between the demand and supply of day-care provisions. To assume that places, if available, would be demanded for 25 per cent of the 3–6 year-olds was hardly an exaggeration. However, the Ministry did not recommend a large-scale investment in this sector, but favoured a selective approach. First and foremost, day-care institutions ought to be directed towards what was called the 'need of special groups', exemplified by children with handicaps and children from single-parent families. Referring to the Child Protection Act, the Ministry stated that the provision of day care was a responsibility of the local authorities. The Ministry did not intend to submit a proposal to Parliament recommending state grants for this purpose (St. meld. 89, 1961–2, p. 16).

As for running costs, the Ministry proposed that earmarked state grants should be given to the local authorities to be distributed to day-care facilities, and local authorities were to take more direct responsibility for local day care. State subsidies were to be linked explicitly with state control and approval; for example, concerning priority of children, level of parental fees, standards for fee exception and so on (St. meld. 89, 1961–2, p. 16). This recommendation meant an expansion of state control over several aspects of local day-care activities.

When the Storting debated the Ministry's report, the recommendations received general support. State policies were to be selectively oriented towards special groups of children and restricted to centre-based services (day-care institutions) only. While the state was not to subsidize the establishment of day-care structures, it was to provide a nation-wide regular scheme of transfer payments to subsidize running costs. As a matter of principle this decision represented an important expansion of state responsibilities for early childhood care and education. From 1959–60 a special code for day care was entered in the state budget, and made permanent from 1963 (Grude 1972). The subvention scheme was not, however, linked with a general national plan for the development of services for pre-school children. The further expansion of day care was made to depend upon voluntary local initiatives, public and private.

State policies for the early childhood years in the 1960s contained two basic ingredients, supervision of centre-based day care and subvention of the running costs of such facilities. From 1962 to 1972 annual subsidies increased from NOK 250,000 to 20 million. Still, provision of services was modest. The number of children accommodated was doubled, from approximately 7,000 in 1962 to 14,700 in 1972, which at that time represented less than 5 per cent of the children under statutory school age (Leira 1985). The introduction of a system of permanent subsidies expanded state responsibility and underlined the supervision and control element in state intervention.

As time passed it became clear that the expansion of state grants did not result in 'a new deal' for the development of public day care. Provision was left to private initiative, with some support from local authorities. State subsidies for running costs did not represent an inducement sufficient to encourage local provision. This carrot was not really attractive enough for local authorities, and there was no stick attached. Throughout the country a shortage of day-care facilities for pre-school children was reported. Although increasing, demand was not well organized, either locally or centrally. Political support for day care varied from one local authority to the other, but it was not a top priority anywhere. For economic reasons, local authorities were not tempted to make large-scale investments, as they were still to defray the larger share of day-care costs. Moreover, collective day care, staged by professionals, represented a challenge to parental upbringing. According to Norwegian tradition, children were to be cared for at home and it was the responsibility of the mothers to look after them. At the time such attitudes had wide popular support, but the extent to which they represented barriers to local day-care development cannot be ascertained unless detailed local research is done. Certainly, the motherhood models implied in popular socialization ideology gave no strong impetus to the introduction of public programmes for early childhood education and care.

In the party programmes for the period 1949–61 Labour supported the public provision of day care, notably as a relief for mothers working at home. Leaving day-care provision to local decision-making, cost-consciousness and local motherhood morals meant that little was done in practical terms to promote this idea. The modes of state intervention chosen, that is, regulation and subvention of running costs but not of establishment costs, came to underline selectivity as the state's main strategy in the policies of early childhood care and education. Implicitly, if not explicitly, the policies adopted represented a support of the gender-differentiated family, and the domesticated mothers' care.

The Day Care Act of 1975

The mid-1970s saw an epoch-making change in the history of state politics of early childhood education and care in Norway. The shift is closely associated with a new approach in welfare state policies towards the pre-school years, as witnessed in the codification of state responsibility in Lov om barnehager of 5 June 1975 (Act governing day care). The ambition of the lawmakers was to make state-sponsored day care available to all pre-school children whose parents wanted it. Thus in principle the Day Care Act represented a break with the selective approaches favoured in previous state policies. Provisions for early childhood education and care were to be incorporated in the range of services regarded as general entitlements. Legislation signalled a radical reorganization of childcare services and an expansion of the state's sphere of influence vis-à-vis the family. Initiated by a bourgeois coalition government in 1969, legislation was introduced by a Labour government in 1975 and gained cross-political support.

What the main motivation for expanding state responsibilities was is not easily deduced. Interpretations of family, motherhood and childcare policies underline different aspects of state policies: for example, the wish to improve future labour (an interpretation of motherhood policies suggested by Barrett and McIntosh 1982); to discipline and control mothers (Donzelot 1980; Lewis 1980); to cater to the demand of the labour market (Borchorst and Siim 1987); or to extend the Social Democratic experience of citizenship to the younger generation (Myrdal 1935). Obviously, leaving provision to the voluntary associations, with some assistance from local authorities, had not proved sufficient to comply with demand. More efficient measures were called for. Did legislation signal that children had become too important to be left to benevolence?

I shall not go into detail about the intentions of collective actors. A growing concern with and interest in early childhood care and education is discernible in Norway during the 1960s. Attitudes to motherhood and childhood changed. Gradually services for the very young came to be regarded as a legitimate field of interest and involvement of the public sector. The notion that this area was to be more closely integrated with national politics increasingly won acceptance. Certainly, as seen in a demand perspective, time for state intervention was more than ripe.

Demand for extrafamilial childcare by far exceeded supply, the most important reason being the rapid rise in the employment of mothers. The voluntary associations providing day care, the professionals dealing with pre-school children, and an increasing number of employed-mother families, some of them articulate, called for increased state involvement in early childhood education and care. The economy voiced a demand for mobilization of the labour reserves (see ch. 5 for a more comprehensive discussion of changes in demand). Within the political parties a concern about women's issues, and women's votes, was growing, and was created to no small extent by women's greater political activity and visibility in public life.

From the late 1960s the Women's Movement in Norway brought women's issues and concerns into public debate more vigorously and vividly than ever witnessed before. The personal was made political, as issues such as abortion on demand, women's right to paid work, and access to childcare provisions were aired publicly. The abortion law forwarded in 1974 lost by one vote, and was reintroduced and passed in 1975. Abortion on demand was instituted in 1978 after heated debates. Questions concerning gender equality were moving up on the political agenda. The Equal Pay Council of 1959 was replaced by the Equal Status Council in 1975, and the Equal Status Act was passed in 1978. The legislation contained new definitions of motherhood and women's rights, as did also the Day Care Act. Not surprisingly, lawmaking was embedded in prolonged political controversy and conflict.

The changes in the family as regards its caring and earning capacity – brought about mainly by the employment of mothers – actualized questions concerning the organization of caring for young children. Who was to do the childcaring when mother and father were both away at work? The shortage of high-quality childcare centres and an increasing demand for extrafamilial resources with which to care for children were regarded as issues of concern both to employment policies and to equal status policies.

The centre-conservative coalition government, which had on different occasions expressed its interest in provisions concerning early childhood education and care,[9] appointed a committee of seven men and five women in 1969 to deliberate questions concerning the provision (establishment and running) of future day-care institutions for children. Committee members came from, among others, the main political parties, from childcare and educational expertise, from voluntary associations providing day-care services and from the government administration. The Labour government, in office from 1971 to 1972, added to the socialist representation on the committee.

The committee was instructed to 'assess whether existing guidelines concerning building and running of day-care institutions for children are educationally and socially satisfactory and also as seen from the wishes of parents, for example as regards employment outside the home. Furthermore, the committee is to assess the need for further developments, and in this context is to make recommendations concerning arrangements for establishment and running costs, and present estimates of the need for qualified pre-school teachers. Whether to introduce separate legislation for day-care centres ought to be assessed, likewise the co-ordination between public day care and the public school system, in particular the connection with pre-school classes and recreational centres' (NOU 1972:39, *Førskoler*, p. 7, my transl.). Later in 1969 the committee was specifically asked to prepare a proposal for an Act governing day care, which was published as part of the committee's final report. The committee programme for the future national policies for childcare included services for pre-school children and for the younger school children. (My analysis deals with the deliberations concerning pre-school children only.)

Following the committee report from 1972 (NOU 1972:39), the Ministry of Government Administration and Consumer Affairs prepared a report for discussion in Parliament with a proposition for an Act governing day care. The Storting debated the Bill and the Day Care Act was passed in 1975. Contrasting the recommendations made by the 1969 committee with the proposals of the Ministry and the debate in Parliament gives evidence of considerable discrepancy in policies for generational reproduction. Analysing the different documents in context therefore helps to bring out more clearly the 'profile' of state policies and the inherent contradictions as regards which family and motherhood models to support.[10]

My analysis does not deal with all aspects relevant to day care considered in these documents. My interest centres on day-care legislation as evidence of a restructuring of the state–family relationship, and particularly the relationship of the state to mothers. Focus is therefore on how state responsibilities for early childhood care and education were defined, as elucidated by the sets of decisions concerning the implementation of the universalist ambition: which parts and which shares of everyday childcare for the under sevens did the state include as coming under its jurisdiction and which were left out? Which categories of children and families gained access to the public day-care services? What were the modes of intervention and the measures adopted? And, which were the family and motherhood models promoted?

By the early 1970s, public involvement in day-care provision was taken for granted. Emphasizing the obvious collective interests connected with the quality and content of the early childhood years, and with the living conditions of the youngest members of society, the committee preparing the Day Care Act strongly advocated the strengthening and expansion of public investment in the provision of day care for pre-school children. Public day care, the committee asserted, contributes to the common good of children, and psychological, pedagogical and social research confirm the positive effects for children that result from the experience of high-quality day care. In principle, services for early childhood education and care were to be made available to all children. Until supply was sufficiently developed, children with special needs ought to have priority of access (NOU 1972:32, p. 12). The committee report consistently argued in favour of a universalist approach to day-care provision. This position was grounded in an assessment of the needs of society and of the benefits to children of high-quality pre-school education and care.

From being a social policy measure provided for the few, and aimed mainly at children at risk, early childhood education and care was to be integrated into a comprehensive educational system and to encompass in principle all children of pre-school age. Stating the objectives of national policies for pre-school children in such terms was far more ambitious than anything the state had so far ventured to do. The universal aims were to be reached by stages, the committee envisaged. They laid out a set of recommendations concerning the modes of intervention necessary to fulfil the ambitions stated, and outlined the aims of a national long-term plan for day-care development.

Developing the arguments in favour of increased public responsibility for day-care provision, the committee moreover considered its effects in promoting greater equality between women and men both at home and at work, and also the need of single parents, and the wish of parents staying at home with children to be relieved of some of their childcare obligations. Considering the costs, they underlined that the provision of comprehensive systems of everyday childcare might contribute positively to the community, and that investment in childcare could give an economic net gain for society in the long run.

How to negotiate the public/private division of responsibility was an underlying theme in the committee's deliberations. The report presented a perspective on early childhood care and socialization in which the obligations of the state (central and local government) and the commitments of parents were carefully balanced. In principle the committee considered everyday childcare and education as an interest common to and a responsibility to be shared between public authorities and the children's guardians. 'The main responsibility for the children's upbringing lies with the parents', the report stated, but it also pointed out that societal involvement in child-rearing had increased, first and foremost with the development of the public elementary school system. State-sponsored day care was to give children more equal opportunities from early in life.

Committee deliberations concerning public and private responsibility did not deal with the state–family relationship exclusively, but also included for consideration the 'market forces', witnessed in the widespread use of private childminding. For the first time, recommendations were made to place private childminding within the jurisdiction of the state.

The committee recommended the introduction of one common term to encompass all forms of day-care services to pre-school children, and advocated the term 'pre-school', presumably to underline the inclusion under 'life-long learning'. This was more than symbolic. In the early 1970s facilities for children were offered under a variety of names, 'day-care institutions', 'kindergartens', 'pre-schools', indicating a difference in origin, and to some extent in content. What were termed 'daginstitusjoner' ('day-care institutions') were the only full-time institutions, and used for the most part by children from families with special needs. The introduction of a single term to encompass all types of institutions emphasized a wish to homogenize the provisions for pre-school children and to eradicate the class stamp that was still discernible. A common set of quality standards was to be applied to all provisions. Regardless of their earlier identification, these standards were to integrate education and care within each institution, attributing equal importance to both.[11]

The committee majority regarded pre-school education and care as an educational investment to be integrated with a comprehensive educational system stretching from crèche to college. In fact, the plan recommended for day-care provision was largely adopted from educational policy: local authorities are charged with the provision of elementary schools. Provision is mandatory, but state-sponsored. Unlike the school system, which is free and where attendance is compulsory, day-care attendance was not to be made obligatory, nor was provision to be free for consumers.

Among the committee's recommendations, two are of special significance when it comes to redefining the responsibility of the state vis-à-vis the family, and the mothers in particular, and these are the only ones I deal with in any detail. Both follow from the universalist aims outlined for state-sponsored day care, and both represent an introduction of new features into state policies; the one was to make provision of day care mandatory, the other to control the informal markets in childcare.

First, and the central recommendation of the committee, which represented a radical break with current policies in the field, was the proposal that the planning and provision of day care was to be made mandatory for the local authorities. To this end another important recommendation followed, that state subsidies to day-care provision be substantially increased (which was not a new mode of intervention but an important expansion of measures already in use). Second, the committee recommended that the private childminding 'business' be included under state jurisdiction. If agreed to and acted upon, these recommendations together would have radically expanded state (local and central government) responsibility for the early childhood years, and significantly altered the opportunity situation of mothers. This was not what happened.

In a report prepared for the national assembly, the Ministry of Family and Consumer Affairs, headed from 1973 by a Labour minister, dealt with questions concerning the national policy on early childhood education and care, presenting a proposition for a law governing day care (Ot. prp. 23, 1974–5, Lov om barnehager). This report included the recommendations made by the 1969 Day Care committee, including the comments on it made by various bodies who had received it for 'hearing'. The Ministry also gave its own recommendations to Parliament for a decision. Following the debate in the Parliamentary Committee, in this case the Social Affairs Committee reinforced by members of the Committee on Education and Ecclesiastical Affairs, the national assembly made the final decision on day-care legislation.[12]

The parliamentary debate about the proposition for the Day Care

Act did not elaborate on the broad societal framework within which the 1969 Day Care committee had grounded its recommendations. The Parliamentary Committee report and the subsequent debate in Parliament saw state-sponsored day care primarily as an educational benefit, a professional supplement to primary socialization within the family, and provided in the best interests of the child (Innst. O. nr 69, 1974–5; Ot. forh. 27. mai 1975, em. *Ot. tidende* 1974–5, vol. VIII, pp. 522–70). Whether state-sponsored day care was to have a mandatory Christian (Protestant-Lutheran) value basis was the hot topic of the debate. Gender equality and the economy's demand for labour were not central issues. However, Labour and notably Sosialistisk Venstreparti (a socialist party to the left of Labour) voiced support for the employed-mother family, while the bourgeois parties favoured a family policy (including day care) that maintained the traditional gender-differentiated single-earner family (see ch. 5).

The law passed as Lov om barnehager (Act governing day care) was less comprehensive in scope and content and on vital points differed from the law proposal forwarded by the 1969 committee. Yet the legislation did introduce a new phase in state policies for pre-school children when compared to earlier practices. Most important in material terms was the general acceptance across parties to increase state subsidies for day-care provision, both by increasing the state's proportion of running costs and by expanding the possibility for loans at reduced interest in the State's Bank of Housing in connection with the erection of new structures.

Important, too, was the change in attitudes. Passage of the law, with support from all parties but one, Fremskrittspartiet (a then small, right-wing party strongly committed to tax reductions), represented a breakthrough for the notion that early childhood care and education were to be included among the regular, state-sponsored personal services. In principle, the idea that state-sponsored day care was to be made available for all children gained general support, no small challenge, considering that only 7 per cent of the children under school age had access to state-sponsored day care in 1975. The national assembly moreover agreed to a plan for the development, stating that 50,000 places were to be made available by 1977, and 100,000 places in 1981. However, neither the Ministry nor Parliament concurred with the recommendations made by the committee concerning the modes of intervention to be used in reaching the stated aims. Most importantly, the Ministry did not support the provision of day care being made mandatory for the local authorities. This was not considered as an 'expedient measure'. Neither did the Ministry want to extend state responsibility by recommending the introduction of a system of licensing for private childminders. In the final process of decision-making, Parliament followed the Ministry.

I shall return here to the two recommendations of the 1969 committee central to my analysis, whether to make day-care provision mandatory for local authorities or not, and the question concerning the licensing of private childminders working for pay, and examine in greater detail the political discourses evolving around these issues. The rejection of the initial committee proposals significantly affected the definition of the state–family relationship, and the public–private division of responsibility for the early childhood years. The first question is obviously of great importance, in principle, as a test-case of the pledge to universal provision. Moreover, it was a matter of political and economic concern for central and local government. Furthermore, decision on the issue signalled which family forms – and motherhood models – legislators were prepared to support.

The second question is perhaps more easily bypassed as of minor importance. However, I shall argue, as regards the delimitation of welfare state responsibility, decision on the issue is a matter of principle, and of considerable political significance. Is state responsibility to encompass all children not in the care of their parents, or just those that are at any time admitted to public day-care facilities? Whether the state claims responsibility for all forms of extrafamilial childcare, or restricts its sphere of influence to the high-quality, state-sponsored schemes only, does make a difference.

Mandatory provision or voluntary

The recommendations proposed by the 1969 Day Care committee (in NOU 1972:39) presented a concept of national childcare policies in which rigorous state control and generous government spending combined were to promote day care as universally available, in fact as an entitlement for children. In the later decision-making processes this radical scheme was replaced by a liberal concept of national policies for early childhood care and education that in practice left it to the local authorities to decide whether they wanted to provide day care or not, and, if so, how many and what form of services to provide.

The basic decision for policy-makers in the preparation of day-care legislation was whether or not to make provision mandatory for local authorities or to rely on voluntary provision. The 1969 committee, as discussed above, recommended that local authorities be charged with wide-ranging responsibilities for the planning, establishing and running of day-care services for pre-school children. Local authorities were to be instructed to prepare a programme for day-care provision based on surveys of local demand. Provision was to encompass as a minimum the number of places corresponding to the number of children 'who come from single-parent families, and those whose parents are employed outside the home, or who for other reasons are in need of day care' (NOU 1972:39, p. 18).

The Ministry agreed to charging the local authorities with the superordinate responsibility for the development and running of local day care (proposition for the Day Care Act, no. 3). In the comments to this paragraph, the Ministry observed that the local authority 'is under a general obligation to provide a number of places that corresponds to its plan for development' (Ot. prp. nr 23, 1974–5, p. 53). Obviously, this responsibility was not meant to imply very definite obligations, when the comment further states: 'this obligation is not by law associated with specific time limits or rapidity of development'. As stated above, the Ministry did not wish to make provision mandatory, but recommended that planning be made obligatory, which meant that the local authority should be instructed to make up schemes for development. Provision was to remain voluntary (Ot. prp. nr 23, 1974–5, p. 53).

The majority in the Parliament Committee concurred with the Ministry's assessment. Planning and preparation of development plans based on analysis of demand was to be made mandatory. To make the provision of day care mandatory for local authorities was not considered expedient (Innst. O. nr 69, p. 6).

Let us now turn to the licensing of childminders: the 1969 committee took the initiative in forwarding for open political debate the meaning and importance (numerically) of the private childminding business. Voicing concern about that part of childminding activities 'which is performed by minders lacking qualifications and who are under no guidance or supervision' (NOU 1972:39, p. 83), the committee stated that 'legal authority is urgently needed so that local government may intervene when the childminding situation is unsatisfactory'. They also called for a system of registration and licensing of private childminders 'so that a competent authority may assess whether a person is qualified to care for the children of others' (NOU 1972:29, p. 83, my transl.). In line with this view the committee called for the licensing of private childminders by local authorities in their proposal for day-care legislation (NOU 1972:39, part V, p. 91).

This recommendation by the committee was certainly not to be interpreted as a repudiation of professional childcare. On the contrary, the report expressed a profound preference for professionally provided day care, and did not seek to incorporate the informal, popular or 'lay' day-care arrangements into the blueprint for the future day-care structure. Considering the widespread use of informal arrangements, the committee aimed at some public regulation and quality control of childminding activities in an interim period, until state-sponsored, professional day care was sufficiently developed. Then, as demand stopped, the private business would come to an end (NOU 1972:39, p. 83).

Discussing the Day Care committee's recommendation on the licensing of private childminders, the Ministry presented an estimate of the number of informal childminding arrangements, showing that these represented the most common form of extrafamilial childcare, by far outnumbering state-sponsored services (cf. ch. 5; see also table 6.2). Even so, the Ministry did not wish to include these activities under its jurisdiction. To recommend the licensing of private childminders was declined because of the difficulties involved in making control efficient (Ot. prp. nr 23, 1974–5, p. 25). However, the Ministry did mention possibilities for obtaining some control over private childminding: the local social welfare committee (sosialstyret), if it so wished, might provide guidelines for private childminding. The local committee dealing with questions concerning health and hygiene (helserådet) might assist parents who wished for an assessment of standards of health and hygiene at the child-minder's premises. Moreover, the local child welfare committee (barnevernsnemnda) had the authority to terminate activities considered as unsatisfactory (Ot. prp. nr 23, 1974–5, p. 25). (The Ministry did not, however, point out that these measures had been available for a long time and were unused or proved futile.) Expressing the hope that development of public day care would make it easier for parents to have their demand for state-sponsored childcare met, the Ministry assumed that private activities in this field would be continued. No indication was given that the Ministry shared the concern of the 1969 committee as regards the quality of private childminding. On the contrary, the Ministry found that such arrangements 'in many cases function well, [as they are] based on neighbourly relations, kinship and so on' (p. 25, my transl.).

Rejecting the recommendation for licensing, the Ministry pointed to the difficulties in making 'market' control efficient. Most probably this was a difficult task. However, the Ministry offered no real response to a question of principle concerning the appropriate delimitation of state responsibility for pre-school children. The authorization of private childminders may perhaps be ruled out, as being irrelevant to state-sponsored day-care provision. To exclude the question as being of no interest to the formulation of a general policy for the early childhood years is less convincing.

The Parliamentary Committee discussing the Ministry's report and proposition for legislation agreed with the recommendations forwarded. They called attention to the outlined possibilities for control, which were assumed to be sufficient, and saw no need to introduce a system of authorization for private childminders (Innst. O. nr 69, p. 7).

Compared with the decisions actually made favouring the development of day-care centres, the rejection of the proposal to license childminders may appear as insignificant. If alternative, state-sponsored facilities could be provided rapidly, then private childminders would soon be out of business. But this was not what happened. As state-sponsored day care in Norway developed rather slowly in the ten years following the adoption of the law, the uncontrolled market in childminding remained a cornerstone in the provisions for early childhood care and socialization (Leira 1985; cf. table 6.2). The Ministry of Government Administration and Consumer Affairs had observed in later reports to Parliament that the private arrangements for childminding were still numerous (St. meld. 93, 1980–1; St. meld. 50, 1984–5). The possibility of intervention to regulate or control such activities was not discussed either in these reports, or in a later document dealing with national policy for early childhood education and care up to the end of the century (St. meld. 8, 1987–8). In short, the state had no wish to interfere with the private market set-up in everyday childcare.

The debate concerning the authorization of private childminders brings out an important aspect of the public–private division of responsibility as regards early childhood education and care. In this perspective, what is excluded or ruled out may be as enlightening as what is chosen for inclusion. As regards extrafamilial childcare, state intervention was to be modest, childminding was to remain largely a private concern, left to the family or to the mothers. The result was a policy of restricted scope, when compared to the universal ambitions for provision contained in the formulation of national policy as well as when quality-control of supply was the issue.

Universal principles – marginal results

Contrasting the legislation for early childhood education and care proposed by the 1969 Day Care committee with the final text passed as Lov om barnehager of 5 June 1975 (Act governing day care) highlights two different concepts of welfare state relationship to the family. The shared premise of the texts is the pledge to make state-sponsored day care available to all pre-school children. There is also agreement as to responsibility for provision: a division of labour within the public sector which charges the local authorities with provision, supported by state grants and subject to state approval. The differences lie in the definition of state responsibilities, in the modes of intervention recommended and in the measures found expedient for the implementation of national policy aims.

In line with the universal aims stated, the 1969 Day Care committee wished for legislation to encompass all forms of paid, extrafamilial day care. To this end, licensing of private childminders was added to the basic recommendation that day-care provision was to be made mandatory for local authorities. The measures recommended were for a combination of 'carrot and stick', in that mandatory provisions were imposed, but with state control and generous grants attached. In questions of provision the universalist principles embodied in its proposal for national policies concerning the early childhood years were to be placed above local autonomy.

The policy approach instituted in actual legislation offered a set of recommendations to which few obligations were added. The law provided a liberal framework, making local planning of day-care provision mandatory for the local authorities while actual provision was to remain voluntary. Each of the about 450 local authorities was to decide whether or not day care was to be provided within its area, in what forms and for whom. The emphasis on local autonomy implied that selectivity was still basic in the state's approach to early childhood education and care. Selectivity was further underlined by the decision not to include the private arrangements for childminding under state jurisdiction.

The two legal concepts point to some striking differences as regards the definition of the relationship between the state (local and central government) and the family, which underline state intervention in the early childhood years as sensitive and controversial. The 1969 committee was appointed by a conservative-centre coalition government, while a Labour minority government introduced the bill. Party constellations hardly explain the differences in policy approach to early childhood education and care. If anything, Labour was more in favour of collective childcare than the non-socialists. Why, then, was the committee's proposal not accepted?

As an expert body committed to the idea of making state-sponsored services for pre-school children universally available, the 1969 committee made their recommendations without making much of a concession to the political climate and which proposals stood a chance of mustering a Parliamentary majority. This was, of course, a main concern of the Labour minority government. Whether a more interventionist legislation might have gained a majority may be debated, but the recommendations of the 1969 committee were controversial. For several reasons, ideology and economy being important among them, the expansion of state intervention proposed met with opposition. The government's preoccupation was not just with the other political parties, but also with opposition from within, for example, from local branches that did not want a law that made day-care provision mandatory.

Responses to the hearing on the 1969 committee proposals offer some insight into the conflicts of interest over day-care provision. Preparing its report on day-care legislation, the Ministry of Government Administration and Consumer Affairs invited a series of the parties involved in questions concerning day care to comment on the recommendations of the committee. This invitation included all the ministries, and the Norwegian Association of Local Authorities (Kommunenes sentralforbund), which, with the consent of the Ministry, invited all the local authorities to participate. The Trade Union Congress and the National Association of Employers were represented, as were professional associations and voluntary associations involved in day-care provision, the Equal Status Council, and a number of women's organizations (Ot. prp. nr 23, 1974–5, p. 9).

Two categories of commentators are of special interest to my analysis: the providers and the consumers. On the provider side, the most important 'collective actors', that is, the local authorities, the voluntary associations and the professions, were well represented in the hearing. (The Association of Local Authorities was particularly efficient, almost half of the comments coming from local authorities.) Consumers' interests were less well represented, which is not surprising considering that they were hardly aggregated and institutionalized, and considering that the hearing system, as practised in Norway, favours organized interests.

Some of the associations invited to comment combined provider and consumer interests, for example, the National Housewives' Association. In the early 1970s the trade unions represented the interests of unionized day-care staff, but not the interests of the membership as parents and consumers of day-care services. Families with pre-school children, presumably the predominant consumer category, hardly acted collectively, if organized at all prior to the adoption of the law. Whether parents' associations were invited to comment I have not been able to ascertain; no comment from anyone in the capacity of parent is cited, however. Obviously, among those invited to participate in the hearing, the organizations representing the provider side had more political influence than those representing consumers.

The extent to which the Ministry in its report was influenced by these comments and what the relative importance of the different categories of commentators was are not my concern here. I am interested more in the views and wishes expressed by different categories of commentators, and whether these were accommodated in the Ministry's recommendation. In the following I deal only with those comments cited by the Ministry in connection with the proposal for the Day Care Act, Ot. prp. nr 23, 1974–5. I do not assume any simple 'causality' between the comments produced in the hearing and the Ministry's proposals. Rather I assume that the document presented by the Ministry is a balancing of interests in which consideration is given to providers and to consumers, and particularly to the economy and to the political aims of Labour, the party in office, tempered with the realities a minority government has to face.

The extent to which provider categories had common interests is not possible to deduce from the citations made. What is clear, however, is that some had specific interests. Local authorities commonly did not support the idea of making the provision of day care mandatory (Ot. prp. nr 23, 1974–5, p. 19). The professional pre-school teachers and their colleagues were concerned with professional quality standards for services (p. 19). The voluntary associations supported the recommendation of increased state subsidies, and so on. On the licensing of childminders, the National Association of Local Authorities, the only body quoted on the subject, was not in favour of mandatory authorization, but suggested a voluntary option (p. 25).

In the end, on the issues examined here, the Ministry's recommendations accommodated the wishes of the main providers, either as a concession to intensive lobbying, as a result of what was considered politically possible, or as an outcome of views basically shared. Debating the proposition for the Day Care Act in the Odelsting (the section of Parliament that introduces legislation), the Minister in his opening statement referred specifically to the strong opposition from the local authorities. This, he added, was not directed to day care as such, but to making provision obligatory (Ot. forh. 27. mai 1975, em. *Ot. tidende*, 1974–5, vol. VIII, pp. 548–9). With the exception of the Socialist party to the left of Labour (Sosialistisk Venstreparti), the Parliamentarians joined the Ministry's recommendations, as shown above. The Day Care Act did not make provision mandatory, and the informal childcare markets were not to be supervised or controlled.

To summarize, the 'winners' were the local authorities, the voluntary associations, the professionals, all of whom had strong interests in provision. Local autonomy was to be the dominant principle of day-care provision. Local authorities accordingly were to decide what local policy to pursue on day-care questions. The voluntary associations which had played the role of entrepreneur in the early provision of day care were guaranteed state support for running costs and cheap loans for getting established. For the pre-school teachers, the most professionalized of the occupations involved in early childhood education and care, a virtual monopoly on 'good' day care was confirmed in that state-sponsorship was to be extended only to those services that were organized and run by professionals. All other forms of day care were exempted from state intervention, approval or support.

The outcome as seen from a consumer's perspective was mixed, indeed. The ambition of policies to make state-sponsored services universally available was a concession to the families who wanted public day care. However, as demand far exceeded supply in 1975, the state offered only vague promises to the families who wanted services there and then. Parents and children demanding public day-care services did not represent well-organized interests, as noted above, and their wishes often conflicted with those of the providers to be, the local authorities, many of whom did not welcome the cost-demanding reform. Whatever the more decisive influences were that eventually shaped the final decision-making, a conspicuous aspect of national policies is the lack of compatibility with the interests, wishes and actual everyday life patterns of families with pre-school children. The political history of early childhood education and care shows state policies as ambivalent; the aims of state intervention signalled a large-scale facilitation of mothers' childcare commitments, a promise that was not translated into comprehensive programmes for the early childhood years.

The decade following the passing of the Act governing day care witnessed a significant increase in public transfers to early childhood education and care. Table 4.1 gives an overview of the number of children accommodated in state-sponsored day care from 1970 to 1990.

Compared with the 1975 status of provision, the number of places in 1990 showed a considerable increase from approximately 30,500 to 139,400 places (see table 4.1). The results are less impressive, however, when compared to the universalist ambition or to registered demand.[13] From 1945 up to the late 1990s demand has persistently exceeded supply. According to government estimates, demand in the late 1980s averaged approximately 60 per cent of children aged 0–6 years (St. meld. 8, 1987–8). The level of supply of the late 1980s, accommodating

Table 4.1 *Children in State-sponsored day care, 1970, 1975, 1980, 1985, 1990*

	Year				
Children in state-sponsored day care	1970	1975	1980	1985	1990
Number of children	12,711	30,479	78,189	98,454	139,350
Per cent of all children 0–6 years	2.8	7.0	20.9	27.5	35.9

Source 1970, 1975: SSB 1977: *Barneomsorg 1976*, NOS A 978, table 31, p. 43.
Source 1980, 1985: SSB 1987: *Barnehager og fritidshjem 1986*, NOS B 722, table 2, p. 17.
Source 1990: SSB 1991: *Statistisk ukehefte* nr 23/91, table 1, p. 1.

approximately one-third of the pre-school population, had sufficed to meet the demand level of the 1960s. By 1990 demand was still well ahead: 64 per cent of pre-school children did not have access to state-sponsored day care, 14 per cent were accommodated on a part-time basis, and only 22 per cent had full-time attendance, 30 hours or more per week (Statistisk sentralbyrå (1991), *Statistisk ukehefte* 23/91, table 6, p. 4).

The mediocre results obtained are closely linked with two of the strategies chosen for the development of day care: charging local authorities with provision, but with no obligation to offer supply to meet the demand, and restricting state sponsorship to professional services only, which meant that private childminding was largely outside state jurisdiction.

The concession to local autonomy in the 1975 legislation and the liberal 'atmosphere' of the law produced a mixture of intended and unintended consequences. The importance attributed to local decision-making in questions concerning the care of pre-school children no doubt facilitated the acceptance of state-sponsored day care by local authorities. However, as no requirement for provision was made, the legislation opened the possibility for local authorities to opt out, which is what some of them did. By the early 1980s some of the local authorities had not produced plans. A few had no state-sponsored day-care services whatsoever. Considerable shortage of supply as compared with demand was the situation presented in the reports prepared for Parliament by the Ministry (see e.g. St. meld. 93, 1980–1, and St. meld. 8, 1987–8). Basing national policies on the aggregated decisions made by more than 450 local authorities did not result in systematic progress as envisaged in the Ministry's long-term plan, which had gained the support of Parliament.

Moreover, local autonomy resulted in problems with distributive justice in the sense of providing equity of access. Access to state-sponsored day care varies across regions, between younger and older children, and the use of services differs between social classes (Leira 1987a; Gulbrandsen and Tønnessen 1988). For ideals and realities to be disparate is certainly no news in the political history of welfare state services. However, among parents, access to high-quality day-care was widely welcomed as advantageous to young children, surprisingly perhaps, considering that it was an experience unfamiliar to the great majority of the population in the mid-1970s. Furthermore, the idea of universal availability was accepted. Expectations were rising. State-sponsored day care came to be regarded as an entitlement, and consequently during the continuing shortage as an entitlement denied some children and parents because of insufficient political support. The rapid spread of the dual-earner family increased both demand and political pressure for more efficient dealing with the issue (see ch. 5). In this political context the gap between political principles instituting universality of provision as the aim and the selectivity of actual provision touches on issues of political legitimation.

In the Norwegian welfare state the use of state grants to provide personal services has gained legitimacy either by universal access to services or by a positive discrimination of groups with special needs. The actual provision of state-sponsored day care up to now does not correspond to any of these 'models'. As pointed out above, state-sponsored day care is not made available to all children. No child has an undisputed right to attend public day care. Moreover, considering the great variation in day-care supply across regions, age groups and classes, it is not at all evident that state-sponsored day care has been made available to those children and families whose needs for it are the greater.

The guiding principle of national policies for early childhood care and education which was to make services universally available contrasts with shortage of provisions and selective everyday practices. Day-care policies illustrate a general point: to achieve cost-demanding national aims by way of voluntary, local decision-making without offering strong incentives is very difficult indeed.

Fifteen years of experience with day-care legislation shows that consumers, still largely unorganized, have had an insignificant influence on provision. Central government has not so far been prepared to intervene in order to change this pattern by making day-care provision mandatory. If providers' interests won the game over day-care legislation, consumers' interests lost.

Childcare, mothers and the state

The introduction of national policies for early childhood education and care in the post-World War II period in Norway represented a change in the welfare state concept. These policies aimed at giving a new and improved content to childhood and reconstituted the state–family relationship. They also implied a new approach to the carer aspect of motherhood. Which models of motherhood did welfare state policies promote? This chapter has examined the post-war redefinition of state responsibility for early childhood education and care as manifested on two issues of central importance to motherhood and mothers: one is the definition of state responsibility as universal or selective in principle, the other is the implementation of the universal principles in practical policies, and concerns the relationship of means to ends, of demand to supply.

During the post-war decades, national policies shifted from being mainly selectively oriented to becoming mainly universal in ambition, aimed at the pre-school population at large. This change in the aims for the state-sponsoring of early childhood education and care projected new images of motherhood, that were, however, set side, even contradicted, by the measures instituted to reach the stated aims. The outcome of day-care legislation was a matching of universalist principles to selective political practices, a mix that points to conflicts of interest, as noted above. The measures adopted in childcare policies gave modest support to the universalist ambition, and did little to facilitate the new approaches to motherhood rapidly emerging in everyday life. Norwegian family patterns changed from the late 1960s as mothers took on greater responsibility for economic provision. As acknowledged in all the documents preceding legislation, the gap between demand and supply was very wide. Numerically, the children of mothers employed outside the home had furnished the most important underpinning of the estimates made concerning the future demand for day care. The needs of the dual-earner and single-provider families for extrafamilial childcare were thus accepted, but the policies adopted did not comply with their interests.

Norwegian policies dealing with the pre-school years show no real commitment to an empirically grounded image of motherhood that took into consideration the comprehensive changes in mothers' everyday lives (see ch. 5). Rather, day-care policies seem to have been modelled on the presumption of an ever-present, home-based mother, even at a time when the majority of mothers were heading for the labour market to work for pay. Ever since the passing of the Day Care Act and up to the late 1980s, the great majority of employed-mother families have been left to find private solutions to the childcare problems created by structural change.

National policies for early childhood care and education do not easily lend themselves to an interpretation indicating that the state encouraged these new approaches to motherhood. The state benevolence towards new models of motherhood, hinted at in the Labour Party programmes from the early post-war years, evaporated in practical politics, and society's collective interest in the fostering of new generations was played down. In the period 1945–75 and in the decade that followed, it was never seriously considered that the responsibility for early childhood education and care should be left to the parents alone or to the market. But to a considerable extent this was the result of the ways in which state policies were made operative.

If the 'welfare state' is characterized by the use of the public purse to defray the costs of social reproduction, the fostering, care and upbringing of young children were not the top priorities of the expanding welfare state in Norway. Among the welfare state reforms, day-care legislation was introduced late. The political history of early childhood education and care in Norway does not show a strikingly interventionist welfare state at work. Initiated in the early post-war period, thirty years elapsed before there was a real 'take-off' for day-care policies. These policies aimed high but hit low. Neither do the results of day-care policies portray a welfare state that adopts an institutional approach to provision. Pre-school education and care is far from entirely 'taken over' by the state. The shift from private to public dependence underlined in recent analyses of Scandinavian reproduction policies (Hernes 1984; Borchorst and Siim 1987) is not a striking feature of Norwegian policies concerning the early childhood years.

The universal ambition of policies for early childhood education and care projected a vision of welfare state childhood that also contained a redefinition of motherhood, a liberation from domestication and a widening of opportunities. This vision of motherhood presented in the comprehensive educational reform programme of the early post-war years was not translated into practical policies. Even the demands for labour of the post-war reconstruction period did not represent an incitement sufficient to change the family and motherhood ideals embodied in the domesticated mother and the nuclear family. When more active state policies were at last adopted, leaving day-care provision to local authorities represented no strong initiative on the part of the state to introduce new motherhood models, or to support the fast increasing employed-mother families. Evidently, money mattered in local authorities' cautious, even negative, decisions about childcare supply. However, family ideology and 'motherhood morals' cannot be overlooked, as local authorities often preferred mother-based childcare within the nuclear family to state-sponsored services.

I shall return to a discussion of the relationship between the Norwegian welfare state and mothers in chapter 5, after a more detailed examination of the policies concerning mothers who combine employment and caring commitments.

5 Mothers, markets and the state

The 'modernization' of motherhood

The generation of Norwegian women born in the first decades after World War II came to introduce new models of behaviour in almost all fields of everyday life. The most dramatic changes are seen in new approaches to motherhood. The 'modernization' of motherhood encompasses women's increased control over fertility and social reproduction; it is manifested in family and everyday life, and in economic and political participation.

Figures do not in themselves give the content and meaning or the quality of social change. Yet, excerpts from the basic statistics of 1960 and of 1990 do give an indication of some of the structural changes to which women have contributed, and which in turn present new frames for women's lives. Figure 5.1 illustrates some of the striking new trends. In Norway as elsewhere in the Western industrialized societies, women of the 1970s gained a degree of reproductive control unknown to earlier generations. The use of oral contraceptives and the right to legal abortion, on demand from 1978, gave women a control over pregnancies and births that has had far-reaching influence on adult women's lives. A greater proportion of women actually have become mothers in the 1980s than in earlier decades, but the number of children per mother is greatly reduced. Shortening the span of the child-bearing and rearing years and increasing education have facilitated women's employment.

Labour market participation obviously is more important to women of the 1980s than to their mothers. Marriage is less important as a framework for raising a family and as regards the channelling of women's labour to home or market respectively. Mothers of the 1980s depend less on husbands for economic provision and more on the state and the market than did the mothers of the 1960s. New trends in lifestyles exemplified by the dual-earner family, cohabitation without marriage and increasing divorce rates have changed the structure of everyday life and the contexts of family relations. More women are

97

Table 5.1 *Data on Norwegian women, 1960 and 1990*

	1960	1990
Total fertility rates[a]	2.88	1.9
Women's share of labour force, per cent[b]	23	45
Percentage of women among students in universities and colleges		
1965 and 1985[c]	32	50
Women among MPs, per cent[d]	8	34
Women in Cabinet[e]	1 of 13	8 of 18

[a]*Source* 1960: Moen (1981, table 3.2, p. 36); 1990: The Equal Status Council (1991).
[b]*Source* 1960: Ljones (1984, table 3, pp. 96–7); 1990: The Equal Status Council (1991).
[c]In 1965 there were altogether about 33,000 students in universities and colleges in Norway, of which approximately 10,400 were women. In 1985 the number of students was 93,600, of which 47,000 were women. (The increase is to some extent due to a change in registration, in that more schools were registered as colleges in 1985 than in 1960.) Source 1965 and 1985: Institute for Studies in Research and Higher Education, Working paper 9/87, *Students and Graduates*, table 96, 1987. Central Bureau of Statistics of Norway, *Educational Statistics*, Survey, 1 Oct. 1980.
[d]*Source* 1960: Haavio-Mannila et al. (1983, appendix 4, table 4, p. 261); 1990: The Equal Status Council (1991).
[e]*Source* 1960: Haavio-Mannila et al. (1983, appendix 5, table 1, p. 265).

active within the formal political system at all levels, as members of political parties, in municipal and county councils. Women have increased their proportion in Parliament and at Cabinet level.

The alterations are comprehensive and point to a continuous experimentation with new sets of strategies for managing everyday life, induced by necessity or choice. New practices are more visible in women's activity patterns than in men's. Still very great differences persist in women's and men's time-use, and as regards economic independence, participation in public life and in the structuring of family obligations. The model of adult equal behaviour advocated by Liljeström (1984) in which there are two parents, two economic providers, two citizens and two persons having an equal amount of leisure time still seems utopian, given the data-sets available on the time schedules and opportunity situations of Norwegian women and men (Lingsom and Ellingsæter 1983).

The changes introduced by welfare reforms and by reproduction technology, labour market developments, public policies and by women managing their everyday lives are multifaceted and complex. The effects are not unambiguous. National policies are sometimes internally inconsistent or contradictory. Changes have very different consequences for different categories of women. Labour market opportunities for some

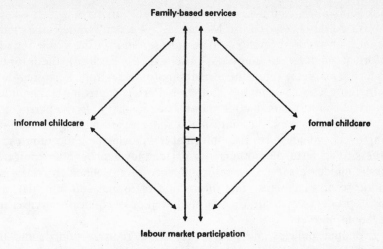

Figure 5.1 Combinations of childcare and employment in employed-
mother families

women imply greater differences between groups of women. Policies towards mothers as both earners and carers are also contradictory, promoting conflicts of interest for individual women and at an institutional level as well, between the family and the labour market.

In this chapter I shall address some conspicuous aspects of the 'modernization' process. Examining the relationship between mothers and the welfare state, I deal primarily with the changing position of women as earners and carers, as evidenced in mothers' employment and in their provisions for early childhood education and care, that is, in their relationship to production and to social reproduction. Which models of motherhood are developed in mothers' relationship to the market? What are the strategies pursued by mothers who combine earning and caring? And what is the welfare state approach to mothers as earners and carers?

Figure 5.1 illustrates the combinations of childcare and wage-work most common in employed-mother families in the post-war period in Norway. In principle, employed-mother families, whether dual- or single-earners, may combine jobs with formal childcare services, or with informally provided childcare; they may rely on family-based provisions, or on a combination of different forms of childcare. As the welfare state expanded, the triangle to the right became the main model of welfare state ideology. In everyday practice the interactions shown in the left triangle still dominate. This 'shadow' or informal counterpart to the welfare state promise is made up of the informal enterprises of mothers and minders to supplement or substitute for shortages of state-sponsored supply (see ch. 6). Mothers who take up formal employment depend on public provisions for childcare, and on the women-made, informal childcare economy. As observed above (ch. 4), the informal childcare markets protect the formal supply system from collapsing.

In those cases where the mother is herself a private childminder, informal childcare and labour markets are conflated. In the perspective of individual actors, the informal childcare arrangements of some employed women are the informal employment opportunities of others. The level of mothers' formal employment and the range of public childcare services greatly influence local demand for informal childcare arrangements. The interaction of formal and informal processes produces an institutional differentiation of childcare services and of labour markets.

Economic policies and policies for social reproduction delimit the activity arenas accessible to individual actors, but do not predetermine actors' total range of opportunities. Individual actors create new alternatives. The 'modernization of motherhood' introduced by the mothers who joined the labour market, and the flourishing informal economy in childcare going with it, are expressions of change in the labour market (economy) and also in women's reactions or responses to motherhood.

The aggregate of individual choices and enterprises concerning the combination of job and childcare commitments influence labour markets, welfare state services and everyday life. As mothers took up gainful employment, the demand for extra familial services for childcare increased. New models of motherhood were made possible by public 'take-over' of some childcare responsibilities. What is less often observed is that the formal employment of mothers has also depended upon an informal production of childcare services. An aggregation of individual activity produced structural change.

In the following section I present the changes in the earner aspects of motherhood as shown in the formal economic activity of mothers in the period 1945–85 in Norway, dealing mainly with the last twenty years of the period. Returning thereafter to the political history of early childhood education and care I examine the interplay of labour market and childcare policies: what was the welfare state response to the demand for public day care following the increase in mothers' economic activity? What was the political institutionalization of the employed-mother family? In the last sections, commenting upon the striking non-involvement of the welfare state in the childcare problems of employed mothers, I trace the development of informal childcare markets and discuss the dynamics of the woman-made informal economy developed around everyday childcare. The generation of informal markets in childcare and other forms of care shows processes different from those underlying informal markets in other fields, I argue. The importance of these markets to mothers and minders is discussed, and formal and informal labour markets are shown to be mutually dependent.

Labour market participation of women in Norway

Class differences were pronounced in women's pursuit of economic opportunities in late nineteenth- and early twentieth-century Norway. Working-class women strove for jobs and for better pay, and some supported the idea of a 'family wage', while women of the upper echelons of society fought for the right to education and to enter the professions. The right to be employed was particularly important for the women who did not marry, who were widowed or deserted. Upon marriage, however, most women who could afford to left employment. This was the common pattern from the late nineteenth century until the 1970s (Ljones 1979; 1984).

The years between the two world wars saw a drive to oust married women from employment. Unemployment was increasing. As a scarce commodity, employment had to be rationed, it was argued, and preserved for those who needed it most, the male economic providers of families. In the 1920s the fight to end married women's employment was initiated by the Oslo branch of the Labour Party and followed up by Landsorganisasjonen (The Norwegian Federation of Trade Unions). Opposition was voiced from within the party and the unions, notably by women. In 1936–7 these policies on married women's employment were withdrawn, but reintroduced by the Trades Union Congress in 1940 (Lønnå 1977). As only 2–3 per cent of the married women were employed in the inter-war years (Ljones 1979), the number of women who lost their jobs was not dramatic. Only a few men actually gained jobs from this decision. The symbolic effect, however, was considerable.

The grave social problems constituted by male unemployment were not solved, but absorbed in the war-time economy of the early 1940s. Unlike what happened during World War II in the US and the UK, there was no mass mobilization of women to the labour market in Norway during the 1940–5 war years. Not until the expansion of the welfare state in the 1960s was underemployment and unemployment of Norwegian women significantly diminished.

Welfare state policies affected the carer aspects of motherhood (as shown in ch. 4), and also the earner aspects. In principle, there were two ways in which the state could act to influence mothers' economic provision: either through economic transfers or by expanding the job opportunities for women, for example, by stimulating the public sector labour market. Lov om barnetrygd (the Child Benefit Act) from 1946 illustrates the first approach, as do the specific transfers established by law in 1964 (Lov om enkje- og morstrygd, later incorporated in the National Insurance Scheme) aimed at widows and unmarried mothers.

Direct large-scale intervention in the market to secure jobs for women was not considered. However, the modernization of motherhood, the process demonstrated by the number of women who left full-time house-wifery to join the formal labour market, was encouraged indirectly by the national economic policy in general, and by the expansion of the range and scope of welfare state benefits and services in particular.

Child benefits were introduced in 1946 to help cover the costs of children's upbringing and were made payable directly to the mothers. They have never been of an amount that matched the income gained from paid work. A 1985 allowance did not pay for a full-time place in state-sponsored day care. Child benefits represented a recompense for mothers' work of great symbolic significance, but of minor importance as a contribution to their economic-provider capacity.

Norway is the only Scandinavian country which has instituted a special entitlement for single providers. Paying benefits to single parents, of whom approximately 90 per cent are women, to help them stay with their children as long as the children are very young does perhaps represent more of a 'cash for care' approach. Through the National Insurance Scheme, the state compensates for the lack of a husband/father as economic provider, and as such replaces income from market-based employment (Lov om folketrygd of 1966, ch. 12). This allowance has made it possible for unsupported unmarried, widowed or divorced women to have a small income of their own, which may be one reason why very few babies born to Norwegian single mothers are given up for adoption. As the transfer payment is modest, the feminization of poverty in Norway is witnessed among single mothers who depend on this benefit as their main income. The benefit acknowledges the carer aspects of motherhood, but does not encourage mothers to combine childcare and employment. If mothers receiving benefit report more than a minimum income, the benefit is reduced or lost (P. Knudsen 1988).

To the majority of mothers, whether married or single, the state transfers have not been important in enhancing their income-generating capacity. When it comes to emphasizing the economic-provider aspects of motherhood, the expansion of job opportunities in both the public and private sectors of the labour market has been of far greater significance. This development accelerated in the 1960s.

The early post-war years, the period from 1945 to 1960, has been called the prime time of the conventional nuclear family in Norway (Skrede 1984a). Access to the labour market was strongly gender-divided, as was the occupational choice and the payment offered. Upon marriage, women commonly quit paid work, or stayed on until the first child was born, when they left for a prolonged period or for good. Some form of income-generating work, outwork, seasonal work or informal work in family business or on family farms was, however, common among married women in many districts. Only very few mothers in the late 1940s and 1950s held a 'normal' work contract representing forty-eight hours of work outside the home per week.

Among the married mothers of young children those most likely to hold jobs outside the home were the ones at the top and at the bottom of the educational ladder: the professional women, of whom there were few in 1945–60, and the women whose education had ended after seven years of elementary schooling. The census from 1950 reports that a total of 5.4 per cent of the married women aged 15 years and over were in paid employment. Ten years later the 1960 census registered 9.5 per cent of married women as employed. Single mothers were much more likely than married mothers to be wage-earners. According to the 1960 census, only 5 per cent of married mothers with children under school age were gainfully employed, as compared with 60 per cent of those previously married, and 69 per cent of the unmarried ones (Selid 1968, p. 51).

In Norwegian society and in the government administration as well, ideological barriers against encouraging married women's employment seem strong. The number of women actually engaged in paid employment decreased in the 1950s (Bull 1979). Commenting upon the history of the post-war years, Bull (1979) observes that economic necessity did not any longer mobilize women to labour force participation, as the families in the 1950s could afford to have one economic provider only. Traditional family values embracing the home-based mother/housewife flourished. Moreover, Bull also mentions the considerable practical difficulties mothers had to handle if they wanted to take up paid employment, in particular the lack of day-care services and a negligible supply of part-time jobs.

However, the lack of interest is puzzling since labour shortage was regarded as an impediment to war-time recovery. A foreign expert assessing the results of the reconstruction programme found the neglect of the labour reserves among married women surprising. He observed, too, that neither day care nor part-time jobs were offered to facilitate women's labour market participation (L. R. Klein 1948, quoted in Tornes 1986, p. 14). In Norway, the wish to preserve the domesticated-mother family apparently was stronger than were the demands of the economy.

Examining the labour market and employment policies of the post-war period, Tornes (1986) calls attention to this discrepancy between the economy's demand for labour on the one hand, and the lack of interest in the labour reserves among married women on the other. In economic planning, married women's domesticity was apparently taken for granted. No concerted action was taken to encourage or facilitate their employment, a fact which Tornes regards as an expression of the 'housewife ideology' of the 1950s and 1960s (1986, pp. 14–15).

The impact of an ideology that favoured the home-based mother is reflected also in the tax policies of the period, giving special concessions to the families that conformed with the gender-differentiated family model. Not until 1959 were tax laws changed to allow for separate taxation of spouses. (Skrede 1984a).

According to the 1950 and 1960 censuses, the families with young children, like the rest of the families, display a strikingly conventional gendered division of labour. Father is the breadwinner and economic provider. Mother is the home-maker, responsible for household main-tenance, housework, caring and upbringing. However, also within this overall setting, it is important not to neglect the economic contributions of women's paid and unpaid labour to the family's subsistence and level of living. To a considerable extent the economic impact of women's work is a function of the structure of local economies; the importance is more pronounced, for example, in rural economies dominated by small, labour-intensive farms. Women's work is, of course, crucial in local economies dependent upon a combination of trades, such as fishing and farming or lumbering and farming, which demand the men's prolonged absence from home. Women's work was also essential in the families of men serving in the merchant fleet. Within other economies, too, the contribution of women's work in production and processing of food, and of clothes for consumption in the household, for exchange or sale, is also considerable, as are a competent woman's skills in budgeting and household management.

The division of labour associated with the isolated nuclear-family concept (Parsons 1955; Holter et al. 1975) easily minimizes or mytholo-gizes the everyday life of a considerable proportion of Norwegian families in the early post-World War II period. Feminist research from the 1970s indicates an under-registration of women's paid work in the censuses (see Hagen and Skrede 1976), and emphasizes that women's income-generating activity was more extensive than demonstrated by

Table 5.2 *Women's labour force participation rate, 1973 and 1988, Denmark, Norway, Sweden, United Kingdom*

(percentages)

	1973	1988	increase
Denmark	61.9	78.3	+ 16.4
Norway	50.6	72.8	+ 22.2
Sweden	62.6	80.1	+ 17.5
UK	53.2	63.5	+ 10.3

Source: OECD *Employment Outlook*, July 1990, table G.

Table 5.3 *Part-time employment in 1986. Denmark, Norway, Sweden, United Kingdom*

	Total employment	As a proportion of: Male employment	Female employment	Women's share in p/t
Denmark[a]	23.8	8.4	43.9	80.9
Norway	28.1	10.3	51.3	79.2
Sweden	23.5	6.0	42.8	86.6
UK[a]	21.2	4.2	44.9	88.5

[a]Data refer to 1985.

Source: OECD *Employment Outlook*, September 1987, p. 29.

the censuses. Thus the general division of labour by gender is not disputed, but qualified in important respects. More generally, I shall maintain that the form and content of the gender division of labour within the nuclear family differs across social class and across local economies and that the economic importance of women's work to the family economy is a question for empirical validation.

Throughout the 1970s and early 1980s there was a net increase in employment in Norway, constituted primarily of women, many of whom worked part-time (see tables 5.2 and 5.3). Men's participation rates have not been much changed during this period; thus women's share of the labour force has grown, reaching 45 per cent in 1990, compared with 29 per cent in 1972. The increase in the labour force mainly means that paid labour is distributed among more persons. Because of reductions in working hours and expansion of part-time work, the annual number of hours worked has not increased much in the period (see Strømsheim 1983 for a discussion of the work-force expan-

Table 5.4 *Unemployment rates by sex, 1975, 1983, 1985. Denmark, Norway, Sweden, United Kingdom*

(percentages)

	Women			Men		
	1975	1983	1985	1975	1983	1985
Denmark	5.1	12.3	8.9	4.7	10.7	5.9
Norway	2.9	3.8	3.1	1.9	2.9	2.1
Sweden	2.1	3.5	2.9	1.3	3.4	2.8
UK	1.4	8.0	8.8	4.3	13.3	13.4

Source: OECD *Employment Outlook*, September 1987, table L.

sion and working hours stagnation). Women's share of unemployment has also increased. In the period 1975–85 the proportion of unemployed women surpasses that of men, but has not reached 4 per cent of the female work-force (table 5.4).

Increasing their economic activity, women became somewhat more equal to men as far as income-generating work was concerned. In this respect gender roles became more symmetrical. However, women's labour market participation differs distinctly from that of men. Occupational segregation, reduced working hours and a certain amount of discrimination in pay mean that few women earn a 'family wage' sufficient to support themselves and their children. As measured by type of job, hours in paid work and rate of pay, the typical male worker is still the 'model worker', on whose form of labour market participation such concerns as work contracts and employment related benefits are moulded.

Horizontal and vertical labour market segregation by gender is more pronounced in Norway than in the majority of the OECD countries (OECD 1975; 1985; Skrede 1984b; 1986) and may well have contributed to keeping women's wages down. However, identifying certain expanding branches and occupations as 'typically female' has also preserved entrance to the labour market for a considerable number of women. The persistent segregation of jobs by gender, I hypothesize, may even have modified opposition and outright resistance to women's formal employment, as it is clearly evident that women up to now have not seriously challenged 'male preserves' and men's dominant position in the labour market.

Neither the Norwegian Equal Pay Council from 1959 nor the Equal Status Act of 1978 which advocates the principle of equal pay for equal work have eradicated sex discrimination in pay (Rødseth and Titlestad 1984). In some branches the differences in hourly wage between women and men holding similar jobs have actually increased in recent years. (*Dagens Næringsliv* 1988). The most important factors in determining women's average level of earnings are part-time and generally low-paid jobs. Part-time work is the only offer in several fields, others have to offer part-time work in order to attract qualified staff. In 1986 women constituted 80 per cent of the part-time workers in Norway (see table 5.3). Part-time employment is of very different significance in women's and men's job lives. Among women in the labour force, part-time work is a primary feature, whereas men who work part-time represent a minority of the male work-force. Working part-time in paid work is generally considered to be a consequence of women's greater share of unpaid, domestic work. Survey data indicate that for a considerable proportion of the labour force actual working hours do not coincide with personal preferences (Ellingsæter 1987).

Gender inequalities become even more evident when waged and unwaged work are considered together, as was done in the Norwegian time budget analyses from 1970–1 and 1980–1. On average, women work as many hours per day as men do, but women get paid for a smaller proportion of their work (Lingsom and Ellingsæter 1983). Nevertheless, it is significant that women's economic dependence on individual men has been reduced. The long-term implications of this, for example for the division of resources and the power structure in households, remain to be seen.

Women's attitudes toward the combination of wage-work and motherhood were also in the process of transformation. Answering survey questions in the 1960s and 1970s women voiced the opinion that they wanted to work for pay. A desire to earn money of one's own and a need to escape from the isolation of a life at home were the reasons most commonly given by those who wanted a change (SSB 1969). Though the women's response hardly carried the force of Ibsen's Nora Helmer of *A Doll's House* almost a hundred years earlier (which the precoded questionnaire did not allow for anyway), indirectly their answers illuminated the sadder aspects of 'situation housewife'. Public debate was divided on the issue of mothers in employment, but in the early 1970s it was not at all unusual to encounter the opinion that a mother's place was in the home.

Questions concerning mothers in employment were also raised in social research. In the influential analysis *Women's Two Roles: Work and Home*, Myrdal and Klein (1957) outlined the emerging structures in the labour market participation of women, and strongly supported the opportunity for married women to join formal employment, notably in the phases of life when mothering and nurturing obligations were less demanding. The title of the book indicated, however, that the authors accepted a split in women's roles, as distinct from those of men, and an imbalance in parental obligations to offspring. This view, though widespread, was not unanimously accepted at the time.

The Scandinavian debate of the 1960s in many respects anticipated the debates on domestic labour and gender inequality that gained wider audiences in the 1970s. The assumption that biological motherhood was necessarily tied to the menial tasks of housework was contested. The additional responsibility for children's welfare implicitly allocated to women was also questioned, and it was argued that caring for children was a moral challenge for all human beings, and a human activity not by necessity linked with women's capacity for procreation (Dahlström et al. 1962; Grønseth 1966; see also Holter 1970). During the last ten to fifteen years opposition to the employment of married women has declined, influenced by the reality of women's economic activity, by the activities of the Women's Liberation Movement, and by government policies promoting equal status between women and men.[1] As noted above, the persistent segregation in jobs may also have contributed to the modification of general attitudes, as it became clearly evident that women were not going to 'invade' men's positions in the labour market.

The most striking feature of the Norwegian labour market of the 1970s was the rapid recruitment of married women and even of mothers of very young children to formal employment. To a considerable extent, underemployment and unemployment among women was being absorbed. Hence the 'pool' of labour reserves available for unpaid and/or informal caring decreased. The effect of this migration of married women and of mothers of young children has been described as a 'revolution' of labour market structure (Ellingsæter and Iversen 1984; Hernes 1984; Skrede and Tornes 1986).

For mothers to remain in employment while their children were below statutory school age (which is seven years in Norway) was unexpected and most unusual in the 1950s and 1960s. By 1980 this was what most mothers did, mainly on a part-time basis (table 5.5), following patterns established earlier by women in the neighbouring countries. Mothers of young children were the fastest-rising group in the labour market. From 1976 to 1990 the participation rates of mothers of children under three years rose from 40 per cent to 69 per cent, while those of mothers whose youngest child was aged 3–6 years increased from 48 per cent to 74 per cent. The majority of these mothers worked part-time. The extent to which mothers of pre-school children would opt

Table 5.5 *Married mothers in employment by age of youngest child, 1976, 1980, 1985, 1990* (per cent)

Year	All married women with children	Age of the youngest child			
		0–2	3–6	7–10	11–15
1976	53	40	48	64	67
1980	62	48	58	71	75
1985	71	55	70	75	81
1990	77	69	74	82	86

Source: Ellingsæter 1987 (in which the registration practices used in the national labour market surveys concerning mothers' employment are appraised).
Source 1990: the Equal Status Council 1991.

for full-time employment if such jobs and full-time childcare provisions were available locally is not known. However, in recent years an increasing proportion of mothers with pre-school children work full-time and they make up approximately 40 per cent of the mothers in employment in 1987 (Ellingsæter 1987, table 6, p. 58).

The labour market participation of mothers in this period varies not only in accordance with the age of the youngest child, but also in accordance with the number of children, and years of schooling of the mother. Having the second child is what affects women's activity rates most strongly. The difference between mothers having two, three or four children or more is not as significant as that between mothers with one child and those with two or more children (Ellingsæter and Iversen 1984). The more years of education mothers have, the more economically active they are likely to be. Throughout the post-war years mothers' employment opportunities have also differed across local labour markets.

The cause of the new trends in women's economic activity from the 1960s onwards has been much debated (for a review of the Scandinavian discussion see Anttalainen 1984). An important factor in Norway was a restructuring of the demand for labour, and a tightening labour market with a corresponding need to mobilize labour reserves. From the late 1960s, the expanding welfare state increasing the supply of health, education and social services made a great impact on women's job opportunities by creating jobs in local labour markets and in fields traditionally regarded as typically women's work. Employment policies were not explicitly aimed at mobilizing married women or mothers to formal economic activity. Married women were recruited mainly because they represented the only labour reserve segment of any significance. To invite large-scale immigration in order to recruit labour, the only alternative, was not seriously considered. Though hardly a prime objective of welfare state policies, the economic-provider part of mothering changed and took on new forms. Increasingly, the content of 'motherhood' was expanded to include not only childcare, domestic work, household production and management, but also commitment to job obligations.

The influx of mothers to the labour market has profoundly changed the structure of Norwegian families, and has considerably transformed the labour force. Two out of three families with children of pre-school age are dual-earner families. One-third of the labour force is made up of parents of children aged 0–10 years (Leira 1983). Commitments to care and to material provision are basic elements in parenthood. During recent decades Norwegian society has witnessed a new approach to the gendering of parenting. The changing gender differentiation is largely brought out, as I have shown above, in mothers' practices. Norwegian mothers of the 1980s combine earning and caring commitments, child-care and employment, to an extent hitherto unwitnessed.

Welfare state, working mothers and childcare

The economic policies of the 1960s and 1970s, and particularly the expansion of welfare state services, more or less intentionally mobilized mothers to labour market participation. But what was the welfare state approach to the childcare commitments of the mothers who expanded their earning activities? Gradually, the Norwegian welfare state had influenced family forms, the structure of the mother-child relationship and the content of motherhood by a series of welfare state measures adopted to this end, but also by its non-intervention or modest involvement, for example in the development of childcare facilities for employed mothers.

Contradictions in welfare state motherhood policies are displayed in the ways in which the state affected mothers' economic situations and their childcare arrangements. In this section I shall turn to the political history and examine in greater detail the welfare state planning for and response to the changing models of motherhood. My 'case study' focuses on mothers who combine earning and caring commitments and the political institutionalization of the concept of the employed mother in national policies concerning early childhood education and care.

Toward the end of the 1950s, prior to any significant change in the employment rates of married women, the political debate in Norway anticipated an increase in women's formal economic activity. The labour market participation of mothers of young children was also expected to rise. The government-appointed committee from 1959 (the Lyseth committee) which reviewed the provision of day care for pre-school children devoted considerable attention to the problems employed mothers faced when combining employment and care, and strongly recommended that local and central authorities intensified the support of day-care provision, *inter alia* to facilitate the employment of mothers (see ch. 4). Managing the childcare of employed-mother families was obviously regarded as the women's or the mothers' concern. The change envisaged in women's economic activity was not expected to introduce changes in fathers' earning and caring commitments. This perspective probably reflects the dominant philosophy of the time, in which gender equality was conceived as necessitating a change in women's behaviour only: women were to act more like the men.

Participation rates of mothers of pre-school children were actually very low in the 1950s. Calling attention to the increase in women's economic activity in other countries in Western Europe, the Lyseth committee, however, anticipated that this situation would soon be altered. Among the factors assumed to promote the economic activity of mothers, they mentioned a proposed reduction of weekly working hours, changes in taxation that were to reduce the tax burden of dual-earner families, a diminishing male/female wage differential and an increase in the number of well-educated women. As domestic work was rationalized, taking up waged work would be easier for women. Moreover, extrafamilial provision for day care was more important than before because the character of women's paid work had changed. Mothers employed in industry, in commerce, in transportation or as professionals could not be expected to combine employment and childcare as women working on farms and as domestic servants had often done (Innstilling fra komitéen til å utrede visse spørsmål om daginstitusjoner m.v. for barn, 1962, pp. 23–4 and pp. 34–5).

In its report on childcare policies presented to Parliament in 1962, which discussed the arguments of the Lyseth committee (St. meld. 89, 1961–2), the Ministry of Government Administration and Consumer Affairs addressed the expected increase in the employment of mothers. Married women's employment outside the home is a general feature of modern societies, the Ministry observed, and continued: 'The development that has taken place in society as regards women's position and the family's structure and way of living has created a special need for day-care institutions with long opening hours, i.e. day-care centres and crèches that are able to take care of the children of married, employed mothers. Therefore emphasis is on providing conditions that will, to a greater extent than before, enable married women with children to choose whether or not they wish gainful employment outside the home' (St. meld. 89, 1961–2, p. 9, my transl). Evidently, the Ministry, like the Lyseth committee, regarded childcare services as useful to employed mothers (notably the married ones, see quotation above). Childcare does not appear to be an interest essential to the fathers, or important to their employment status.

Thus, the employed-mother family's need for childcare services was clearly recognized. The Ministry presented an estimate of the need for day care in which the children of mothers employed outside the home constituted the largest single category of the 'need-base'. However, a sharp distinction was drawn between which forms of need were to be supported by state subsidies and which excluded. Giving priority to children who were physically or mentally handicapped and to children of single providers, the Ministry did not propose to include the children of employed married mothers among the prioritized categories for whom public day care was to be provided (St. meld. 89, 1961–2, p. 16). Parliament did not object to the priority recommended by the Ministry (Innst. S. nr 11, 1962–3). Hence the demands of employed mothers for childcare relief was to be solved outside state-sponsored schemes.

The remaining years of the 1960s marked a period of moderate progress in the provision of state-sponsored day care (see ch. 4). Less than 3 per cent of the pre-school children had access to public day care in 1970 (see table 4.1). The labour market participation rates of mothers were rapidly increasing, however. Thus the gap between demand and supply of public day care was considerable when in 1969 the centre/ conservative coalition government appointed a new committee to review state involvement in early childhood education and care. (For an analysis of the recommendations of this committee on questions of principle concerning the modes and scope of state intervention, see ch. 4). In this section I examine only the considerations and recommendations concerning the need to provide day care for children of employed mothers. Fragments of the social and political issues of the period give a tinge of the context in which the committee framed its report.

Labour market developments in the late 1960s contributed to a growing interest in and concern with the status of day-care provision. The Norwegian labour market was tight. Married women constituted the only domestic labour reserve, as I have argued above. Labour market policies, for example as outlined in government reports to Parliament,[2] presumed a mobilization of these reserves. A survey conducted in 1968 indicated a willingness among the reserves to head for gainful employment, although a considerable proportion of mothers with young children reported that lack of childcare facilities represented a hindrance in this respect (SSB 1969). Questions concerning equal status between women and men were considered as political issues in the early 1970s to an extent not witnessed before, and legislation was forwarded to promote gender equality as noted above. An increasing proportion of families with pre-school children were dual-earner families. In 1972, when the Day Care Committee published its final report, 28 per cent of the mothers of under threes and 40 per cent of the mothers whose youngest child was aged 3–6 years were in employment. It needed no stretch of the imagination to predict that the majority of families with pre-school children was soon to consist of employed-mother families.

In its report the Day Care Committee underlined the growth in women's employment from 1960 to 1970, and observed that the increase in the labour market participation of women was three times that of men. Furthermore, it stated: 'a decrease in the number of children per family, labour-saving devices in the household and better education among women contribute to processes of change in the ways in which women's role is regarded. A greater number of the younger and better-educated women demand [the right] to be both employed *and* a parent' (NOU 1972:39, p. 49, committee emphasis, my transl.). The committee noted that the demand for employment and parental com-mitment to be made compatible was voiced primarily as 'a demand that society makes high-quality opportunities for development available for children during the periods in which the parents cannot themselves provide the care'. (p. 48, my transl.).

Emphasizing the benefits of high-quality, state-sponsored day care for children the report, in addition, saw day care as facilitating mothers' employment, supporting family economy and as promoting gender equality. The demands of production for labour were not equally underlined. However, when the committee assessed the need for day-care supply, children of employed parents were by far the largest category.

In 1975 the Ministry of Government Administration and Consumer Affairs presented Parliament with its recommendations for state inter-vention in early childhood education and care and a proposition for a special Act to govern questions concerning the provision of day care. On central issues (as noted above, ch. 4) the Ministry disagreed with the recommendations made by the Day Care Committee, but conceded that improved access to day care was a prerequisite for the increased labour market participation of married mothers (Ot. prp. nr 23, 1974–5, p. 13). The report underlined the origins of modern day care in the traditions of the early children's asylums, established to care for the children of working-class mothers who had to earn their living, and in the Fröbel kindergartens, which represented an educational approach rooted in pedagogy and developmental psychology. Modern day care, the Ministry stated, was to integrate and to perpetuate both traditions. However, as this dual aim (that is, to provide both education and care) might contain a clash of interests, clarification of the aims of day-care policies was necessary. 'The focus', according to the Ministry, 'is to be the child and the needs of the child, so that when the needs of the child clash with other societal needs, consideration for [the needs of] the child must be decisive' (Ot. prp. nr 23, 1974–5, p. 13, my transl.). More specifically, the Ministry mentioned opening hours, localization and quality standards as potential areas of conflict of interest between the parents' demands for care and what was conceived as the best interests of the child.

The Ministry came out very strongly in defence of day care as a child-oriented device, almost to the virtual exclusion of other interests. State-sponsored day care was not to be subsumed under the political aims of other Ministries or of interest groups, such as employed parents, or of the labour market's need for labour. Acknowledging that conflicts of interest may exist between the aims of day-care policy (as defined by the Ministry) and labour market policies, the Ministry stated that solutions had to be found by means other than by adjusting day-care policies (p. 13).

As a potential area of conflict, day-care opening hours were given special attention. According to the Ministry, considering what was in the child's best interests, opening hours ought not to be expanded to cover more than the nine to ten hours per day that was common (in those few institutions that were open full-time – my addition). Conflicts between what was considered best for the child as regards hours of day-care attendance and the actual working hours of parents had to be resolved by means other than by expanding the opening hours. The Ministry advocated reduced working hours for parents, flexible working hours and/or a general reduction of working hours (p. 13).

Puzzling, however, in this analysis, is the basic but unstated premise that what is best for the child can be determined without the situation of child and parents being considered together. Moreover, what is 'best' for the child is discussed without situating the child in a specific family context, for example that of the rapidly increasing dual-earner family. In terms of real-life choices parents had the following options if parents' working hours exceeded day-care opening hours: to arrange for private childminding to supplement the public day-care services; to leave the child without an organized caring scheme; or for parents to reduce working hours. Some parents, but not all, were free to choose whether to be in employment or not, or, when in employment, to decide upon the number of hours to work. The solution offered by the Ministry to the problem posed when parents' working hours and day-care opening hours did not coincide was to propose a restructuring of labour market agreements, mainly outside the influence of individual parents and of the Ministry, as well. Defining standards for opening hours according to the best interests of the child, but with no regard for the child's total situation does not indicate that the Ministry was particularly concerned with the changes in family patterns or with the lot of employed mothers and their children.

Employed parents were important, however, when it came to providing empirical foundations for estimates of the need for day care. The report presaging the Day Care Act gave an assessment of needs based upon the number of 'parents who are in a life situation or wish to be in such a situation that necessitates collective day care' (p. 17, my transl.). Among the family forms considered, the dual-earner family was by far the most numerous. As a moderate estimate, the Ministry assumed that in the early 1970s there were about 85,000 children under school age (close to 20 per cent of children aged 0–6 years) whose parents were both in employment. Of these children 65,000 belonged to families in which both parents had a wage-working week of twenty hours or more. Extrafamilial day care was needed for approximately 5,000 pre-school children whose mothers were in an educational programme, and for at least 10,000 children from single-parent families (p. 17).

Only a tiny minority of these children were accommodated in state-sponsored day care at the time. Altogether 12,700 children aged 0–6 years, i.e. 2.8 per cent of all children in the age bracket, were admitted to public day care, full-time or part-time. Approximately 2,500 children from single-parent families were actually accommodated, while places as noted above were needed for 10,000. Around 5,000 children from dual-earner families had access to public day-care. Accommodation was needed for at least 65,000.

The Ministry estimated that the difference between demand and supply represented 66,000 places, and in addition that another 15,000 places with shorter opening hours were needed. Furthermore, the Ministry referred to social surveys in which it was reported that a considerable number of parents (these were most likely mothers) wanted employment, provided that childcare could be satisfactorily arranged.

The need for labour presented by other Ministries in previous reports to Parliament was also considered. In a 1974 report on the budding petroleum industry the Labour government had stated its aim as the increasing of employment by 0.8 per cent per year until 1980 (St. meld. 25, 1974–5). To achieve this growth the labour reserves among married women had to be activated. Having outlined this general background, the Ministry of Government Administration and Consumer Affairs assumed that the increase in employment necessitated an increased supply of day care, and recommended that 100,000 places be made available by the end of 1981 (Ot. prp. nr 23, 1974–5, p. 18). The proposed expansion was largely founded on the number of children living in employed-mother families. However, as shown in chapter 4, the measures approved in the promotion of state-sponsored day care were too meagre to produce the number of places aimed for. What forms of day care to be provided and for whom was made discretionary for local authorities. Central control was insignificant. The estimate of needs was thus not transformed into obligatory national policy.

There is a striking contradiction or an ambivalence in the Ministry's approach to the employed-mother family's obvious childcare problems. On the one hand, these families demonstrably need extraparental childcare. Accordingly the Ministry presents a quantification of places needed if the children from these families are to be accommodated by public services. On the other hand, this acknowledged need (or demand) is to be met only in so far as the local authorities wish it. As shown in chapter 4, local authorities argued strongly against making day-care provision mandatory. A concern with costs was pronounced. A concern with undermining the family's responsibility for its offspring could also be discerned. The Ministry's stand on mandatory provision and on licensing of childminders, which was to recommend neither, does not indicate any strong support of the dual-earner family, or of the employed mother, whether single or married. In short, the Ministry saw no need to co-ordinate day-care policy with the situation of the family nor with labour market policy. Neither the demands of production for labour nor the needs of the employed parents for childcare were to be dominant influences in public day-care provision. The Ministry focused on the needs of the child in the abstract, without considering the emergence of new family forms.

In the parliamentary committee's written statement concerning the proposition for the Day Care Act, they agreed that satisfactory child-care was a precondition for the employment of mothers and fathers in two-parent families, and of single parents (Innst. O. nr. 69, 1974–5, p. 3). However, the committee was not prepared to make large-scale efforts to improve the situation of dual- and single-earner families. As for the conflict between day-care opening hours and parents' working hours, the committee was not inclined to expand opening hours because it was not in the best interests of the child (p. 4). The parties to the left wanted the Ministry to hasten the preparation of work-hours reform, and saw the need for reduced hours for parents. The parties to the right and centre expressed a clear preference for part-time day care, and advocated caution in the use of full-time services (p. 4).

Employed parents' interests, needs, or demands for services were of minor concern. Nor was the economy's demand for labour mentioned. Unlike the 1969 Day Care Committee, the parliamentarians did not argue in favour of day care as a means of promoting gender equality. A minority statement from the centre and conservative parties defended the traditional family form, arguing that families ought to have more freedom of choice; families should not for economic reasons be forced to have two earners (p. 3).

Conflicting views on which family and motherhood models to support came up when the proposition was later debated in the Odelsting (the section of Parliament where legislation is introduced). The Labour Minister in charge of questions concerning day care addressed the conflict between working hours and day-care opening hours, and the minority's fear that the demands of the labour market would cause the welfare of children to suffer. It was important, he said, that working conditions were adjusted to the needs of families with young children, and the Ministry was at work on the issue (Ot. forh. 27. mai 1975, em. *Ot. tidende*, 1974–5, vol. VIII, p. 548).

The ethical foundation of day care was a main concern in the debate. Ideologically the basic question was whether state-sponsored day care was to have a mandatory Protestant-Lutheran value basis, as this was the religion of the state Church, which is what the bourgeois parties favoured and the socialists did not. Family ideology also played a part. The socialist parties, notably the Sosialistisk Venstreparti, to the left of Labour, advocated state-sponsored childcare not only as good for children, but also as a means of facilitating parents' and mothers' employment. It was due time to relieve women of the 'serfdom' of domestic labour (MP Henriksen, Ot. forh. 27 mai 1975, p. 540). Commenting on opening hours, MP Kvanmo, also from the Sosialistisk Venstreparti, pointed out that work-hour reforms had not yet been instituted. They might help mothers of the future, but were of no use to working mothers here and now. She also underlined the class aspects inherent in the questions concerning day-care opening hours. Working-class women did not have the same working hours as the women of the middle class. If day-care policies did not face up to the facts, day-care centres would remain institutions for the middle class (p. 561).

The bourgeois parties, on the other hand, favoured a traditional family form, and argued for parents' freedom to choose whether to work outside the home or not. A member of Høyre (the Conservative Party) reacted negatively to the government's prognosis concerning the economy's demand for labour. He did not object to married women's employment, he said, but considered that the demand for labour had to come second to the needs of the child (MP Andersen, p. 529). This view was echoed in the arguments of other bourgeois MPs.

A member from Senterpartiet, one of the centre parties, advocated the introduction of wages for caring, 'omsorgslønn', in order to equalize the situation of single- and dual-income families, and to give families greater choice with respect to having one parent at home or paying others for childcare (MP Sælthun, p. 533).[3] Although phrased in gender-neutral language, the proposal does not escape the impression that the traditional gender-differentiated family was at issue.

The ambivalence and opposition to employed mothers expressed in the debate is perhaps not surprising when considering the challenge they represented to the traditional family patterns and values and to the traditional gendered division of labour. For some of the parliamentarians, to preserve the traditional family was more important than addressing the very real childcare problems of a growing number of families with children of pre-school age. The legislation instituted did not contest this view. Neither the Day Care Act of 1975 nor later amendments give special concessions to employed-mother families. Mothers' labour was collectivized to an extent not matched by collective childcare services. Employment policies and childcare policies, the policies of production and those of social reproduction, were not synchronized.

The emergence of the modern dual-earner family in Norway did not presuppose a public supply of day care. Large-scale public day care was introduced too late, and expanded too slowly to be of any great importance in furthering the development of the dual-earner family in the 1970s. This lack of co-ordination between the two processes, the collectivization of childcare and the modernization of motherhood represented by the mothers who took up formal employment, is not always acknowledged. In the Norwegian debate the assumption is often made that the development of state-sponsored collective childcare has represented a precondition for the increasing labour market participation of mothers of pre-school children. In some of the largest cities this may have been the case, particularly in Oslo, where local authorities supported the provision of collective day care from early on. The assumption is not validated, however, if comparisons are made on a nation-wide basis, contrasting the employment rates of mothers with the provision of state-sponsored day care. When national policies for early childhood education and care were implemented, the facilitation of the earner capacity of mothers was not a major concern.

Labour market policies of the 1970s planned for a mobilization of the labour reserves represented by the mothers of young children, but did not incorporate the caring commitments of this labour into its overall scheme. The increased importance of the economic-provider aspects of mothers' parental obligations did not much influence the policies concerning early childhood education and care. Day-care policies proved singularly inefficient when it came to meeting the demand of the most rapidly increasing family form, the employed-mother family (see also ch. 4). To provide care and socialization for children under school age remained a responsibility of the family, for the most part of the mothers, even in the families where both parents were in full-time employment.

From the 1970s Norwegian legislation affecting work environment and worker protection increasingly acknowledged the status of the 'worker-parent', and has made some concessions to the dual commitments of this category of workers. Basically, the questions concerning conflicts of priority of either employment or childcare commitments may be approached in two ways: either by modifying the market's demand for the worker's time, or by producing extrafamilial childcare services. The Norwegian Work Environment Act has adopted the former approach and addresses the caring commitments of employed parents as questions concerning presence of workers at the workplace (see ch. 3). The law deals with daily working hours and with entitlement to leave of absence in specific situations.

According to the Work Environment Act, employed parents are entitled to leave of absence, retaining job security, following the birth of a child. Maternity leave is given with wage compensation, paternity leave is unpaid. When breast-feeding, mothers are entitled to daily pauses, or reduction of working hours. Employed mothers and fathers have the right to leave of absence when the child or the childminder is ill (for details, see ch. 3). Moreover, employed parents are entitled to reduced daily hours when the child is under school age, retaining job security, but without wage compensation, provided that the arrangement does not cause considerable inconvenience to the employer.[4]

These entitlements provide interesting evidence of something rarely seen in Norwegian society, that the demands of social reproduction are given priority when they conflict with the demands of production. The legislation signals that labour market organization has to make some accommodation for the reproduction of generations. However, in sum, the reforms appear to be piecemeal, and modest, as the intervention of the state was restricted to needs for care stemming from relatively rare events in the employed parents' lives. To include the requirement of everyday childcare under this legislation has not been considered appropriate, and the everyday need of employed parents of pre-school children for adequate childcare has not been met.

The development of the modern dual-earner family in which both parents go out to work outside the home when the children are very young represents a relatively new feature in the post-World War II period in Norwegian society. Up to the mid-1980s this development has for the most part implied alterations in women's behaviour, because the co-ordination of job and childcare commitments is commonly ascribed to women. The problems created by structural change, the lack of compatibility between labour market and family organization, were more or less explicitly defined as private problems to which the employed-mother families had to find individual solutions.

The situation of the employed mother bears out contradictions inherent in welfare state policies. The equal status policy of the Norwegian government, which has strongly emphasized the rights of married women to employment and economic independence, has supported and legitimated the changing behaviour of women. Welfare state expansion has stimulated the recruitment of women to gainful employment. However, functioning as employers, central and local government have not planned for the caring commitments of the new work-force (Leira 1991). An overall assessment cannot escape the conclusion that public intervention to provide childcare facilities for the children of employed mothers has been mediocre.

Mothers, minders and markets

During the 1970s and 1980s Norwegian mothers have changed the content and contexts of motherhood. The development of more diversi-fied approaches to motherhood has contributed to an institutional differentiation of labour markets and of provisions for early childhood care and education. The expansion of the economic-provider aspects of motherhood is linked with the 'collectivization of childcare' introduced by state-sponsored day-care facilities, but less explicitly so than in other countries where labour market and childcare policies have been more synchronized (see ch. 3). In the transformation taking place as regards

Norwegian mothers' economic activity in the 1970s and 1980s, the interconnection of mothers' employment with an informal economy of childcare provision was more important than the efforts of the state (Leira 1985). This informal economy is generated by the interplay of the economy's demand for labour, and by labour's demand for childcare provision, each in turn influencing the earner and carer aspects of motherhood.

In the Norwegian literature, private childminding has until recently not usually been regarded as 'employment', 'occupational activity' or as 'work' (Leira 1979; Sverdrup 1984b). Considered as 'employment', childminding appears as ambiguous, particularly when the minding is being carried out in the childminder's home. Whatever the degree of formalization of the private childminding agreement, a common feature of this form of employment is the lack of characteristics commonly associated with wage-work, such as separation of the arenas of 'work' and 'home', the lack of routinized, predictable operations, the lack of interactions with fellow workers, and so on. Childminding does not have the formal, organizational characteristics of 'a job' (Acker 1990). On the other hand, private childminding has many features in common with mothers' dealing with their own children and with general aspects of housewifery and home-making. Norwegian vernacular captures this in the term commonly used for a private childminder, 'dagmamma', which literally translates as 'day mother'. The allusion of kinship may indicate an effort to familiarize family external childcare. The reference to 'mother' lends to the term a connotation of a mother replacement or 'substitute'. Encompassing at the same time outwork and unpaid housework for own kin, private childminding is embedded in the everyday domestic responsibility of the childminder and often with her maternal care for her offspring as well. To articulate the boundaries between motherhood and employment in such relationships is often difficult, which may to some extent explain why private childminders do not necessarily regard their employment as a 'job' (Leira 1983).[5]

By considering childminding as part of the overall day-care structure on a par with the formally organized state-funded services as I have done, the multitude of private childminding arrangements are placed in a labour market context. One of the earliest descriptions and attempts at empirical documentation of private childcare is provided by the Ministry of Government Administration and Consumer Affairs in the report to Parliament presaging the Day Care Act in 1975, discussed above. The Ministry did not identify the production of informal services as 'labour market' activities, but pointed to the interconnection between mothers' employment and the use of informal childcare arrangements.

In total the Ministry assumed that there were about 66,000 children whose parents were dual-earners or students, or single providers who were not accommodated in state-sponsored day care (Ot. pr. nr 23, 1974–5, p. 18).

On the forms of childcare actually used for children who were not accommodated by state-sponsored services, the Ministry observed: 'Common to the approximately 66,000 children [from dual-earner and single-earner families mainly] who are not accommodated in state-sponsored day care is that the parents have managed to arrange for childcare one way or another, with the help of relatives, childminders [non-registered] or non-approved day-care centres' (p.18, my transl.). Implicitly, the statement outlines the composition of informal labour markets in childcare, and the institutional differentiation actually taking place. However, as seen in chapter 4, according to the Ministry's recommendations such informal arrangements were not included in welfare state policies for early childhood care and education.

Reporting to Parliament on the status of day-care provision in 1979, the Ministry estimated that altogether 70,000 to 80,000 pre-school children were catered for by 50,000 to 60,000 private childminders, and that approximately 90,000 children were 'looked after' by relatives and neighbours or by the parents bringing the children with them to their jobs and arranging for parent shifts or reduced working hours (St. meld. 93, 1980–1, pp. 16–17). According to other assessments of private childcare, the figures estimated by the Ministry are too high.[6] Reanalysing the data, I found that approximately 60,000 families reported the use of private, extrafamilial, childcare arrangements and estimated that the number of private childcare providers was 15,000 to 25,000 if they each minded children from two to three families (Leira 1979, see also Sverdrup 1984b). Yet, when considered in a job context, private childminding was one of the major job categories for women.[7] And, as noted above, the informal services by far outnumbered the public provision of childcare.

Later, in 1984, the Ministry assessed the scope of private childminding, but expressed little concern over the quantity or quality of such arrangements (St. meld. 50, 1984–5). In a later report on provision of early childhood care and education, which outlines the aims of government policies towards the turn of the century, private childminding is not mentioned at all (St. meld. 8, 1987–8, *Barnehager mot år 2000*). Day-care policy is conceptualized as referring to state-sponsored services only, while the numerically more important informal childcare arrangements are excluded from consideration. Day-care policies proposed for the remaining years of the century thus do not address the everyday situation of the majority of employed parents of pre-school children. In 1989, the Labour minority government announced initiatives to formalize parts of the informal childcare markets (St. meld. 4, 1988–9), and in the same year members of Parliament recommended that private childminding be supervised and controlled.

Mothers, markets and the state

According to Norwegian data, women acting as mothers and minders are the central agents in the shaping of an informal infrastructure in childcare. A high level of regular employment among mothers combined with a shortage of public day-care provision have mobilized labour reserves among other groups of women. At the level of individual actors, the informal, family external arrangements are produced by mothers who are willing to be recruited to formal labour in co-operation with other women who, on an informal basis, agree to care for the formally employed mothers' children. Individually, the private, informal arrangements for childcare may appear as insignificant, created as they are on an *ad hoc* basis for relatively short spans of time, and embedded in the organization of everyday life. When added together, the aggregate of all actors and arrangements presents the contours of a comprehensive informal economy in childcare. The sum of arrangements describes labour market segments with more actors involved than in the formal childcare economy.

The development of the modern Norwegian dual-earner family in the 1970s has depended largely on the conservation of a more traditional family form, in which the women retain the home-maker's role, perhaps not exclusively but to a decisive extent. The use of informal arrangements for childcare supports and maintains the formal employment of mothers. Mothers (and fathers) who comply with the economic-provider aspects of parenthood by taking on formal employment depend upon the informal childcare markets to meet their caring commitments, and, vice versa, the informal childcare markets are constituted by the formal labour market demand for mothers' labour. A tight formal labour market in some sectors stimulates the development of informal labour markets in childcare that absorb unemployment and underemployment among women. Thus the competition for jobs is reduced, and the shortage of regular salaried work becomes less noticeable. In a labour market perspective, formal and informal employment are mutually dependent.

I contend that the dynamics promoting the informal economy of childcare are different from those developing within other sectors. The 'black' marketing in auto repairs, building and construction, rehabilitation, petty commodity production and in some forms of personal services competes with goods and services offered for sale in regular markets according to approved procedures. The supply of 'shadow' market goods and services (the provision of personal care not included) is not in the Norwegian context an expression of scarcity of regular provisions, but represents a competition for market share, using the price mechanism. Customers are attracted by competitive prices, which in turn offer sellers an improved market position. As compared to transactions within formally organized markets, the deal may appear to be profitable for both seller and buyer.

The informal economy developing around provision of care for vital needs for persons who are not able to manage on their own presents a different picture. The main issue in these cases is not to make a good bargain, but to gain any access to needed services at all. The social and material driving forces generating an informal economy in childcare are linked with the scarcity of regular, approved provision. Within the context of the welfare state economy the shadow labour markets in childcare do not indicate any general recession or stagnation. Rather, I shall argue, they are the outcome of local political priorities and decision-making processes over which central government has chosen not to exert much influence. The informal economy in childcare does not necessarily result from public poverty, but certainly from the priority of public authorities. Public services for early childhood care and education are strongly rationed and distributed according to needs-testing. Formal markets have not been capable of producing services at selling prices. Thus the informal labour markets in childcare emerge in a situation in which the welfare state responsibility is undermined or fragmented.

In the 1970s, Norwegian society witnessed a restructuring of the labour market and of family patterns that challenged the gendered division of labour and called for a redefinition of the accustomed boundaries between the welfare state and the family. Women played a significant part as change agents in these processes. Entering the labour market in large numbers they altered the composition of the labour force and the economic provision patterns of households as well. In women's tripartite income maintenance system, where marriage and family, labour market and social security were the main institutions, the relative importance of the marriage contract declined, while that of the work contract and state-guaranteed economic transfers increased (Dahl 1976; 1984).

To no small extent the increase in women's general economic activity is associated with an expansion of welfare state services. The welfare state recruited women to be its service managers and producers, thus implicitly if not explicitly encouraging the economic-provider aspects of womanhood. As a 'carer state' the welfare state depended on women's labour, but did not question the assumption of labour as a free and mobile commodity nor address the individual caring commitments of this new labour (see, for example, NOU 1978: 6). The concept of the 'wage-worker' did not include caring. Neither labour market nor family policy dealt specifically with the employed mothers' demand for child-care. The interplay of welfare state economic policies, which in effect supported the employment of mothers, and family policies which did not created a vacuum, an empty space in the provision of services for childcare which allowed an informal economy to flourish.

The importance of state intervention in changing women's social position has been much discussed in Scandinavian feminist research. Hernes (1984; 1987) Siim (1984), Borchorst and Siim (1987) all argue that welfare state reforms have been of great significance, and point to the state's economic support of women in Denmark, Sweden and Norway through jobs in the public sector, via social security entitlements and through the provision of social and personal services. Hernes argues that the state under different circumstances has formed alliances with women to promote welfare state interests and to support relief of women. All the same Hernes (1984) characterizes the Scandinavian welfare state as 'tutelary' in its relation to women, because women have never attained the opportunities equal to those of men in shaping the policies influencing women's lives. Siim (1984) contends that a partnership was formed between women and the Danish welfare state (see also Borchorst and Siim (1987). Dahlerup (1987), on the other hand, finds the welfare state rather 'unplanned' in its approach to women. Woman's subordinate position in society has been a 'non-issue in Western politics', Dahlerup concludes (1987, p. 123).

My analysis of the Norwegian data from the period 1945–85 gives little evidence of an alliance or a partnership being established between employed mothers and the welfare state. State intervention in childcare policies was not particularly oriented towards the employed parents' need for childcare. Rather, 'reproduction policies' focused on the needs of the child. First and foremost, state-sponsored childcare was provided as a contribution to early childhood socialization and development, not as a contribution to mothers' employment.

The policies of production and those of social reproduction signalled contradictory approaches to motherhood. The expanding welfare state created jobs for women, thus endorsing the development of the earner aspects of motherhood. Labour market policies did not incorporate comprehensive concessions to the carer aspect of motherhood. As employer, the welfare state may be considered a main force behind the change in women's economic activity. But state initiatives or reforms were not what made mothers' employment possible. Welfare state policies only marginally addressed the incompatibility of labour market and family organization. Policies for early childhood education and care were implemented with virtually no concern for the changes in mothers' economic activity. The concept of the 'employed mother' that was to typify the majority of Norwegian mothers of pre-school children in the 1970s and 1980s was not politically institutionalized. State-sponsored childcare was not supplied to meet demand, and formal markets did not provide childcare. In this institutional impasse mothers did not wait for the state to help, they developed coping strategies of their own. What made new models of motherhood possible was the concerted entrepreneurial efforts of mothers and minders investing in small-scale childcare arrangements.

The 'modernization' of motherhood, as shaped by the mothers who took up employment while their children were very young, and the woman-made informal childcare economy that goes with it reflect processes of societal change that have far-reaching consequences, not only for family practice, primary socialization, the structuring of everyday life, but also for labour markets and the level of functioning of the welfare state. The social reconstruction of motherhood in everyday life was not preceded by a political reconceptualization of motherhood models. By and large, welfare state policies played a minor part in instituting change. In this case the change agents were the mothers.

Motherhood policies 1945–85: a discussion

The conceptualization of day-care policies shifts throughout the postwar years, as do attitudes towards mothers' employment. The context within which policies were framed also changed from the deprivation of the early post-war years to the affluence of the early 1970s, when day-care legislation was instituted. The political staging was altered from 1961 when Labour lost absolute majority in Parliament. From then on the party was either in opposition or heading Labour minority governments.

In the following discussion about the welfare state and Norwegian mothers, I distinguish between the earlier post-war years, from 1945 up to roughly the early 1960s, and the later period, dealing in the main with the debates presaging the 1975 Day Care Act. In my discussion of both periods, focus is on the conceptualization of the employed mother in political discourse and on the approach in national policies towards this model of motherhood, particularly as seen in day-care policies. Looking at the first part of the post-war period, the interesting questions are why mothers' labour was not mobilized for the post-war reconstruction, and why day care was not provided to this end. In the latter part of this period under consideration, the situation has changed (chs. 4 and 5), and the pertinent question now is why the very considerable demand for childcare represented by the employed-mother families has not been addressed. My study does not provide the complete answer to these questions. I offer some hypotheses and draw attention to areas of interest for further research.

Neglected as labour

The very modest interest of the state in the provision of day care for pre-school children in the early post-war years is perhaps most plausibly explained with reference to war-time recovery and the reconstruction of the economy, which demanded sharp priorities of investment. The basic necessities had to come first. Other desirable reforms had to wait.

The provision of day care for pre-school children was not perceived as a basic necessity. Discussed in the Labour Party working programmes as a relief for home-based mothers from their drudgery, and also by a government-appointed committee as a part of comprehensive educational reforms, provision of day care was clearly desirable, but a cost-demanding reform that was not very urgently needed. Considering the grave problems with housing and with the provision of almost all sorts of services, this is not strange. If this was the frame of reference within which day-care policies were planned, the slow development of such services is hardly surprising.

However, from a different perspective day care might have been given high priority. From the end of the war and throughout the 1960s a shortage of labour was reported. In an assessment of the reconstruction economy it was underlined that labour shortage and lack of foreign currency were the two serious impediments. The foreign commentator, L. R. Klein, was surprised that women's labour reserves had not been mobilized and that day care and part-time jobs were not offered to facilitate their entry into the labour market (L. R. Klein 1948, quoted in Tornes 1986, p. 14). When placed within the context of the economy as a means of mobilizing the labour that was high in demand, day-care provision was certainly a desirable, even an economically profitable, investment.

From this perspective the interesting question is why women's labour was left at home, and why measures such as day care were not instituted to help meet the demands of the economy. Was the labour shortage not that serious? Or, perhaps the 'planned economy' of the reconstruction did not perceive women as 'labour', as Tornes (1986) suggests? Or, was day care not conceptualized as an instrument of economic policies, even though the war-time mobilization of women and the war-time nurseries of the US and the UK were known. If we assume that Klein's observations were not completely off the mark, what could be more important than the recovery of the economy? Was it the preservation of the domesticated-mother family?

Further analyses of the economic and labour policies of the period might possibly shed light on some of the questions I have raised and help clarify the complex interplay between the economy, and motherhood and family ideologies in the planning of post-war reconstruction.

If the domesticated mother was the model of the planners, what about the mothers themselves? As noted above, labour market participation of mothers was very low throughout the 1950s and so was the demand for day care. The comparatively few mothers who were employed from necessity or choice did not represent an organized hard-hitting demand. Some organized demand, e.g. that of the Housewives' Kindergartens, did not advocate an untraditional motherhood model. Like the Labour Party programmes they regarded day care as a relief for mothers (and advantageous to children) but not as a means of liberating mothers from domesticity.

The extent to which the more influential women's organizations regarded the provision of day care as a precondition for mothers' employment is not easily assessed. The archives of some of the organizations, in particular those of the Labour Party Women's Secretariat, and their journal, and also other women's magazines, might possibly furnish more information on women's reactions to state-sponsored day care and to employment.

Neglected as mothers

The neglect of the employed mother family in the early post-war years is perhaps explained by the minimal importance of that family form in Norwegian society at the time. By the mid-1970s all this had changed. From the late 1960s the employed-mother family was rapidly on the increase and from 1969 the government appointed a committee to prepare day-care legislation. A consideration of the new family forms that began to emerge seemed plausible, but in the final phase of lawmaking the childcare commitments of the employed mothers were turned into a non-issue. The Norwegian welfare state was not prepared to make special concessions to the demands for day care represented by the employed-mother families.

This lack of response to the employment of mothers is puzzling, particularly when one considers that the Norwegian Labour Party, like the other Social Democratic parties in Scandinavia, was otherwise committed to working-class interests and to social equality. In fact, the Norwegian Labour minority government was considering an Equal Status Act when the Day Care Act was passed. The simple answer is, of course, that other issues were more important to the lawmakers than the interests of the mothers. Which were the interests that set aside the employed mothers' demands? Why was the concept of the employed-mother family, which was soon to represent the majority of families with children of pre-school age, not politically institutionalized? I do not pretend to give more than fragments of answers, and shall only point out some areas of interest for further research.

In the early 1970s mothers' employment was ideologically not a neutral issue; neither was a day-care policy that aimed at encompassing all children. Traditional family forms and values were challenged. The ideological conflicts over motherhood and family forms were sharpened as new models of motherhood were on the increase, and the defence of both traditional and new family forms intensified. Support of state-sponsored day care and of mothers' employment was more pronounced within the parties to the left, while the centre and conservative parties were generally more reserved towards both issues. If the Day Care Act was to gain passage, the Labour minority government had to mediate between the different motherhood ideologies entailed in the different attitudes of the two largest party constellations, those to the left, and the centre and conservative parties.

The conceptualizations of early childhood education and care, or 'day care' for short, in the proposal for a Day Care Act and in the parliamentary debate, indicate a wish for a broad consensus over day-care policies. Did the wish for consensus contribute to the playing down of employed mothers' interests? If this is the case, focusing as Labour did on collective childcare as a principally child-oriented device and making no special concessions to the employed-mother families become more comprehensible as a gesture towards the reduction of political tension.

Hardly anyone objected to this conceptualization of day care, and it was certainly most difficult to oppose a reform that aimed at protecting the best interests of the child. The bourgeois parties accepted this formulation but underlined the parents' rights to choose whether one of them or both were to work outside the home (something the Labour Party could not possibly object to), and some of the bourgeois MPs advocated the institution of economic transfers to parents to ensure that the choice was made a reality.

In these different formulations of the objectives of childcare and family policies, Labour played down the image of the welfare state invading the private sphere of the family, and the bourgeois parties their defence of the traditional family form. Rephrasing their ideologies, the main party to the left as well as the main bourgeois parties established a common political platform over day-care policies. The interests of the parties were accommodated in this staging; the interests of the employed mothers were not.

And the question lingers on: why should a drive for political consensus entail a conceptualization of day-care services that excludes the interests of its main potential beneficiaries, the employed-mother families? The question is all the more intriguing as the neighbouring countries, Denmark and Sweden, adopted conceptualizations that considered the demand of the economy for labour as well as the demand of the employed-mother families for day care.

Possibly, as mentioned above, demand was less strongly articulated in Norway, and possibly the women's organizations were more divided on the issue of day care and mothers' employment than was the case in Denmark and Sweden. More detailed examinations of the making of policies in the three countries might reveal more of the similarities and differences in approach. In Norway, examination of the motherhood and family ideologies of the different parties in the post-war period might offer an interesting insight into the processes of policy-making.

In 1975, when the Labour minority government forwarded its proposition for the Day Care Act, the provision of day care was left to the local authorities. With the support of the party to its left, Labour might have mustered a majority for a proposal making day-care provision mandatory for the local authorities. However, opposition from the local authorities and others, and from within the Labour Party itself, was too strong. The proposal was discarded prior to the introduction of the bill. By leaving the provision of day care to the discretion of local authorities, the controversial issues were being transferred from the national stage to a multitude of local arenas.

The relative weakness of demand possibly explains part of this process. Those wanting state-sponsored day care were not represented by nation-wide organizations or by professional lobbyists. Women's associations were divided on the issue of day care and mothers' employment in the mid-1970s, some of the day-care 'activists' advocating day care as relief for the home-based mother, not as a service for the employed one.

Concern over the economic situation of local authorities had an influence on the provision of day care not being made mandatory. Still, in the mid-1970s the idea that the provision of day care might prove profitable for the local authorities was rarely heard. In retrospect it would seem that the relationship between the economic situation of local authorities and the provision of day care is highly variable. Some of the poorer counties have a better supply of services than the more prosperous ones, some of the sparsely populated areas accommodate a larger proportion of pre-school age children than do some of the urban areas (Leira 1985; 1989). The economic situation is only one of the many factors influencing the local decisions on day-care provision.

More detailed local studies comparing and contrasting the priority given to day care in different types of local authorities and within structurally similar ones might clarify the interplay of economic reasoning and the dominant local motherhood and family ideologies. Including for analysis the local interpretations of the relationship between central and local government over questions related to day care, local studies might produce a wealth of information about the processes that generate new local approaches to employed mothers and to day care for pre-school children, and new definitions of local authority priorities.

In the mid-1970s, Labour as the largest of the political parties was prepared to support Equal Status legislation that upheld women's (and mothers') right to paid employment. The Party was not, however, prepared to give equal support to the childcare needs of this new labour (Leira 1991). This paradox calls attention to interesting areas for further research concerning the interplay of the economy and of family and motherhood ideology in the formulation of policies concerning areas of vital interest to mothers.

6   Modes of mothering

Introduction

In the previous chapters welfare state efforts to initiate or promote new models of motherhood are analysed, while in this chapter I explore the mothers' making of motherhood as shown in their strategies to combine earning and caring commitments. The following examination assumes, as does much social research from the 1970s and 1980s, that market-based and non-market-based work needs to be analysed in context (Leira and Nørve 1977; Wadel 1977; Ingelstam 1980; Pahl 1984).

This approach underlines the importance of reconceptualizing 'work' so as to include non-market activities, and to make explicit the interrelationships of market to non-market work. Moreover, I find that the studies point towards the need for analysing 'care' and 'work' within a common conceptual framework. Without such a perspective the welfare state restructuring of the 'public' and the 'private' cannot be grasped. The welfare state changes the institutional differentiation of caring and transforms personal responsibilities into public concerns. As professionalized employment, 'care' is conceptualized as 'work'. However, other forms of care also entail work. Caring for very dependent persons is work embedded in a personal relationship. Looking at 'care' as 'work' across institutional differentiation makes everyday strategies to reconcile earning and caring commitments more easily visible.

In the first part of the chapter I use survey data to identify the principal forms of motherhood as practised by Norwegian mothers in the 1970s and 1980s. The development of the modern dual-earner family in Norway, I shall argue, has been dependent upon the conservation of a more traditional family form. Through the organization of private childcare arrangements, different types of households become mutually interdependent.

In the second part of the chapter I present an ethnographic study of everyday mothering, where I focus on the processes that generate different forms of motherhood. The everyday perspective is essential, I maintain, to the analysis of institutional differentiation of work and care, and also to the analysis of mothers' earning and caring strategies (cf. also Smith 1988). The division of labour and resources within families, I shall show, is in mutual dependence with a division of resources between families. My study demonstrates that mothers are most instrumental in creating new approaches to motherhood. Drawing upon my analysis of mothers' different earning and caring strategies, in the final section I discuss everyday practices as elements in structural change.

Caring and earning: employed-mother families

The development of the dual-earner family as the dominant family form in Norway from the 1970s implied greater economic equality between spouses. At the same time the organization of everyday life grew more complex. Co-ordination of time, domestic tasks, jobs and childcare posed problems for households. With an increase in the number of hours spent by parents in 'production', the time resources available within the family for 'social reproduction' were restricted. When the mothers joined the labour market in large numbers the problem of who was to care for the children had not been solved. Expanding the earner aspects of motherhood underlined the importance of childcare arrangements.

Socio-cultural interpretations of childhood and motherhood necessarily influence the ways in which society and family respond to childcare needs. The reluctance of many Norwegian local authorities to offer childcare services, even after the Act governing day care was passed in 1975 (see ch. 4), expressed a mixture of monetary and moral concern. Obviously the provision of day care would entail considerable cost to the public purse. Moreover, state-sponsored childcare was regarded by some local politicians as undermining the moral commitments of the family and was therefore opposed. Responsibility for the upbringing of offspring, it was argued, ought to remain with the parents. Mothers' duty was to stay with their children, not to leave them to others. In many regions the public provision of day-care services was successfully delayed. However, the defence of the conventional nuclear family and of the gendered division of labour strongly associated with this family form largely failed. Challenging the prevailing normative construction of motherhood, mothers changed their everyday practices.

Norwegian surveys from the 1970s and 1980s present two major 'models' of motherhood, the employed mother who works outside the home for pay, and the one whose main involvement and occupation is in home-making, with negligible or no formal income-generating work attached. The mothers heading for employment were the trendsetters. From 1975 to 1990 the shift in family form, as noted above (ch. 5), was towards the employed-mother family, which became the major family form. By 1990 two out of three mothers with children under 3 years were in the work-force.

Basically, the reduction of maternal resources for childcare could be compensated for in two ways: either by a rearrangement of time resources within the family, or by providing additional resources from outside. The idea that the fathers' employment patterns could be changed and that the parents might share the childcare and housework more equally between them has attracted attention, but has not had much impact on the organization of everyday life. The increase in the labour market participation rates of mothers was not accompanied by a corresponding decrease in the participation rates of the fathers. On the contrary, fathers with young children work longer weekly hours than other men (Ellingsæter 1990). The picture of the 'average father' provided by time-use data indicates that during the 1970s fathers became somewhat more involved in domestic routines, and spent more time caring for their children. In no way did this substitute for the mothers' care. Rather the caring activities of the fathers supplemented the caring of the mothers (Lingsom and Ellingsæter 1983). In 1980–1 married men with children under 7 years of age spent less than half as much time on household work and family care as women did (Lingsom and Ellingsæter 1983, p. 84). Even in the families where mothers were employed full-time, father was rather remote as child-carer. (It should be noted, though, that this type of survey data is not well suited to identifying those families where fathers do take a more active role in child-rearing and domestic work.) An interesting analysis of children's work hypothesizes that children aged 10–12 years may represent more important childcare assets in dual-earner families than the average father does (Solberg and Vestby 1987). Recent studies from Britain give evidence of mothers' coping strategies that are in many ways similar to the Norwegian experience (Brannen and Moss 1988; 1990; see also New and David 1985).

When the Norwegian mothers' exodus to the labour market started in the late 1960s, state-sponsored day care was a scarce commodity. Twenty years later, in a period that has seen mothers' employment steadily rising, public day-care facilities are far from sufficient to meet demand. The mothers who experimented with new approaches to motherhood, leaving full-time housewifery behind, did not wait for the state to prepare the way. In co-operation with other women, employed

Table 6.1 *Mothers' employment and childcare*

Forms of childcare	Mothers' employment		
	Formal	Informal	Non-employment
Family-based			
Informal			
State-sponsored			

mothers developed coping strategies of their own. As I have shown in earlier studies, the combination of childcare and employment commitments rests on an institutional structure in childcare in which the parents, public sector services and private, informal supply of services represent the cornerstones (Leira 1979; 1985). For a more detailed examination of motherhood models, the combinations of childcare and employment shown in table 6.1 offer a starting point. The combinations shown in the table give nine different ways of structuring motherhood. Considering in addition mothers' working hours and day-care opening hours, the variety of informal childcare and combinations of the different forms of childcare complicates the picture even more.

Having examined the development of mothers' employment in chapter 5, I shall next deal with the main combination of employment and childcare in the period ranging from about the mid-1970s to about the mid-1980s. Survey data from 1973 and 1985 present overviews of the intermixture of employed mothers' labour market participation and childcare arrangements (see table 6.2). The response range of parents to the 1973 and 1985 questionnaires on jobs and childcare also illustrates aspects of the transformations of family patterns and provides a rudimentary typology of approaches to modern motherhood. Table 6.2 shows the different combinations of earning and caring of mothers in 1973 and 1985.[1]

As different sampling procedures were used and questions and precoded answers framed somewhat differently, the results of these studies are not directly comparable. Yet, as 'snapshots' of the different combinations of labour market participation and childcare provision of employed parents at certain points in time, they do offer an indication of the relative importance of the various combinations, and of the direction of institutional change. The use of extrafamilial childcare increased from 1973 to 1985, particularly among employed-mother families, which

Table 6.2 *Combinations of earning and caring: dual-earner families, 1973 and 1985*

(per cent)

| Forms of child care | Mothers' employment | | | |
| | 1973 | | 1985 | |
	Employed	Not employed	Employed	Not employed
Family-based	51	82	13	77
Network-based	18	10	11	6
Market-based	19	2	37	1
State-sponsored	11	4	36	15
Other	2	3	3	1
Total	101	101	100	100
Number of respondents	242	494	320	293

Source 1973: SSB, *Boforholdsundersøkelsen* 1973, table 116, p. 114.
Source 1985: Bogen (1987), table 2.9, p. 9, table 3.3, p. 54.

was expected. Slightly more surprising is the increased use of extrafamilial childcare in families where mother is home-based.

Looking at the remaking of both earner and carer aspects of motherhood I shall focus on the employed-mother families. Among these families both surveys report different models of motherhood; that is, different ways of making jobs and childcare compatible. Most common were:

– employment combined with informal childcare,
– employment combined with state-sponsored childcare,
– employment combined with family-based childcare.

The childcare 'histories' of mothers in employment usually include experiences with all these forms, family-based childcare in the first months of a child's life, followed by private arrangements, and possibly access to state-sponsored childcare for a child aged 3–6 years. Some families combine private and state-sponsored childcare.

In 1973 two features of the childcare-employment intermixture were striking: first the large proportion of employed mothers who reported non-use of any childcare arrangement outside the family (51 per cent); and, secondly, the relative importance of the private, informal arrangements for childcare among employed mothers (37 per cent). The use of state-sponsored facilities was not impressive (11 per cent), which is not so strange, considering that state-sponsored day care, as I have pointed out, was not planned for mass consumption until after 1975 (Leira 1985).

A national survey of the use of childcare conducted in 1975 gives interesting additional information about how the Norwegian dual-earner families with children aged 0–11 years coped with childcare and employment (SSB 1976). Among these families more than half reported that the mothers worked reduced hours. In 15 per cent of dual-earner families, work and children were managed through what has been termed 'parent shifts' (Kalleberg 1983), which means that the parents did their waged work at different hours and split the nurturing between them. More than one in ten of the mothers said that they brought their children with them to work – an empirical illustration of women's dual workload in everyday life.

Among the families who used external resources for childcare, private arrangements were much more common than the use of public day care. The survey data pointed to a great variety of private, extrafamilial childcare provision. Family networks played an important part in such arrangements. Grandmothers, friends and neighbours were often mobilized for childminding. Private childcare was also organized by, for example, employing a nanny, an au pair girl, or a non-registered childminder (Leira 1979).

Ten years later, the intermix of jobs and childcare was based on the same elements, but the relative importance of the different childcare arrangements had shifted (Bogen 1987). For employed parents to manage childcare on their own, in addition to job commitments, was far less common in 1985 than in 1975; only 13 per cent of dual-earner or student families did not make use of extrafamilial childcare arrangements in 1985. Of these families the majority reported parent shifts. The use of state-sponsored services for early childhood care and education showed a substantial increase; 36 per cent of the families had access to state-sponsored day care. However, the expansion of state-sponsored services apparently had not eradicated the informal markets for childcare provision. Informal arrangements, that is, the use of nannies, childminders, relatives, friends and neighbours for childcare, made up 48 per cent of the childcare arrangements. If the 1985 study gives a fairly accurate picture of the situation, the informal childcare services have maintained their share of the total childcare market, and may even have expanded.[2]

Obviously, the combinations given in table 6.2 are not equally available to families, nor equally acceptable. Class differences most likely are important, but no systematic evidence exists on this matter. For example, use of paid domestic help, the more expensive of the childcare arrangements, is an option only for families with above-average incomes. Mothers with more years of education are more likely to take up employment soon after giving birth, which possibly indicates greater acceptance of childcare outside the family. Some mothers may prefer network-based childcare to centre-based, and so on. Commonly, in Norway as in Britain, mothers who want employment do not have a choice of form of childcare, particularly as regards care for very young children (see Brannen and Moss 1988). The motherhood model usually formed in employed-mother families in which formal employment is combined with the use of informal childcare is generated by women who opt for different combinations of employment and care. Who are the mothers and who are the minders?[3]

Mothers and childminders

The private childcare that I refer to presents a 'mixtum compositum' of arrangements. It includes care by grandmothers, neighbours, friends, au pair girls, nannies and childminders. Being interested in different aspects of private childminding, I have classified arrangements according to the character of the relationship between mother and minder, and according to the form of remuneration involved. Thus, I make distinctions between 'close' and 'distant' relationships or between 'social network-based' and 'market-based' relationships and between paid childcare and unpaid, exchange-based childcare. In 1985, the great part of the informal child-care was market-based (see table 6.2). The extent to which unpaid services are reciprocated in kind or by exchanges of services has not been registered in national surveys. Network-based childminding does not exclude payment, Norwegian studies report (SSB 1976; Hansen and Andersen 1984; Opdahl 1984; for an overview, see Leira 1985). If we are to take the survey responses at face value, relatives, friends and neigh-bours do get paid in cash for childcare services. In this perspective everyday practices permeate the distinction between social networks and informal labour markets.[4]

However, it is not always clear how the distinction between different forms of private childcare is drawn. In the remainder of the section I use the terms 'private childcare' or 'private childminding' to include all forms of extrafamilial childcare arrangements not approved or registered by public authorities.

Norwegian statistics do not usually identify respondents by ethnicity or social class. No overviews are given on mothers' employment and child-care by ethnicity. The surveys utilized for table 6.2 do, however, give some indication as to similarity or dissimilarity in social background between mothers and childminders. These studies show that mothers and minders are fairly often related by kin, or associated by social-network relationships. In the 1985 study discussed above, almost one in four of the private childminders was recruited through kinship, friendship or neighbourly relationships. For this category a relative status homogeneity between mothers and minders is likely. Whether network-based childcare is more frequent among families of working-class or other social backgrounds is not reported. Based on earlier Norwegian studies of families with young children (Holter et al. 1975), one might expect working-class mothers to develop or maintain support networks based on family and kin, and middle-class mothers to be more likely to base support networks on friends. Private childminding, however, as a composite totality, is made both within class and across class backgrounds.

The diversity of arrangements is illustrated in a small-scale study of childminders and mothers which I carried out in Oslo (Leira 1984, unpubl.).[5] Among the thirty-five childminders interviewed, I found that only two were related by kin to the child cared for. Still, childcare arrangements made through network mediation were common. More than half of the mothers and minders had met through the introduction of common friends, neighbours and acquaintances. The minders were usually older than the mothers, and generally had the longer motherhood experience. The mothers usually had more years of education, but all the childminders had more than just elementary schooling, and all had previous experience in formal employment. If we disregard for a moment the difficulties involved in determining women's class position, 'within-class' arrangements were more common than 'cross-class', probably because of the network mediation. In some few cases mothers and minders 'swapped', that is, friends would exchange the childminding for one another. Some mothers who had used a childminder for their first child left their jobs and took up childminding when their second child was born. The mothers who held on to their employment often were upwardly mobile. Childminding, in a job context, represented downward mobility.

Among the childminders interviewed, childminding was commonly combined with mothering one's own children. Three of the women had no personal mothering experience prior to childminding, two were grandmothers, the rest had young children at home.

A professionalized approach to childminding was represented in my study by the pre-school teachers who had left formal services to work on their own. Usually, however, childminding was not considered as 'work', but as 'helping others'. For some women childminding was deliberately planned as temporary, an in-between activity, for example for mothers who took a year's leave of absence to facilitate the beginning of school for their offspring. Newly divorced mothers who needed money might take up childminding while looking around for better-paid jobs. The majority of the minders interviewed had several years of experience as childminders, while twenty had been in the business for five years or more, with thirteen years as the maximum reported. Childminding had become an informal carer career, representing for the minders an addition to the household economy, and also moments of gratification, presumably sufficient to make the job worthwhile. Long-term material returns were non-existent, as informal childminding did not add to the merit list, either to seniority, or to social security benefits.

Cash for care in a mother–minder relationship is not just a 'cross-class' phenomenon; it also takes place in the 'within-class' relationship. As noted above, Norwegian studies report that network-based childminding is sometimes carried out for pay, sometimes unpaid (Leira 1985). Whether middle-class mothers and minders are more likely to exchange cash for care than working-class mothers and minders is not known. To find cross-class arrangements involving middle-class mothers paying working-class minders is obviously more likely than the reverse.

Even very close kin are reportedly paid for childminding. In one respect this represents a 'commercialization' of close personal relationships. But this is only part of the picture. When cash is introduced in exchange for care between mothers and minders whose relationship is personal and close, the meaning of money, its symbolic importance, takes on a different character. Even in close personal relationships the 'material' meaning of money may of course be very important. The money may be needed for what it can buy. Mother and minder acknowledge the value of the minder's labour as being cash convertible in the regular labour markets. In addition, paying for childcare symbolizes respect for the carer's labour and time, and shows that the other's involvement is not taken for granted.

A mother paying her own mother or sister or friend for childcare in one respect is 'paying them off'; a strategy perhaps for balancing and delimiting anticipation of reciprocity. Yet, payment may be a precondition for a negotiable arrangement, facilitating the voicing of wishes for both parties. 'Commercialization' may provide the 'coping stone', the leverage which keeps both childcare arrangement and the personal relationship from deteriorating.

Caring for someone else's child involves more than money, time and labour. It also entails a minimum of personal contact between mother and minder, a minimum of reciprocal trust, respect and some degree of compatibility between the two. Evidently, this is important to the mother, who depends upon the minder for the child's well-being and upbringing. She also depends on the minder for her income. This composite dependence balances the relationship. Economically the mother is the stronger, but the minder is essential to her coping with her situation.

Implicitly, table 6.2 indicates the institutionalized cross-pressures surrounding present-day Norwegian motherhood. In employed mothers' everyday life the incompatibility of job and childcare time structures meets with limited public efforts to soften the conflict. The reconciliation of structural incompatibility is privatized, resolved by individual initiatives. The childcare arrangements of employed mothers call attention to the contradictions in the welfare state over which motherhood model to endorse.

Mothers who take up employment challenge the division of labour in caring embedded in the traditional welfare state concept. They are also confronted with considerable segments of Norwegian popular opinion as to what is the best way of mothering. An attitude survey from 1985 gave 80 per cent support to the statement: 'More women should stay at home when the children are young' (Leira 1989, my transl.). No one was asked to consider fathers' obligations to children in this respect.

Combinations of childcare and employment are often difficult to manage and a strain on time and energy. 'This society is not made for mothers', as one of my informants succinctly concluded in her story of how she had to give up her job because childcare arrangements broke down. In the words of a recent British study, mothers are 'trading motherhood against employment' (Brannen and Moss 1990).

Although Norwegian society also shows support of mothers' employment, few employed mothers are allowed the experience of not facing the cross-pressures, materially and morally. Employed mothers generally work less than full-time. The extent to which this arrangement represents necessity or choice is not known. It seems very likely, though, that flexible use of mothers' time for income-generating work is one strategy for keeping daily schedules from collapsing, which reduces mothers' income and underlines the primacy of fathers/husbands in economic provision.

In addition to the survey of actual use, the 1985 Norwegian study asked for mothers' preferences for different forms of childcare. Quite a few of both the non-employed and the employed mothers wanted accommodations other than the ones actually reported. Of the non-employed mothers who had no extrafamilial help with the children, 54 per cent wanted help (Bogen 1987, table 3.4, p. 55). Among the employed mothers, 60 per cent wanted state-sponsored day care (actually used by 37 per cent), while comparatively few, 14 per cent, wanted a paid childminder (actually used by 32 per cent). As for network-based childcare, parent shifts and other family-based arrangements, only minor changes were reported between wishes and actual arrangements (Bogen 1987, table 2.9, p. 31).[6]

The demand for mothers' labour and mothers' demand for childcare facilities, on the one hand, and the shortage of approved day care and availability of informal resources, on the other, have contributed to an informal economy in childcare in which mothers and minders are the principal actors. The importance of informal childcare in the overall childcare structure is largely neglected in Norway (see chs. 4 and 5), as is its importance to family economy. Private arrangements for childminding are perhaps so much taken for granted that they are not remarked upon. Or, like so much of the work done by women, childminding is inadequately understood, or ignored, and its importance to the economic and social functioning of society is underestimated (Balbo 1982b). The lack of information on the parental status and childcare responsibilities of the labour force, particularly of men, in the official statistics may well be seen as an expression of the dominance of the 'public domain', which systematically undervalues the 'private' arenas of domestic life and reproduction.

In everyday life the modern dual-earner family frequently transfers some of the childcare tasks to other households, where childminding becomes incorporated into ordinary work strategies. The great demand for women's labour and the scarcity of organized childcare produce a mutual interdependence between 'traditional' and 'modern' family forms, and between formally employed women and those women who take care of their children for them. This is shown in a study I conducted on women's earning and caring strategies (Leira 1983).

A neighbourhood study

In the late 1970s I was engaged on a small-scale study of an urban neighbourhood exploring the strategies women developed in order to combine employment with childcare.[7] The ways in which dual-earner families with young children coped with their work and care were strikingly complex and varied. This was particularly true of the mothers' labour and use of time. My analysis also showed the ways in which these families depended upon each other. A general shortage of organized extrafamilial childcare was crucial in generating exchanges between households. Childcare arrangements were sometimes the only transaction which linked two or more households. In other cases childcare occurred within a general flow of informal exchanges. Where both parents were in full-time employment they depended for childcare upon other families who spent their time resources differently. In effect, the division of time-use and economic activity *within* one household depended on certain exchanges or transactions going on *between* this household and one or several neighbouring households, and vice versa.

The focus of the study was on the processes that generated the linkages, exchanges and interdependence between households, and the influence of social relations upon these processes. Possibly the perspective chosen conveys an impression of complete harmony, which, of course, does not represent the totality of neighbourhood relations (Gullestad 1984; McKee 1987). Disagreements, conflicts and rivalries between neighbours, negative sanctions and socially isolated persons were also features of neighbourhood life. For my research, however, co-operation was more interesting than conflict, as the close personal relationships and the informal social organization among young neighbourhood women played an important part in shaping the women's strategies for combining earning and caring activities.

The fieldwork was carried out in a stable inner city neighbourhood in the centre of Oslo, a city with a population of approximately half a million people. Periods of observation, including some participation in everyday activities, were followed by semi-structured, and later in-depth interviews. The main respondents were fifteen women, aged between 25 and 45 years, all of them living with a husband or cohabitee, and one or more children. Observations and information from this study, supplemented with a follow-up in the early 1980s, were used in the following presentation of neighbourhood life.

The local context: an inner city neighbourhood

This inner city neighbourhood is situated as an enclave surrounded by traffic-laden streets, offices, schools and shops. The residential area consists of six blocks of apartment buildings constructed during World War I. In the neighbourhood the small shops, the playground, the church and the bus stops are arenas for frequent chance meetings.

By necessity, outdoor life is communal. Apartments have no individual outdoor areas such as gardens, balconies or terraces. For the residents of a given complex the large courtyard is collective property, and a centre of local contact and information. Courtyard activities form essential strains in the texture of neighbourhood daily life. Children play, women carry their laundry to the block's launderette, neighbours stop for a chat on the way to or from the entrances.

The pleasant outdoor areas are well kept and inviting, with generous lawns, old trees and brightly coloured flowerbeds. The different activities do not compete for space. Three generations of neighbours are accommodated in the courtyard design, with tables and benches, drying racks for the laundry, and large areas specially equipped for children's play. Making specific plans for contact with neighbours is certainly not necessary. The women who come outdoors during summer to sit on the lawn bring their coffee pots and knitting and signal their social accessibility. Rarely does someone remain sitting alone for long. During daytime, children, old people and young women are the occupants of the courtyard, young men are seen only infrequently.

The neighbourhood is a stable one, few families having moved either in or out during recent years. The majority of residents are old people. Families with children of pre-school age comprise less than one-tenth of the households. Among the families studied, occupational status is relatively homogeneous. Dual-earner families are common. The men are skilled workers in industry, craftsmen, mechanics, technicians. The young married women hold traditional women's jobs, for example as cleaners, shop assistants, secretaries and subordinate positions in the social, health and welfare services. In addition, they are responsible for the greater part of the household routines, family management and childcare.

In conversations with residents, a feeling of belonging is often conveyed. Norms constituting good neighbourly relations are clearly expressed and nonconformity sometimes underlined with mild sanctions, joking or irony. Neighbourliness is a graduated relationship, constructed by the influence of personal attachment and forms of reciprocity developed in local exchange. Relations between neighbours are personal, which does not imply that they are always positive or close. However, one neighbour's welfare is seen as the concern of another. As 'noblesse oblige', so it is with neighbourly relations.

My study of this neighbourhood contradicts the observation by Bulmer (1984, p. 86) based on English studies of neighbourliness that there is 'no basis for functional interdependence between modern neighbours other than proximity or kinship'. Later in the same passage he adds: 'There is no positive sense in which people regularly need each other's services in day to day matters.' Focusing on men in the neighbourhood, my conclusion might, perhaps, have been a similar one. The everyday practices of the young women I studied, on the other hand, gave multiple evidence of reciprocity, mutual exchange and functional interdependence.

Feelings of local attachment and neighbourliness do not necessarily develop in a residential area. In a study of daily life in an old section of another Norwegian city, Gullestad (1978) emphasizes the importance of dissimilarity in resources within a relatively class-homogeneous population for the development of a positive social milieu. However, in my neighbourhood, the relative similarity in resources among homebound women appears as basic to the development of reciprocity and relations of exchange. My study raises the question of the importance of a traditional sexual division of time-use and labour for the development of a locally based informal organization. Obviously, in this neighbourhood women represent the crucial but often overlooked factor necessary for the development of 'good' neighbourly relations: the presence of persons with enough time at their disposal, and with a willingness, because of duty or for pleasure, to establish an informal net of contact and co-operation with others.

In this residential area as in many others the 'social function' of small children was amply demonstrated, offering as they did an opportunity for mothers to establish contacts. Having had neither relatives nor friends in the area, on moving in, mothers had turned to one another when needing some help or assistance with the children. Some of the women and the households had developed frequent contact, and some young women had become friends. Everyday life suggested considerable co-operation and sharing between these women. They (and sometimes also their husbands) exchanged goods and services in a continuous re-allocation of tasks and resources between the households. Within this social context I have examined women's everyday practices and their strategies for coping with the demands of childcare and employment.

All of the young families in the neighbourhood were employed-mother families in the sense that the mothers were in paid formal and/or informal work. About one-third of the women were in full-time formal employment. The rest worked part-time. In all the families the mother had the main responsibility for the children. Even if she did not do all the caring herself, she was the planner, organizer and co-ordinator. The father and older siblings formed part of her childcare resources, to be used within the family or in exchanges with other households. However, mothers made use of different strategies to combine earning and caring commitments. Thus, from my observations of time-use and modes of mothering, two different household forms could be distinguished, one comparatively 'modern', the other more 'traditional' in the approach to childcare and employment. Modern households were characterized by a strong employment orientation among mothers, and by the use of extrafamilial childcare. The economic-provider commitments of mothers (and fathers) structured everyday time-use. Mothers of modern households were employed in the formal sector of the labour market, as were the fathers. Care of children during daytime was organized so that it would not interfere with the parents' job obligations.

In the traditional households, childcare and home-making attained priority in the mothers' everyday schedule, but not to the exclusion of economic provision. The mothers' use of time was oriented towards the needs, real or imagined, of the household, and in particular, the children. Paid work, carried out at home or at odd or inconvenient hours, was organized so as not to interfere with the normal schedule of family life. Being physically present in the home and available for the children was a central element in these women's conceptualization of mothering. According to their stated norms, it was 'good for the children' to have mother 'waiting at home'. The household-oriented, traditional women were those who displayed greater complexity and variation in their daily work patterns. In my study special attention was therefore given to them. The co-existence of 'traditional' and 'modern' households within the area was, however, essential for the development of a neighbourhood subculture.

In my analysis of local women's earning and caring strategies, several forms of work were considered. Distinctions between forms of work were based on the institutional context of the task, to which was added a consideration of the types of contracts or norms of reciprocity that regulated the exchange (Gouldner 1960). Among forms of work commonly found, were the following:

 (i) unpaid work carried out within one's own household;
 (ii) regular employment;
 (iii) paid, irregular work ('shadow' or 'hidden' work, that is, work carried out for pay but not reported for taxation);
 (iv) unpaid work mediated by social networks including neighbours, friends and relatives and organized as specific exchanges, generalized exchanges or as one-way transfers, with no recompense registered.

Since all of the women who lived in traditional households were engaged in some kind of formal or informal employment, being household-oriented in no way precluded working outside the home. When the women worked for pay, jobs were chosen not according to personal preferences or job status, but out of consideration for the well-being of the family and the caring commitments. Jobs had to have flexible hours, or else had to be done at the time of the day when the fathers would be at home to look after the children. A job might be acceptable to a woman if she was allowed to bring her children along. Preferably, the job should be located close to home, so that no time was lost in travelling. Jobs offering such conditions were abundant in the districts surrounding the neighbourhood, and several of the women went out to work together. Usually, the priority given to mothering and household tasks meant downward occupational mobility for the women. Many of the young women had cleaning jobs late in the evenings or in the early mornings in offices and institutions within walking distance. Some were home helpers for old people during school hours, or part-time shop assistants. Others did different kinds of outwork.

'Shadow work', that is, paid work not reported for taxation, was also common in the local women's work patterns. Private arrangements for paid childminding, and informal paid services carried out for elderly people were numerous. (These activities are in themselves highly respectable, but are considered irregular in so far as the taxation authorities are not notified.) The local 'shadow market' for childminding was largely established by social-network mediation. Neighbourhood women minded other neighbours' children and childminders were sometimes passed on or 'inherited' by the linkages of the women's networks. Irregular childminding provisions were arranged in a more businesslike manner, too, frequently by way of notices in the local shops, or by advertisements in newspapers. Often, but not always, relatives and friends were paid for childminding. Locally paid childcare was not regarded as a 'job', but as 'helping' others, even when personal profit accrued in the process. Like the regular wage-work, irregular paid work was organized so that it did not interfere with mothering and housewifery. Often looked upon as temporary activities, 'shadow work', for example in childminding, had developed into careers more permanent than originally intended. The job histories of the 'veterans' among the private childminders covered more than ten years of experience.

The household-oriented women also co-operated and participated in a wide repertoire of unpaid exchanges with their neighbours, ranging from job-sharing and baby-sitting to personal counselling. Assumptions of reciprocity, whether of a specific or non-specific kind, seemed to underlie several of these exchanges. The unpaid work in the neighbourhood also comprised one-way transfers, as demonstrated in services performed by young women to help elderly neighbours. Giving help and care to old people in this way accorded with norms of local life, and was positively sanctioned. (For very interesting analyses of the significance of one-way transfers or non-reciprocal giving in women's lives, see Bernard 1975; Ve 1984; Land and Rose 1985.)

Patterns of work and care

Daily life in the neighbourhood gave an immediate impression of a division of labour by gender, seemingly traditional, in so far as the young women spent their days within the area while the men were away at work. This impression was enhanced by the women who spoke of themselves solely as housewives, and nothing more, although their income-generating work was considerable.

The everyday activities of two neighbourhood women, Mrs Hansen and Mrs Jensen, will give an idea of the complexity of the household-oriented women's work patterns. Mrs Hansen's schedule also shows how the household-oriented women's work patterns are interconnected in local support networks and extended systems of reciprocity. The excerpt from Mrs Jensen's work history elaborates on the development of combined earning and caring strategies. Her story emphasizes the interdependence of 'modern' and 'traditional' households, in particular as evidenced in informal childcare arrangements.

Mrs Hansen was 35 years old, the mother of two children aged 8 and 11 years. Her husband worked in an auto repair shop. The family had lived in the area for ten years. Like many of the neighbourhood women, Mrs Hansen worked in a nearby firm, cleaning at inconvenient hours, in the late evening, night or early morning. She was also one of the veterans among the private childminders in the district. When interviewed, Mrs Hansen was minding the child of another family for thirty hours a week in addition to caring for her own children. Moreover, she had agreed to look after a neighbour's child who was in his first year at school 'whenever needed' outside school hours, since both the parents worked outside the home. The latter Mrs Hansen did without pay. The parents were her close friends and there was a steady exchange of services and help between the two families.

During summer Mrs Hansen started a normal day at 5 a.m. Ten minutes later she was scrubbing the floors at a work place nearby. By 7.30 a.m. she was back in her own kitchen making breakfast for the children. Just before she returned, her husband left for his job. By a longstanding tacit agreement regarding the division of labour between the Hansens, getting the children ready for school and making breakfast, like most of the other household chores, were Mrs Hansen's responsibility. The children were sent off to school at 8.30 a.m. At 9 a.m. the 2-year-old child she minded appeared on the steps accompanied by her mother. Mrs Hansen invited the other woman for a cup of coffee, as she regularly did. One of the neighbours came by to make a call from Mrs Hansen's telephone. He too was offered a cup of coffee and joined the women, joking about Mrs Hansen's kitchen being the neighbourhood café. By 9.30 a.m. the two adult visitors had left. Mrs Hansen chatted with the child, while tidying the kitchen, making her lunch and finding her overcoat. And then it was time to take her to the local playground where the neighbourhood children went to play supervised by a playground leader. On the way back, Mrs Hansen stopped at the shop to get her groceries, and to say hello to various neighbours.

Thereafter she spent one and a half hours working in her house, vacuuming, doing the beds, washing the floors, doing the dishes. On her way out she checked whether her old neighbour had picked up his morning newspaper. This had become one of her regular habits after the old man had had a serious accident the previous winter. 'He might have died if we hadn't noticed and called for the ambulance.' She then proceeded to the courtyard. Several of the neighbourhood women were already there with their coffee pots, needlework, newspapers, talking, joking and laughing. The youngest children were playing on the lawn.

At 2 p.m. the children had to be picked up from the playground, and the older children were returning from school. The child of a neighbour joined them, after leaving his books with Mrs Hansen. The mother of the child Mrs Hansen minded, came for her about 3 p.m. Then it was time for Mrs Hansen to start preparing dinner, which was served regularly at 4.30 p.m. when Mr Hansen returned from work. In the evening, after cleaning the kitchen and getting the children ready for bed, Mrs Hansen would return to her cleaning job and finish her day's duties there.

During one normal day, Mrs Hansen did unpaid work in her home ('housework') as well as her regular waged work. Minding another woman's child for pay, without reporting this for taxation, she did work that is considered irregular or 'hidden'. Moreover, on an unpaid basis she exchanged services with her neighbours and was ready to mind a neighbour's child without expecting to be paid for it.

In the work histories of the other neighbourhood women there were many cases of the women acting as 'entrepreneurs', in co-operation creating for themselves income-generating work opportunities inside or outside regular employment. This was done in different ways, for example by the courtyard women operating as informal 'employment agencies', telling each other about vacancies or new jobs nearby. Otherwise, common enterprises included informal job-sharing and the establishment of private work agreements, and most widespread of all, the many informal arrangements for childcare.

The women's entrepreneurial activity is one of the central themes in the case of Mrs Jensen. The following excerpt from her work history also exemplifies the mutual dependencies between women living in 'modern' and 'traditional' households.

Mrs Jensen is 32 years old, the mother of two children aged 9 and 7 years. The Jensen family has lived in the neighbourhood for twelve years. When her first child was born, Mrs Jensen, who worked as a secretary, reduced her hours and became one of the many part-time working Norwegian mothers. Mr Jensen worked in a machine-tool firm. He did not participate much in the daily chores of housework. Only sporadically did Mrs Jensen get any help with the child. Most often she took the baby with her to work. As the child grew older and became more demanding, she found this arrangement increasingly tiring. Encouraged by neighbourhood women, she decided to give up her job and do the minding of a friend's child as an alternative.

Two years later when the child she minded was accepted into public day care, Mrs Jensen agreed to mind the child of a colleague of one of her friends. At that time Mrs Jensen had just had her second child, and the two babies were about the same age. After three more years of combining mothering and informal childminding, Mrs Jensen decided to leave the childminding 'business' and find a 'real' job outside the home. However, when the mother of the second child she had minded asked whether Mrs Jensen would agree to mind the child of a friend of hers, Mrs Jensen was easily persuaded to accept her third childminding engagement.

Later on, Mrs Jensen and the mother of this last child became a sort of local 'information centre' helping other mothers and potential minders to meet. In one case the mother introduced a friend who desperately needed someone to care for her child. Mrs Jensen was asked to help, and brought the question up in her daily conversations with the neighbourhood women. Some days later one of Mrs Jensen's neighbours offered to mind the child.

Years of minding the children of other families had provided Mrs Jensen with an opportunity to earn some money of her own, and in a way which she found more compatible with her tasks as mother and housewife than the job she had previously held. The importance of the social networks in mediating the demand for as well as the supply of childminders was evident in Mrs Jensen's job history. Mrs Jensen appeared to be a key person in the development of other women's caring and earning strategies.

A combination of different work practices like the ones shown by Mrs Hansen and Mrs Jensen are not uncommon among young neighbourhood women. The composition of their work patterns is influenced by the division of work in the household, ascribing to the women the main responsibility for housework and for family management, and by the demand for labour in the local women's labour market. Friendship and neighbourly relations also play a part in the formation of the pattern. In the organization of the two women's everyday schedule it is evident that social relations influence the work practices.

The employment-oriented women combined different types of work, too. The priority of regular paid work in their time schedules necessarily implied a reduction of the 'spare time' available for investment in neighbourhood relations. The local involvement of these women was therefore comparatively restricted. Co-operation with other local women was, however, often in evidence in the provision of childcare. These childcare agreements contributed to the income generation of the household-oriented mothers and at the same time helped secure the regular labour market participation of the employment-oriented mothers.

Exchanges in everyday life

Regular wage work and housework are important elements in most adult women's work patterns. As I have shown in the description of daily activities among women in this area, other forms of work are also important. Both the unpaid work, mediated by institutional contexts such as kinship, friendship and neighbourhood relations, and paid, irregular work must be considered if we are to gain a better understanding of women's involvement in work and care.

The everyday exchanges of practical advice, help and services may be analysed as an informal support system, and a local 'infrastructure' of social services which entails comprehensive arrangements for the minding of pre-school children, the supervision of school children during the parents' hours of paid work, and the care-giving services for old people living in the neighbourhood. The neighbourhood does not, however, provide an exhaustive supply of such services. Yet, the many small-scale activities represent important supplements to, or substitutes for, the formally organized public social services, as demonstrated in childcare, and also in the services rendered to old neighbours.

Looking at the different kinds of exchanges (Sahlins 1969) or at the different norms of reciprocity underlying these exchanges (Gouldner 1960), I have distinguished between three main forms of unpaid neighbourhood work:
– the reciprocal, specific exchanges with a prior agreement as to the equivalence of what is to be given and gained;

– the reciprocal, non-specific exchanges involving a variety of goods and services on both sides;
– the one-way transfers, where reciprocity is not apparent.

Exchanges of goods and services between neighbourhood women are sometimes organized in 'specific reciprocity' (Sahlins 1969), as in the arrangement between two mothers who both have paid part-time work. They have a long-standing agreement about dividing the care of their children between them. When one works the other minds the children and vice versa. In this way both women are able to maintain their employment and to have incomes of their own. Permanent, specific arrangements of this kind are not common in the area. Mothers, however, often made specific exchanges of services demanding short-time obligations, such as baby-sitting or chaperoning of children to numerous leisure time activities, such as school orchestra, ballet, etc.

More usual in the neighbourhood are the reciprocal but non-specific exchanges. Neighbourhood mothers often mind one another's children; finding a baby-sitter at night is no problem. Sometimes the spouses' and the children's skills are also mobilized in the exchange of practical services between households. Older children are used as baby-sitters or they are sent shopping for a neighbour. A husband may be asked to help if the childminder's car has broken down. By sharing or dividing the daily duties of housework and family management between them, the women create mutual relief. Sometimes they also engage in informal job-sharing.

Looking at neighbourhood life as an observer, it has not always been easy to specify what is given and what is received in these exchanges, nor how the gives and takes are balanced, or what is a return for which favour. Neighbourhood women dispose of different sets of resources. One woman may have the time and energy to mind more children than her own, another may perhaps mobilize her husband's skills in carpentry. Moreover, every giving does not appear to be explicitly measured against a very specific gain. The flows between households are perhaps balanced or regulated by some kind of 'mental accounting', as suggested by Midré (1978). A balancing of exchanges may be anticipated as a long-term outcome. The giving creates a mutual expectation of a recompense, or some sort of delayed reciprocity. Helping one's neighbours may thus be seen as the helper's insurance for future returns, if such be needed. A simple 'cost benefit' analysis of this may seem plausible, but can hardly explain the totality of mutual exchanges. In some cases, moreover, work is done, and services performed with returns being neither expected nor given.

The one-way transfers imply no observable immediate or later return or recompense. In this area such transfers were characteristically carried out by the younger women for older neighbours. Direct reciprocation of the favour was not anticipated and seldom given. Satisfaction was derived from the pleasure of giving, and keeping up with the local standard for being a good neighbour.

One-way transfers typically were small-scale services, easily performed by the younger women, yet complicated to manage for the old, and mattering much for their well-being. For example, the young women did some shopping for the older neighbours in winter-time. They cleaned the stairs and acted as intermediaries between old neighbours and the outside world. Services like these were done when asked for, sometimes also when not explicitly requested. Some of the young women kept an eye on elderly neighbours to make sure they were well. This relationship of 'responsibility at a distance' was supported by the norms of the neighbourhood subculture.

The efficiency as well as the scope of the local unpaid work are revealed in the informal and easy mobilization of neighbourly efforts in a difficult situation: a young mother, with children of 8 and 11 years, was suddenly taken seriously ill. All at once the daily life of the family had to be reorganized. As the news spread, friends, relatives and neighbours came to offer help. Within a very short time a new structuring of daily tasks emerged. The husband and children did somewhat more than their usual share of the housework. Neighbourhood women dealt with the rest. They cleaned the floors, vacuumed, did the laundry and brought it back neatly ironed. They also prepared the dinner, did the shopping and stopped by once in a while to cheer up the patient and to see if something else was needed. The sick woman's other work assignments were likewise taken care of. One neighbourhood woman offered to substitute for the patient in her regular paid work. Another woman promised to do the childminding. Within three weeks the woman was well, and the organization of her daily life returned to the normal routine.

To none, save me, did the smooth, yet complex 'take-over' of the patient's everyday activities appear surprising. 'Just the way we are', was the usual comment. However, even if the neighbourhood women generally expected 'the others', or 'the girls' to help in an emergency situation, the range of exchanges and the intimacy between neighbours varied. Neighbourliness was developed by degrees. Personal attachment and forms of exchange influenced the normative construction of the neighbour relationship.

Neighbourhood women had created diversified work practices, catering for their own and each other's everyday needs. Conceptualizing informal social services as part of composite, locally based work patterns, the social activities and social relations which I have described present a perspective on the way women act and work that is different from what is commonly characterized in the terms 'self-supporting social network' or 'informal community care'. The use of such terms tends to marginalize the importance of women's work and time commitments in the production and maintenance of informal service systems. Moreover, the so-called 'well-functioning social networks' are not unambiguously 'good' seen from a woman's point of view. The fragility of such constructions (including those I have described) is often overlooked. As often noted, the establishment of formal social services may lead to a fragmentation of informal support and help systems (see e.g. Lewis 1980). However, a lack of public services may have similar consequences, since the demand for help and care can easily overload the capacities of informal networks. In the neighbourhood studied it is, for example, important that limits are set as to what types and levels of services can be informally provided. Small-scale services are easily effectuated. Comprehensive services can be arranged on special occasions, in emergencies, and on a short-term basis. The total responsibility, for example, for old, helpless neighbours cannot be managed on an informal local basis with no outside support. Informal support networks and exchanges of services in this neighbourhood are closely associated with the presence of mothers with young children. The capacity for informal care-giving is of a transitory character and may easily disappear.

Neighbourhood as exchange

The neighbourhood may be analysed as a complex system of interconnected patterns of earning and caring where childcare is a central element. In mutual dependence women create the conditions for each other's earning and caring strategies. What are the processes in which the coping strategies are generated? What are the conditions producing the linkages and interconnections? The design of the neighbourhood in several ways contributes to neighbourly contact, as noted above, and provides a setting conducive to local interaction and exchange. In addition, two characteristics of the neighbourhood work organization are essential. First, it is necessary that there are *similarities* in the earning and caring experiences among some of the women. Secondly, *dissimilarities* between individual patterns for earning and caring are also important. Neighbourhood exchanges and informal support systems are generated in the transactions among the household-oriented women and in the interconnections between the household-oriented and the employment-oriented women's work patterns. Let me begin by analysing the similar combinations of work, as shown in the work patterns common among the household-oriented women.

The household-oriented women's strategies for combining paid work and childcare are shaped by the mutual effects of several processes. Important are:

(i) a gendered division of domestic labour, traditional in so far as women are given the main responsibilities for childcare, housework and family management;

(ii) local labour market processes which produce a steady demand for women's labour in jobs that do not interfere with housewifery or mothering;

(iii) a neighbourhood subculture where norms of reciprocity and 'good neighbourliness' are pronounced. This culture is developed and maintained primarily by the young women whose co-operative practices are in turn reinforced by the subculture.

Basically, the household-oriented women's everyday activities are structured by gendered divisions in time-use and economic activity within the household. The various combinations of mothers' earning and caring capabilities are greatly influenced by the employment of the husbands and by the husband being the main economic provider. Local job opportunities where inconvenient hours, part-time or irregular work are common do not represent any great challenge to the traditional division of work and responsibility in the household. Such a job does not necessitate renegotiations of the principles underlying the domestic division of labour.

The household-oriented women share a common set of experiences as regards paid work, family management and time-use. Within the framework set by the division of household work by gender, the combined earning and caring strategies of the household-oriented women offered an opportunity to combine pleasure and plight. Accepting 'inconvenient' job hours meant that consideration for one's own good did not collide with the management of family comfort. Jobs of higher status were difficult to find nearby. Moreover, full-time work with normal hours would challenge the division of labour at home, and eradicate basic elements in the women's neighbourhood contact. The well-being of the family was important when housework was combined with 'inconvenient' job hours in the first place. Attending to one's own good was a more essential element when this economic and time-use adaptation was continued over time.

The everyday schedule leaves some time at free disposal, which is often spent in informal local conversations and exchanges vital to the development of the local neighbourhood subculture. The young women appear relatively satisfied with the everyday activities structured around their housework and mothering commitments. In this context the importance of 'significant others' ought to be mentioned. Most often the significant others are neighbourhood women who spend much time together. Participation in courtyard life seems important when 'the girls' keep to their low-status jobs. The close social and personal contacts are undoubtedly highly valued in themselves. In addition, they also provide the basis for a comprehensive mobilization and re-allocation of resources between the women and between their households. The social texture of neighbourhood life may thus have contributed to the continuation of patterns of earning and caring originally planned as temporary, simply because they have become part of a general 'style' in the organization of everyday life.

In everyday time-use the household-oriented women also share a strong local attachment. A common set of norms and attitudes have been developed which reciprocally influence the informal exchanges of daily life. In the neighbourhood many forms of work are closely connected with feelings of neighbourhood identity and with friendship between the young women. This is brought out in the exchanges between young neighbourhood women, but also in their relationship to older neighbours. Social relations and local work organization are mutually interdependent.

In the case of the household-oriented women the division of labour *within* the household is mutually dependent upon a sharing of resources *between* similar types of households. At first glance the well-developed social networks and close personal ties between these women seemed to help conserve a traditional division of domestic and gendered labour. But this was only part of the picture. In the courtyard, private issues were also made public and transformed into matters of common concern. A tinge of apprehension could be noted among the men when they commented upon the women's 'courtyard union'. In some cases power relations within the household were affected as the backing of the courtyard supported individual women in their marital negotiations about the allocation of household resources. The courtyard community gave women a degree of autonomy *vis-à-vis* their husbands. In some respects the equality between neighbourhood women, which was conditioned by the division of labour within the households, was more important than attaining greater formal equality with the men. The neighbourhood women formed the peer group. To become what was at that time known as a 'man in skirts' was not the women's ambition.

Traditional and modern families are linked by mutual arrangements as well. The work patterns of household-oriented and employment-oriented women are interconnected in informal childminding arrangements which presuppose dissimilar work and time schedules within the two types of families. The use of time and the economic activities of the modern families are dependent upon alternative ways of structuring the day within the traditional families, and vice versa.

Mutual dependence becomes even more evident when looking at the individual actors. The work patterns and time schedules of mothers and minders are tied into the informal arrangements for childcare. Mothers make space for themselves – a pocket of spare time – that can be invested in regular employment. Minders create for themselves an opportunity for income-generating work that may be more attractive than other possibilities, if alternatives exist at all. A high level of regular employment among mothers combined with a shortage of approved day-care provision have mobilized labour among other groups of women, whose earning and caring strategies are different.

One might perhaps analyse the totality of local women's earning and caring strategies as produced by such sets of dyadic relations. However, that would be an over-simplification. Sometimes three, four or more women with slightly dissimilar work patterns divide common tasks between them, on a mutual basis. Also, some of the neighbourhood women appear as 'sociometric stars', key persons in as much as they act as mediators in linking other women's work patterns.

Formal and informal social service systems are also linked, as demonstrated in the organization of childcare. As noted above, mothers and minders supplement or substitute for the shortages of welfare state services for children, at a minimum cost to the public purse. Public budgets show formal services as expensive. Informal services on the contrary are cheap. Hence the public interest in community care. For individual carers the case is reversed. Small is not necessarily beautiful (cf. Hirsch 1977; Bulmer 1984). The costs of planning, producing and maintaining informal services are met on a private basis in childcare by mothers and minders who serve as a buffer zone between family needs and the welfare state. Were public budgets to absorb these costs, for example by providing professional care, the public share of 'reproduction costs' would dramatically increase. But the demands for care represented by very dependent people are not met within the welfare state economy. In order to secure the care and welfare of very dependent people the welfare state has also had to depend on an informal infrastructure of services usually provided by women. Informal carer careers support the welfare state.

When placing different forms of work side by side, as I have done here, the complexities and variations in everyday work organization become more apparent. The perspective underlines what is already obvious, that for the day-to-day functioning of the society more work is done and more work is necessary than is registered as paid work. The organization of care-giving work offers abundant examples, showing the importance of private and informal involvement. Everyday life shows public services and private arrangements as intermixed. Though analytically useful, empirically the public–private distinction is blurred.

This analysis of the organization of everyday life leads to several sets of questions. One that is normative and political refers to the division of responsibility for childcare between families and the welfare state. A second points to problems in social analysis when it comes to conceptualizing the 'public' and 'private' domains so that the importance of the one to the other is not obscured. A third issue concerns the integration of new interrelationships of work and care in social policy and in social theory.

Welfare state policies and everyday practices

The structural framework that allows for the development of new individual strategies is created by political and economic decisions concerning the economy, employment and social reproduction. This framework delimits and influences the activity 'arenas' of individual actors, but does not predetermine the individual opportunity situation, nor the individual choice of strategies. Moreover, when aggregated, the sum total of individual choices concerning strategies for combining earning and caring influences the structure of employment, of labour markets and of social reproduction. Everyday action is at work in the making of social structure.

To summarize the reasoning: I have worked with dichotomies of actors at individual, household, market and state level.[8] The basic distinction at market level is between formal and informal market formations. The regular labour market participation of mothers is supported by an informal labour market producing childcare, and vice versa.

The distinction between households is based on the division of earning and caring responsibilities within the household. The 'traditional' household is the one that approaches the division of labour of the 'isolated nuclear family' model most closely. The 'modern' dual-earner household presents a somewhat more egalitarian division of labour, at least when income-generating work is assessed.

The differentiation of women's strategies for combining earning and caring is based on time-use, and refers to the sets of activities which are most important in the structuring of everyday life, earning or caring. Employment-oriented mothers organize daily life around the schedule of job commitments. Household-oriented mothers structure the day around the caring commitments and the schedules of (other) family members. Thus, my classification does not refer to motivation or the individual preferences of women, but rests on observations of women's behaviour; in this case how they combine earning and caring commitments.

The differences in women's strategies are to some extent mediated via negotiations in households. Interactions between women from different types of households contribute to the differentiation between households, and also to the development or maintenance of different labour market segments which are in mutual influence. The interaction of formal and informal markets contributes to the opportunity structure of individual women and influences their choice of action *vis-à-vis* earning and caring.

The differentiation of forms at each level is generated by processes that contribute to mutual dependence within organizational levels and between levels. The employment of some mothers who hold 'normal work contracts' in full-time employment depends upon the availability of other women for childcare. The demand for childcare among formally employed mothers allows the childminders to have some income of their own, while at the same time allowing them to care for their own children. The combination of earning and caring arrangements of the one is in mutual dependence with the dissimilar combination taken by the other. When aggregated, informal childcare arrangements constitute informal labour markets. Everyday practices generate structural change.

Individually, the informal arrangement for childcare appears as insignificant. The totality of such arrangements, however, has reached considerable proportions. Unregistered childminding represents important employment opportunities for Norwegian women, so that one may well speak of the informal or 'hidden' labour markets of childcare. These labour markets support and maintain the regular employment of parents. The formal and informal labour markets are mutually dependent.

The informal economy of childcare is premised upon the co-existence of different family forms. The 'modernization of motherhood' represented by the formally employed mothers was an important precondition for the development of an informal labour market in childcare provision. Important in this respect was also the presence within local labour markets' recruitment areas of forms of households in which the women's strategies for combining earning and caring were different. The emergence of the modern dual-earner family was dependent upon the conservation of a more traditional family form. Different opportunity situations and different coping strategies within a welfare state framework produce a differentiation of motherhood models.

7   Carer state and carer careers

Introduction

The making of motherhood in the post-World War II period in
Scandinavia is profoundly influenced by the interplay of two processes:
one is at work in the restructuring of boundaries between the state and
the family in childcare, the other is demonstrated as a shift in the
gendered division of labour within families, and notably in the increased
economic activity of mothers.

In the Scandinavian countries this motherhood experiment is supported by the welfare state. However, as I have shown, welfare state
policies alone do not account for the reconstruction of motherhood
registered in the years 1945–85. Motherhood is also changed by other
actors, and most importantly by mothers themselves. My examination
traces changes in the material basis of motherhood and in the opportunity situation of mothers. I consider welfare state approaches and
mothers' responses to motherhood. Including the recent political history
of motherhood as well as mothers' everyday practices in the analysis
does not imply that I see 'mothers' and 'welfare state' as actors of equal
stature, power and authority. What I do emphasize is that everyday
action is an important element in producing structural change.

My analysis focuses on two aspects of motherhood, what I have
termed the 'earner' aspect, referring to economic activities, and the
'carer' aspect, which encompasses nurturing, rearing and upbringing.
Social theory usually casts mother as the parent primarily responsible
for childcare, and primarily as a carer-parent. Dealing with Scandinavian mothers as my main case, I do not take issue with the first part of
the argument. The second assumption needs qualification when confronted with the Scandinavian data on mothers' employment. Thus, I
argue that approaching mothers as both earners and carers allows for a
more accurate understanding of the changes in 'motherhood models' in
recent decades. My approach highlights a lack of co-ordination between
the welfare state policies that more or less intentionally promoted the

employed-mother family, and the childcare policies that did not meet the 'new' mothers' demand, though Sweden and Denmark did better than Norway. This approach also reveals a discrepancy between welfare state motherhood policies on the one hand, and mothers' practices on the other, particularly in Norway. The motherhood model favoured by Norwegian mothers was not the one promoted by the state.

Moreover, conceptualizing mothers as both carers and earners calls attention to a contradiction inherent in the welfare state structure in the ways in which earning and caring, or, more specifically, formal employment and informal care are incorporated. Both sets of activities, employment and caring, production and social reproduction, are essential to social life and to society's continued existence. However, the welfare state benefit and entitlement system, what Marshall (1965) termed 'the social rights', differentiates distinctly between earners and carers. A wide range of entitlements are employment-related. Comparatively few are caring-related. Examining access to entitlements, and the processes that differentiate access, I have argued that the welfare state in effect operates with a dual model of citizenship, where the entitlements of citizen the carer do not equal those of citizen the wage-worker. The division of labour which ascribes caring responsibilities to women shows the gendering of citizenship. Moreover, my analysis points to contradiction and ambivalence in the relationship between the women and the welfare state, but also to a mutual dependence. This duality is displayed particularly in caring.

After a brief summary of my findings I shall return to a discussion of the contradictions in the relationship between the welfare state and women, and to the questions concerning the character of the relationship as 'patriarchy' or 'partnership'.

Welfare state and working mothers: summary

Welfare state policies in Scandinavia in the post-war years introduced a reconceptualization of motherhood – more deliberately in Denmark and Sweden, less so in Norway – by providing state-sponsored childcare, and by economic policies that eventually offered employment opportunities to married women.

Preparing day-care legislation and launching state-sponsored programmes for pre-school children in which education and care were to be integrated, the Scandinavian welfare state initiated changes in the boundaries between the public and the private. Including the early childhood years in its sphere of influence the state introduced a new set of principles governing the relation of the state to the family. In principle, state-sponsored childcare was to be made universally available, accommodating all children whose parents required such services. Though not always explicitly stated, this universalist ambition signalled images of the family and motherhood new to Scandinavian societies, implying that the state was to share in everyday childcare responsibilities.

Examining the policies concerning mothers' earning and caring commitments, I find that the notion of a common Scandinavian 'model' of reproduction policies is exaggerated. The results of policies, particularly as witnessed in Norway, also do not fit well with the 'model' of the Scandinavian welfare states as institutional in their overall design. The shortage of day-care provision contrasts with the universalist ambitions originally set for state involvement in the early childhood years. Denmark, Norway and Sweden approach the childcare commitments of employed mothers in both similar and different ways. Although structural similarities are striking, so are the differences. State-sponsored childcare represents a substantially larger share of the total supply of services in Denmark and Sweden than in Norway. Moreover, the policies of the three countries appear to be grounded in different images of the mother–child relationship, and of the relation of family policy to the economy. In Denmark and Sweden the economy's need for labour was integrated into childcare policies to an extent not seen in Norway. Providing large-scale, state-sponsored day care, Denmark and Sweden facilitated the employment of mothers, while Norway gave this 'model' of motherhood only modest support. Not surprisingly perhaps, the countries in which 'good day care' was also seen in a labour market context were more successful in reaching the universalist aims, and in meeting demand, than was Norway, where day-care policies were aimed more exclusively toward the socialization of the child.

Conflicting motherhood ideologies were voiced in the debate preceding day-care legislation in Norway. When the Act governing day care for pre-school children was implemented, practical support of the universalist ambition was less than half-hearted. Informal childminding and social network-based arrangements that represented the bulk of extra-familial childcare in operation when the law was passed were excluded from the state's sphere of responsibility. Local authorities were charged with the responsibility for early childhood education and care, but provision of day care was not made mandatory, giving to the universalist ambition a utopian ring.

Without underestimating the importance of the principle of state responsibility for all young children, day-care provision in practice shows rather limited, or residual, results. Whatever the intention of legislators, childcare remained largely a private concern. To the majority of employed mothers or to those wanting employment, the effect of national day-care legislation hardly represented a new deal.

When the Norwegian Day Care Act was instituted in 1975, mothers' labour market participation had been on the increase for several years. The welfare state did not intervene directly to promote or prevent women's employment. Indirectly, however, the welfare state played an important part in this change. Expanding its services locally, the welfare state recruited women to the public sector labour market, generally because women represented the only domestic labour reserve.

In Scandinavia a connection is often assumed to exist between the policies of production and those of social reproduction in that state-sponsored childcare is perceived as a precondition of mothers' employment. Analysing in context the interplay of the two processes in Norway offers a more complex picture. Mothers' employment was not a special concern of childcare policies. Childcare was not an important issue in labour market policies. Mothers' employment was well advanced when day-care legislation was instituted, a fact that was acknowledged but not addressed. In fact, in the 1970s and 1980s state-sponsored childcare was marginal when it came to facilitating the early employment of mothers. Far more important in this respect was the mobilization of private, informal resources. Childcare provision shows a division of labour within the private sphere more striking than the division of labour between the state and the family.

Legislation concerning employed mothers' (and fathers') entitlements to leave of absence in connection with the birth of a child, and to parental leave when a child or her minder is ill, provides an interesting exception to this overall picture. In such cases the demands of social reproduction are given priority when in conflict with the demands of production. This lawmaking points to a 'budding' partnership between the state and the family, in which the state acknowledges and reacts to the dual commitments in employed parents' lives. Important as this is as a solution offered to parents' practical problems, and as a reconceptualization of the relationship between production and social reproduction, the partnership is, however, restricted to relatively rare occasions in the employed parents' lives. The everyday problems created by the incompatibility of the labour market and childcare structures were not met by a rapid, generous supply of state-sponsored facilities. Introducing entitlements to earn supplementary pension for unpaid childcare acknowledges the importance to society of this work, but offers no solution to employed parents' daily problems with managing jobs and children. The gap between demand and supply is consistent in childcare provision. After a decade of experience with state-sponsored day care, private informal arrangements still accommodate a larger proportion of the employed mothers' children than do the state-sponsored services.

As the gendered segregation of economic provision declined within families, the conflicting demands of production and social reproduction, of labour market participation and childcare commitments became increasingly visible. In Norway these conflicts were not conceived as requiring structural change. The concept of 'the employed mother', which came to represent mothers' predominant approach to motherhood in the 1970s and 1980s, was not politically institutionalized. Rather, the problem of structural incompatibility was left to individual families to solve, in practice, usually to the mothers.

The 'models of motherhood' contained in Norwegian economic and family policies were contradictory. The motherhood model presumed in childcare policies in particular, which largely neglected the rapid spread of the employed-mother family, contrasted with the one adopted by the majority of Norwegian mothers in the 1970s and 1980s. Increasingly mothers opted for labour market participation and for extrafamilial childcare. Mothers managed to introduce new approaches to motherhood without seriously challenging fathers' time-use and work patterns, nor waiting for state support. As state-sponsored services were scarce, and formal markets did not produce services at selling prices, mothers' coping strategies commonly involved the mobilization of informal resources for childcare. Social networks and 'shadow' labour provided services that outnumbered public provision. Up to the 1990s public policies made only marginal attempts to supervise, assist or control this flowering informal economy of childcare. Operating as small-scale 'entrepreneurs', mothers and minders in mutual influence developed an informal infrastructure in childcare, which supported the formal employment of mothers, and created informal employment opportunities for the childminders.

When aggregated, these everyday arrangements constitute an important element in the overall childcare structure, in womens' labour markets and in structural change. What appears in a structural context as institutional differentiation is, however, experienced in daily life as a fragmentation of services, and as a constant tension between demand and supply. At grassroots level the informal childcare arrangements represent an undercurrent of change in womens' earning and caring strategies outside formal planning and policy-making.

Considering welfare state policies as well as mothers' behaviour, I find striking the discrepancy between welfare state motherhood policies on the one hand, and mothers' practices of motherhood on the other.

Moreover, my examination of the political history of Norwegian reproduction policies points to a contradiction in welfare state policies
between the indirect, but important expansion of mothers' employment
opportunities on the one hand, and the neglect of mothers' everyday
needs for childcare facilities on the other. In Norwegian policies the
concept of the 'employed mother' has not received strong support.
Political institutionalization lags behind everyday practices. Welfare
state policies were not developed to promote the combination of
earning and caring that the majority of mothers adopted in their making
of motherhood. My study demonstrates that general statements concerning the Scandinavian model of the welfare state need qualification
when the policies of social reproduction are the issue.

The political history of Norwegian motherhood modifies the assumptions generally made about the welfare state and its intervention in
human reproduction. My examination does not show the family as
stripped of its functions in early childhood care and education. On the
contrary, welfare state intervention is only slight, and the use of private
and informal labour more widespread than is commonly associated with
the welfare state concept.

'Patriarchy' or 'partnership'

Social research has often pictured the welfare state as 'taking over'
social reproduction, or as emptying the family of its functions. Feminist
scholarship emphasizes similar trends when analysing the welfare state
relationship to women as a transfer from private to public dependence
(Hernes 1984). The change is interpreted alternatively as an expansion
of patriarchal structures of domination, or as evidence of a partnership
between the welfare state and women. I shall first look at how the
description fits in with my empirical material, and then turn to questions
concerning the character of the relationship between the welfare state
and women.

The shift in women's dependencies outlined represents an important
feature of welfare state development, but it is far from being the
principal characteristic of all fields of social reproduction in Scandinavia
in the 1980s. This conceptualization does not really convince when
childcare is the issue. Institutional analyses that focus on the state may
easily underestimate the importance of other parties and neglect the fact
that state involvement varies considerably across sectors. Acknowledging the collective interests in childcare, Scandinavian, and particularly
Norwegian, welfare state policies nevertheless imply that substantial
parts of these 'reproduction costs' are to be borne by the family.

From 1945 onwards, state involvement in the early childhood has expanded very gradually in Norway. By 1985, family-based childcare and other private, informal provisions still predominated. Examining the childcare arrangements of employed Norwegian mothers in particular, I find no unambiguous shift from private to public dependence. A restructuring within the private sector, a part-time transfer of childcare responsibilities from the family to other private, informal parties is a more characteristic feature of recent institutional differentiation than is state intervention.

Questions concerning the nature of the welfare state and the character of its relationship to women are central issues in feminist discourse from the 1970s onwards. Does the welfare state improve women's situation in society or does it merely represent a perpetuation of women's subordination in a new form? Detailed empirical examinations of different welfare states provide abundant evidence of women being less well rewarded, cared and catered for than men.[1] Feminist research in the Nordic welfare states portrays women as 'small men' (Dahl 1984). In the UK women are pictured as 'second-class citizens' (Carter 1988).

Feminist discourse is, however, divided when it comes to theorizing the character of the welfare state relationship to women. Piven (1985), in an overview, discerns two conflicting strands of interpretation: one conceives of the welfare state as 'patriarchal' and inherently oppressive (e.g. Seccombe 1974; Dalla Costa and James 1975; Eisenstein 1979); the other puts the welfare state relationship to women in cautious but positive terms, pointing to the possibility of alliances, or of the state promoting 'women-friendly' policies (Hernes 1987), even a partnership being formed between the state and some women around certain areas of common interest (Hernes 1982; Balbo 1982b; Siim 1984; and, more recently, Borchorst and Siim 1987). Conceivably, these different interpretations of what the welfare state represents to women might stem from the different sectors of welfare state policies being considered. However, whether the welfare state is analysed as 'patriarchal' or as offering a 'partnership', the organization of social reproduction is crucial to the argument.

Eisenstein (1979; 1983) contends that the organization of social reproduction in the welfare state, and in particular the ascription of childcare and upbringing to women, is essential in the perpetuation of men's dominance and women's subordination. The welfare state, which has not interfered with the division of childcare by gender, is accordingly conceptualized as a transformation of the power structures that women act within, a shift from what has been termed 'private' to 'public' patriarchy (Brown 1981).

Scandinavian feminist studies, on the other hand, often emphasize the possibility of state intervention in social reproduction as advantageous to women, or as improving women's lot. Hernes (1982; 1984) underlines the importance of the welfare state in providing more (and better) opportunities for women's participation in all walks of life, not only in the domestic sphere. Pointing to the possibilities of alliances between the welfare state and women, Hernes nevertheless emphasizes the 'tutelary' character of the relationship, referring to women as being 'the others', the class of citizens on whom a welfare state not of their own making was imposed (Hernes 1984). In later works Hernes (1987; 1988) underlines the 'woman-friendliness' of the welfare states in Scandinavia, while Dahlerup (1987) presents a more cautious analysis. According to Dahlerup, a lack of consistency characterizes the welfare state women policies. Other Scandinavian analysts also contest the 'patriarchy' interpretation of the welfare state. Siim (1984, pp. 20–1) conceives of the Scandinavian welfare state as establishing a partnership with women in social reproduction. Evidence of this, Siim argues, is shown in the policies towards employed mothers. The state acknowledged the dual obligations of mothers as earners and carers and developed state-sponsored childcare to facilitate this approach to motherhood (Borchorst and Siim 1987).

However, as I have shown, the Norwegian mothers' experience with the welfare state is different from that of mothers in Denmark and Sweden (Leira 1987a; 1989). My examination of Norwegian data concerning the two processes, the collectivization of childcare and the mass employment of mothers, gives evidence of different sets of alliances being made between the mothers and other parties, among them the state, the fathers and, most importantly, other women.

To some extent the different interpretations of the welfare state's approach as either 'patriarchy' or 'partnership' may stem from the rather different politics of social reproduction instituted by individual welfare states. The comparatively 'institutional' politics of the Scandinavian states presents a more comprehensive state intervention than do the more 'residual' approaches initiated by other states also considered welfare states. However, institutional welfare states are not therefore necessarily more oppressive than residual ones.

Opposition to state intervention in social reproduction may have been stronger in 'liberal' welfare states like Britain than in the 'Social Democratic' welfare states of Scandinavia, observes Ruggie (1984) in her comparison of policies concerning employed mothers in Britain and Sweden.[2] Ruggie interprets this as a result of the public–private split being essential to the liberal conceptualization of the state. In the Social

Democratic welfare state the public–private distinction does not hold the same significance. She suggests that a stronger commitment to working-class interests may explain why the Social Democratic Swedish welfare state has made large-scale investments in childcare, something Britain has not done. However, this analysis does not account for the considerable differences between the Scandinavian Social Democratic welfare states in their policies of social reproduction. Keeping the Norwegian case in mind the argument needs modification, as my analysis shows. Arguably, however, the 'Social Democratic' welfare states in Scandinavia – for a variety of historical, political and cultural reasons – have pursued more active policies of 'state feminism' than have other welfare states in Western Europe. State intervention in the private sphere is more commonly accepted, for example as a contribution toward redistribution and egalitarian reforms.

The 'patriarchy–partnership' debate, it seems to me, reflects a difference in analytical approach to the state – and thus different approaches in general. Conceptualizing the welfare state relationship to women in terms of 'patriarchy', gender hierarchies, male supremacy and women's subordination situates the 'woman question' as 'dead-ended', within an inherently oppressive framework. The patriarchal state apparently cannot be an instrument of women's interest. Theorizing the relationship as 'patriarchal' rightly acknowledges the collective dominance of men within important sectors of the state, the market and in the majority of society's institutions, and shows the state as instrumental in upholding men's structural domination and women's subordination. Yet the 'patriarchy' interpretation marginalizes the substantial advance of (the majority of) Scandinavian women in the post-World War II period, and the importance of women's collective actions to this end.

An interesting aspect of Scandinavian political culture is the terms 'state' and 'society' being used rather interchangeably, at least in Norway and Sweden (Hernes 1987; Esping-Andersen 1987). The Swedish welfare state is popularly embraced as 'folkhemmet', literally 'the people's home', a connotation which apparently voices considerable acceptance of state intervention. Pictured as a home, the state, at least potentially, may represent 'us' not 'them'. State power is not thus conceived as inherently oppressive. The partnership thesis – perhaps more inspired by consensus than conflict theories, and by the pragmatic corporatism of Scandinavian politics – portrays a state potentially benevolent towards citizens, women and men. This state does not necessarily side with men only; state intervention may represent a promotion of women's interests, however these are defined.

Conceptualizing the relationship between the welfare state and mothers as earners and carers as either 'patriarchal' or in terms of a 'partnership' does not fit in with the Norwegian evidence. My analysis does not support the interpretation of the welfare state forming an unambiguous 'partnership' with the employed mothers, if a partnership is taken to imply that the state as partner either precipitates social change and acts preventively to meet the problems forecast, or, that it intervenes *post hoc* to offer solutions to the problems emerging. The Norwegian welfare state policies towards mothers in employment display a mixture of measures, a passive partnership at best, with more than a tinge of patriarchal overtones. By providing new job opportunities for women, the expanding welfare state came to support the new family form, the employed-mother family that was rapidly increasing. The duality of mothers' lives as mothers and employees, carers and earners was, however, not addressed. Comprehensive schemes for the provision of collective day care were, as stated above, not really adopted. When employment policies and childcare policies are assessed in context, I find the relationship to be one of ambivalence and contradiction as well as one of mutual dependence, which presents the Norwegian welfare state as Janus-faced in its approach to employed mothers.

Carer state and carer careers

As earners and carers charged with both economic provision and childcare commitments, mothers engage in 'production' and 'social reproduction'. To any society both sets of activities are indispensable. However, as activities of individual actors, participation in social reproduction, or more narrowly, in informal caring, does not equal participation in formal employment when economic independence and access to social rights is the issue.

Assuming that access to social rights constitutes an important element of citizenship, and looking at the differentiation of access to welfare state benefits and entitlements, I have argued that the Scandinavian welfare state was in fact premised upon a dual concept of citizenship, one modelled on the citizen as wage-worker, the other on citizen the carer. The interdependence of these different activity patterns and entitlements was embodied in the nuclear family, in which material provision was exchanged for domestic and family management, social and sexual servicing and care. The employed-mother family challenges this notion of interdependence. Conceptualizing mothers as citizens underlines a contradiction in how the welfare state appreciates employment and caring. Discussing employment and care in a 'social rights' or citizenship perspective, I focus on processes that profoundly affect the gendering of citizenship. I do not deal with differentiation according to class and race.

The image of the welfare state as a carer state is upheld not only by publicly sponsored services but also by an informal 'caring culture' and by a multiplicity of informal carer careers. The present level of functioning of the welfare state service system depends on the women's labour power, in waged care-giving work as well as in unpaid and informally organized care. For example, in childcare, as I have documented, the Norwegian welfare state has accepted responsibility for only a minor part. The greater share is defined as a private responsibility. Childcare, though vitally important to society, is depending heavily on informal services supply.

Thus the formal and informal welfare state that I have presented in the institutional differentiation of childcare also entails a differentiation of carer careers, which distinguishes sharply between formal and informal carers. Welfare state benefits and entitlements generally favour the citizen as wage-worker more than the citizen as carer, and men more than women. This has to do with central assumptions of the welfare state design: one is the hierarchy of work forms, which accords primacy to wage-work, however useless, over other forms of work, however useful. Another – more tacit – is the presumption of private responsibility for care, and the third is the gendered division of labour.

In fact, the first two of the above-mentioned premises constitute 'employment' and 'care' as activities distinctly different as regards access to social rights. The distinction between individuals according to employment and caring commitments structures access to welfare state benefits. Different sets of entitlements are available for those citizens in whose adult lives formal employment is the main activity and the basic source of income, and those citizens in whose adult lives formal employment is of little or no importance. Activities that are unpaid, including activities of vital importance to society, such as informal and/or unwaged care for children, have not been considered as equal to waged work. What matters when access to social rights is the issue is the formal contract of employment and the form of remuneration given. Caring, when carried out informally or unpaid, is not integrated in the welfare state entitlement system on a par with employment. Establishing the possibility of earning entitlements to supplementary pensions for informal carers acknowledges this work as socially useful and necessary to society, but does not radically transform the entitlement system, nor the gendered division of labour in caring. In the welfare state the wage is still the most important entrance ticket to the benefits and entitlements.

If the three premises are not contested, if formal employment is to remain privileged in the welfare state reward system and caring to remain in private hands, ascribed to women as part of their unwaged responsibilities, the inherent inequities in earners' and carers' social rights will prevail, and a gendering of citizenship will remain a feature of welfare state design. The channelling of men to formal employment and of women to informal care, domestic and other unpaid or 'shadow' forms of work thus signifies a gendered division of the welfare benefits available as rights, and a gendering of the connotation of citizenship. As women join the labour market the differences are decreasing, but slowly, and unless legislation is changed they will not be eliminated until women's and men's behaviour patterns and opportunity structures become identical.

The dual model of citizenship is of considerable importance to the citizenship entitlements of women who combine job and childcare commitments. The 'typical' childcarer careers, for example that of mother or minder, entails private informal care, which means that access to social rights is restricted. For mothers and minders full access to social rights is ensured only if their caring commitments are organized so that they do not interfere with formal employment. Motherhood models that imply doing formal work part-time, allowing for interruptions or discontinuous labour market participation, for example to care for young children, mean reduced access to welfare state entitlements, as does informal childminding. Defining childcare as predominantly private and informal and as the responsibility and work of women, combines to provide a differentiation of access to social rights, and to a gendering of citizenship. Only if the employed mother gives employment first priority, in personal time-use, as do the majority of fathers, and does not allow childcare to interfere with full-time employment – which most mothers do not – will she gain full access to the total range of welfare state benefits and entitlements.

What is lacking is a concept of citizenship which encompasses those citizens whose adult lives comprise both economic provision and caring commitments; this is an interesting omission, considering that parents of children aged 0–10 years made up approximately one-third of the Norwegian labour force in the 1980s and an unknown proportion have considerable responsibility for the care of sick or old persons.

By the positive discrimination of those who have held regular employment, and the neglect of public investment in essential care, the welfare state has kept the model of citizen as wage-worker, to the detriment of the citizen as carer. The gendered division of labour, which makes labour market participation more a masculine pursuit than a feminine one, and the hierarchy of work forms ensure that the model of the citizen as wage-worker fits better with the labour patterns character-istic of men, and the model of the citizen the carer fits in with women's work patterns. Linking the hierarchy of work forms with the gendered division of labour, the welfare state favours male time schedules and work patterns more than women's schedules, practices and commit-ments.

Welfare state expansion contributed importantly to women's greater economic independence *vis-à-vis* individual men. Welfare state inter-vention was not, however, made in a form nor in a scope that radically questioned the privileges accorded by the welfare state to the citizen as wage-worker. If the welfare state established a partnership with citizens it was a 'patriarchal partnership', benefiting men's traditional behaviour patterns more than women's. The 'middle-class' character of welfare state provisions has often been noted in Scandinavian sociology. With the benefit of hindsight provided by feminist research, an addition should be made to the point that, although the welfare state meant real gains for Norwegian women, it did not seriously challenge male privilege.

In the 1970s and 80s Scandinavian women's situation in and in relation to the welfare state has changed considerably. The develop-ment of formal welfare state caring supported women's earning oppor-tunities, reduced their dependence on individual men and strengthened the mutual dependence between the women and the state. The welfare state came to depend on the labour of women in this provision of formal social services. As wage-workers and public employees women's stra-tegic position in society – and *vis-à-vis* the state – was improved. In this process, women in different forms of carer career have come to question the traditional division of responsibility and labour connected with caring for dependent others, and envisage new forms of distributions of burdens and rewards, plights and privileges stemming from caring commitments. Increasingly women realize that unless the welfare state design is altered, it is only by acting more as men do that they will gain greater equality as regards benefits and entitlements. Negotiations between the welfare state and caring women are thus situated in new contexts and attain new meanings.

However, this is only one aspect of the relationship. The 'revolution of rising expectations' has also meant increasing popular demands for welfare state services that have come to be regarded as social rights. The demands for care represented by very dependent persons are not satisfied by welfare state provisions. In order to provide the socially useful services, necessary in securing the welfare of the care-needing

sectors of the population, the welfare state has also had to depend on
the activity of the family, and on an informal infrastructure of services
and in a gendered division of labour. Women are usually the ones who
have to cope with the deficiencies of the welfare state services. In daily
life women soften the caring crises. They reduce the strain and pressure
on the public budget. Thus, the gap between individual demands for
care and the formal supply of services becomes less visible. Informal
care provided by women prevents or postpones a legitimation crisis that
shortage of services and entitlement may provoke.

The responsibility to provide for very dependent persons expresses a
contradiction inherent in the welfare state structure between the
normative, ideological basis on the one hand and the welfare state
reward system on the other. Taking care of the care-needing is a basic
value in the welfare state, yet doing the caring is attributed little
importance. To provide for the vital needs of very dependent persons,
be they young or old, holds a more prominent tenet in welfare state
ideology and value hierarchy than in the reward systems of the welfare
state. This contradiction which is displayed in the relationship of the
welfare state to the citizen as carer, that is, most often to women,
represents one of the great political challenges to modern welfare states.

Norwegian surveys convey a picture of a population divided in its
response to welfare state values, women being more in favour of welfare
state provisions than men (Aardal and Valen 1989). On the surface this
represents a paradox, as men have gained more from the welfare state
than women have. However, women may now have more to lose if the
welfare state becomes increasingly dismantled and collectively provided
services are fragmented. Political conflicts over welfare state issues are
sharpened and gendered as are the choices of which values to promote.
The provision of care for very dependent people is increasingly becoming an important issue of political debate and conflict. Who is to care for
whom if the welfare state withdraws?

Welfare states and women's work

The employed mother characteristically combines economic provision
and childcare. Social analysis and social policy need to integrate this
interrelationship of 'work' and 'care' in individual experience and as
institutionalized in society. In the case of the employed mother (or
parent) the importance of examining 'work' and 'care' within a common
conceptual framework is clearly evident. A substantial share of the
Scandinavian work-force combines commitments to both employment
and care for very dependent persons. This empirical characteristic

underlines the necessity to break down or transcend the models of 'work' and 'worker' that ignore or marginalize the interrelationship of labour market organization and labour reconstitution, care for children and sociocultural reproduction. Although mothers in the Western industrialized world have increased their economic activity, the gendered division of responsibility and work involved in childcare provision is still a foremost feature in families with young children. Men's collective choice of non-participation in childcare helps to maintain men's privileged position in society, and in relation to the market and the state.

The responsibility to care for persons who are not able to care for themselves constitutes an element common to the definition of both welfare state and femininity, definitions that are the outcome of social interests and social conflicts. The expanding Scandinavian welfare state changed the social division of labour, but upheld the gendered division of labour in the public domain and in the private sphere, and may even have strengthened it. More or less tacitly it was assumed that women would go on coping with care. In childcare, as we have seen, 'political motherhood', that is, the ascription of rearing and caring to mothers, prevailed as a basic structural element.

As shown in my study, the institutional differentiation of one limited but vitally important field of social reproduction, i.e. primary socialization, early childhood education and care, is the outcome of several processes, of which welfare state intervention is but one influence. Conceptualizing the state–family relationship over the early childhood years as a shift from private to public dependence marginalizes the responsibility and work still ascribed to the family, primarily to the mothers, and underlines the image of the interventionary state. Without underestimating the impact of the renegotiations of responsibilities implied in state policies, I have called attention to other processes that are also influential in generating everyday practices and institutional differentiation.

A detailed examination of the everyday practices of employed mothers displays an intermixture of private and public resources for childcare. My analysis of institutional differentiation underlines the need to deconstruct the concepts of 'public' and 'private', 'formal' and 'informal' if we are to improve the understanding of welfare state functioning, and the inter-relationship between the welfare state and its informal 'counterpart'.[3] Employed mothers' management of jobs and childcare also emphasizes the need for our rethinking the public–private distinction. Combining jobs and childcare responsibilities mothers crisscross between the private arena of the home, the public or private sector job, public or private transport systems and public and/or private childcare arrangements. Everyday provision for childcare, in particular, shows the public–private distinction as hazy. The childcare histories of the majority of the employed mothers in Scandinavia give evidence of a mixture of private and public arrangements caused for the most part by the shortage of public day care for very young children. Some parents and children even combine public and private services in their everyday childcare schemes, because the public day care available does not cover the parents' working hours, or because public facilities are not available to all the children of the family.

This differentiation of childcare services at an institutional level, the mixture of public and private, formal and informal arrangements, is experienced in everyday life as a fragmentation of supply or of services which are insufficiently or not co-ordinated. For those whose everyday life contains both earning and caring obligations this means that extra efforts and resources are demanded – more time, more planning – to put together an array of provisions sufficient to comply with the need for care. Balbo (1982b) has used the parable of patchwork quilting to depict women's everyday work in caring for other people's vital needs. Emphasizing the planned but unassuming character of the work, and its integrative aspects, the term also evokes associations of utility and beauty combined. In an earlier work I have compared women's strategies to integrate the schedules of paid work and childcare to a jigsaw puzzle, where the individual parts sometimes have to be made in the process of constructing the whole, and many different pieces must be fitted together neatly if everyday life is to be made coherent (Leira 1983). The metaphors refer to an institutional differentiation which has to be made explicit if we are to understand the making of motherhood in modern welfare states.

In childcare, a fundamental part of social reproduction, the informal economy constituted by mothers and minders is an essential ingredient. This informal economy represents a structural innovation that fills the lacunae of welfare state services, contributes to individual welfare, and maintains a general level of welfare provision. Socially necessary and useful services are delivered at a minimum cost to the welfare state economy. The costs of planning, producing and maintaining the informal services are met by mothers and minders who supplement or make substitutes for the shortages of the state-sponsored services. However, the importance of informal labour markets to the welfare state economy and to women's employment is underestimated.

Individually, the women-made arrangements for childcare may appear as insignificant, almost trivial, created as they often are on an *ad hoc* basis, as temporary provisions, to meet with pressing demands for care. When analysed in the context of welfare state strategies, the use of informal services has attained a striking degree of permanence. Mothers and minders function as a buffer zone, protecting not only their own interests but also those of the state in procuring vitally necessary care. This division of labour in childcare keeps the level of services up, and the public share of reproduction costs down. Defining motherhood as primarily an individual undertaking, moreover, obscures the considerable collective interests in human reproduction, and the considerable cost to the mothers.

When it comes to the reconstruction of motherhood in post-war Norwegian society, as demonstrated in particular by the mothers who took up both extrafamilial childcare and employment, my analysis does not show the welfare state as the principal initiator or as the predominant instrument of change. Only lately and in a very limited fashion do state policies approach the situation of the citizen mothers who have comprehensive commitments to both childcare and employment. The innovators and change agents are the mothers. This perspective illuminates and confirms an essential theoretical conclusion, in that it brings out the importance of everyday practices in the making of structural change.

Notes

1 INTRODUCTION

1 The term 'working mother' is often used as synonymous with 'wage-working mother' or 'employed mother'. I do not wish to give the impression that mothers who are not employed or in waged work do not work. This is a matter for empirical validation. Unless otherwise specified, however, the term 'working mothers', when used in the text, refers to those who are economically active, and/or in income-generating work.

2 MODELS OF MOTHERHOOD

1 For Norway, see e.g. NOU 1984:26, *Befolkningsutviklingen* (Demographic trends).
2 For an overview of positions, see Lerner (1985), ch. 1.
3 The difficulties in registering and assessing women's work when not paid are discussed e.g. by Skrede (1984b).
4 In addition tax legislation makes some concessions to the dual status of employed parents. Dual-earner families and single providers are entitled to a special tax deduction for expense accrued for childcare.
5 Since 1982 Sweden offers the possibility to earn supplementary pension to persons who care for children under the age of 3 (SCB 1990, *På tal om kvinnor och män*).
6 Cf. Norsk Riksmålsordbok, a standard Norwegian dictionary for etymology. See also Skaara (1979); Wærness (1979); Leira (1979).
7 Of particular importance is Engels' discussion in the *Origins of the Family, Private Property and the State* (Norwegian edition 1970) and the widely quoted preface which juxtaposes the importance of social reproduction with that of production. The making of commodities and of human labour both stand out as activities necessary to the continuation of human society. This posed problems for the Norwegian editor, who in a footnote of his own pointed out that Engels is guilty of an inaccuracy when juxtaposing the reproduction of generations with the production of material provisions ('levnetsmidler') for survival. The note further states that in the book Engels demonstrates that 'the mode of material production is what determines the development of society and societal institutions' (Engels 1970, p. 12, my transl.).

What represents the 'correct' interpretation of Engels has been much

178

debated. To the above-mentioned editor it was obviously important to establish the primacy of material production. Engels himself seems to be well aware that both sets of activities, production as well as generational reproduction, are necessary if a society is to prevail.

8 The domestic-labour debate had no common definition of central concepts like 'domestic labour' or 'social reproduction', and no agreement as to the interpretation of the character of the relationship of 'production' to 'social reproduction'. The initial lack of conceptual clarification was addressed, among others, by Edholm, Harris and Young (1977), who suggested that distinctions be made between biological reproduction (referring to generational reproduction), reproduction of labour (referring to the daily restitution and re-creation of human labour), and social reproduction, which refers to the re-creation of cultural forms and social life.

By and large, however, use of the term 'social reproduction' is highly eclectic. When applied without reference to schools of Marxist thought, 'social reproduction' may refer to a diffusely outlined 'private sphere', to daily life in the household, or to the trading of social and cultural traditions, for example in socialization and upbringing. For an early critique of the economistic and biologistic assumptions of the term 'social reproduction' see Dahlström and Liljeström (1981), and more recently Nicholson (1987).

'Domestic' labour posed problems of a similar kind in encompassing a diversity of activities which needed conceptual clarification and specification. (See Kaluszynska's (1980) witty and challenging review of the many connotations of 'domestic labour'.)

9 This concept is inspired by Prokop's thesis about a special feminine mode of production, 'a mode of production directed towards the satisfaction of needs' (Prokop 1978, p. 21).

10 Caring is not always accepted as representing one form of skilled work. This may have to do with caring skills often being acquired informally in the course of everyday life. Cockburn (1983) suggests that it may have to do with the term 'skill' being a male-connotated term.

11 The affective components in a caring relationship are sometimes difficult to specify, and the interdependence of activity and affection in the provision of care extremely complicated (see Noddings (1984) for a comprehensive discussion of caring within a moral philosophical context; Lessing (1985) for a literary exploration of the theme; and Ungerson (1987), for illustrations from daily life).

Altruism is the attitude most commonly associated with the caring for the very young, the very sick, the very old. However, altruism has different aspects. As a basis of care it may be of a voluntary character, e.g. as shown in caring arising out of a friendship between equals (Ve 1984). Altruism may, however, also take on a compulsory character, as pointed out by Land and Rose (1985), when care is provided in a relationship characterized by the dominance of the cared for and the subordination of the carer.

12 The system of state-sponsored day care comprises facilities owned by public authorities and private bodies (see Leira 1987a, and ch. 3). The private bodies include congregations, housewives' associations, parents' co-operatives, employers, among others. For facilities accommodating more

than a certain number of children it is mandatory to register with the local authorities. If approved, the facilities, whether public or private, are entitled to state subsidies. Some local authorities will also subsidize day care provided by private bodies.

State-sponsored day care comes in two main forms: centre-based care and 'family day care'. The latter refers to childminding in private homes, but organized under public auspices, with public supervision and subsidies on a par with care in centres. Family day care thus offers an example of a different public-private mix than does centre-based care. However, the vast majority of childminding arrangements are all private. Unlike the situation in other countries, for example, the UK, registration or licensing is mandatory only in some cases, which means that the majority of private childminders are not required to register (Leira 1987a).

3 WELFARE STATES AND WORKING MOTHERS

1 Some of the empirical data presented in this chapter, I collected for the Council of Europe Social Research Fellowship Programme 1986/7, Forms of Child-Care; see my report: *Day Care for Children in Denmark, Norway and Sweden* (Leira 1987a).
2 For a more detailed overview and discussion of maternity and paternity rights and parental leave in the Nordic countries, see R. Knudsen (1990).
3 Similar trends in early childhood education and care are registered throughout Western Europe, although the form and scope of public involvement varies (Moss 1988; Thayer et al. 1988).
4 Denmark: Lov om social bistand, nos. 63–4; Sweden: Socialtjänstlagen, sections 12–18; Norway: Lov om barnehager av 5. juni 1975.
5 The Norwegian Day Care Act gives priority of access to children with handicaps, provided they can benefit from attendance.
6 Data on the proportion of children admitted are not easily comparable because registration practices differ, and because services to families also differ. The length of maternity leave and parental leave influences the demand for care for the youngest children, as do options for flexible school start for the older ones.
7 Unlike the situation in the UK, for example, where the use of informal childminding is much debated (see Mayall and Petrie (1977)); Jackson and Jackson (1979); Bryant, Harris and Newton (1984), until recently the relationship between state, informal markets and family in the provision of everyday childcare has not received much attention in Scandinavia. In this chapter, I examine private childminding as an element in day-care structure, I do not address the problems associated with this form of childcare.

4 THE COLLECTIVIZATION OF CHILDCARE

1 According to Saraceno (1984), 'The policies of welfare states which concern children always embody a definition of mothers; and the policies which concern women always assign them responsibility for the children' (p. 352).
2 Until the first college of early childhood education was opened in 1937, in

Oslo, women who wanted a professional background for work in day-care institutions went abroad to study.

3 The Child Benefit Act from 1946 (Lov om barnetrygd), which provided for a monthly allowance made payable to mothers, introduced a redefinition of the division of responsibility between the state and the family, accepting that the state was to contribute to the costs of generational reproduction. As early evidence of a trend that was to gain in importance, that is, of state intervention in matters previously considered as family concerns, it is interesting. From a woman's perspective, it is also important as one of the early 'mother-directed' economic transfers that the welfare state enacted, representing for many women at that time the only income of their own.

4 However, questions concerning day care were not shelved. In the early 1950s the Ministry of Social Affairs recommended the appointment of a committee to examine questions concerning early childhood education and care. Parliament supported the recommendation (Grude 1972), but it was postponed because priority was given to another committee instructed to deal with the professional training of day-care staff (St. meld. 89, 1961–2, p. 2).

5 The Ministry of Social Affairs and the Ministry of Education disagreed as to which Ministry was to hold responsibility for questions concerning day care (Søsveen 1974, p. 85). The shift in location within government administration, it has been hypothesized, was undertaken to eliminate the discussion between the two Ministries as to how day care was to be interpreted and classified, as an issue of educational or social policy (Sande 1984). The shift may also be seen as a wish to integrate day-care policy with more comprehensive family policies.

6 A 'snapshot' from the period gives an indication of how strongly the housing problems were felt: when the king celebrated his eightieth birthday in 1952, he made a speech to the people, stating that he had one main wish, that every Norwegian would soon have access to decent housing (Kong Haakons 80-års fødselsdag, 1952, TV documentary, 20 Aug. 1989).

7 Two of the men of the committee, the chairman among them, were well-known Labour politicians. Among the women were prominent advocates of centre-based childcare, and also some members of the inspectorate dealing with day-care institutions.

8 See Bay (1988) for an analysis of the political debate concerning cash transfers to parents versus provision of day-care services and Leira (1987a) for an overview of the forms of subsidies used for different forms of day care.

9 See St. meld. 55, 1969–70, the long-term plan for the period 1970–3, and St. meld. 45, 1968–9, on labour market policies.

10 Important policy documents from the period used in the present analysis are:
– NOU 1972:39, *Førskoler* (Pre-schools), the report prepared by the committee appointed by the government in 1969 to deliberate questions concerning day-care provision and prepare legislation.

– Ot. prp. nr 23, 1974–5, Lov om barnehager (Proposition for Day Care Act), the document in which the Ministry of Family and Consumer Affairs presents its recommendations to Parliament and the text of the Act.

– Innst. O. nr 69, 1974–5, which contains the report of the extended Parliamentary Committee of Social Affairs on Ot. prp. nr 23, 1974–5.

– Ot. forh. 27, mai 1975, em. *Ot. tidende*, vol VIII, 1974–5, pp. 522–70, a verbatim recording of the debate in the Odelsting, 27 May 1975.

– Lov om barnehager of 5 June 1975 (Act governing day care), the final result of the deliberations in the national assembly.

11 In the later discussion of the committee's recommendations the use of one term to encompass all services for pre-school children was accepted. The Ministry of Family and Consumer Affairs in its recommendation to the Storting proposed that the term 'barnehage' be preferred to 'førskole', that is, 'kindergarten' was to replace 'pre-school'. The Ministry's proposal was accepted by a majority in Parliament. (On the terminological dispute and its many connotations, see Sande 1984.)

12 This procedure is commonly followed in the preparation of new legislation.

13 The meagre results of national policies is perhaps best demonstrated in the fate of the plan for day-care development covering the period 1975–81. The plan, as adopted by Parliament, called for 50,000 places to be made available by 1977 and 100,000 by 1981. The goal of the first stage was relatively successfully completed. The plans for the next stage, however, failed. Not until 1986, almost five years delayed, were the 100,000 places established.

5 MOTHERS, MARKETS AND THE STATE

1 See Ellingsæter (1989) for an interesting analysis of survey data on attitudes towards women's paid employment.

2 See, for example, St. meld. 45, 1968–9, *Om arbeidsmarkedspolitikken* (On labour market policy), St. meld. 25, 1973–4, *Petroleumsvirksomhetens plass i det norske samfunn* (On the impact of the petroleum industry on Norwegian society).

3 Wages for caring have lately been much discussed in Norway. See Bay (1988) for an analysis of political positions on the issue.

4 A detailed overview of the entitlements of parents with young children (*Småbarnsforeldres rettigheter*) is prepared by Direktoratet for arbeidstilsynet et al. (the State Directorate of Work Inspection), latest edition 1989.

5 Similar reactions to employment are reported in Danish studies of women employed by local authorities in family day care (Liebach 1980) and in a British study of outwork (Allen 1983).

6 The estimates are apparently based on a survey of forms of childcare commissioned by the Ministry in 1975, which showed that 61 per cent of families with children aged 0–11 years reported the use of extrafamilial private childcare (SSB 1976). This study gives a detailed overview of the institutional differentiation in childcare and also provides a basis for estimating the number of childcarers involved in private childminding.

7 When private, paid childcare takes place in the home of the child, the carer-person is to be regarded as employed by the parents, according to

Norwegian tax legislation. If it takes place in the home of the carer-person, the carer is conceived of as 'self-employed'. Each category has its own tax and labour legislation. During the 1950s and 1960s the number of domestic servants rapidly declined. In childcare the use of domestic servants, au pair girls, nannies and househelps is numerically less important than childcare based in the childminder's home (see Leira 1985).

6 MODES OF MOTHERING

1 Of the two surveys used for table 6.2, the 1973 survey reports the forms of childcare used by employed and non-employed mothers for children aged 0–7 years. The 1985 survey considers student families together with the dual-earners and registers the childcare arrangements for children aged 0–6 years.
2 The government's long-term plan (St. meld. 4, 1988–9, p. 14) reports an increase in the number of children minded by private childminders from 30,000 in 1983 to 60,000 in 1987.
3 Unfortunately, the recruiting of private childminders to informal labour markets cannot be followed systematically in the same way as labour market statistics trace the development of women's labour market participation. In Norway private childminders are not registered anywhere. Information on the size or scope of the private, mainly informal labour market in childcare provision is derived either from occasional surveys asking parents about childcare arrangements or by reponses to questions concerning forms of employment.
  Legislation in Norway requires that private childminders register with local authorities if a certain number of children are accommodated for a certain number of hours, but this is seldom done. No central register exists on private, non-state-sponsored childminding (Leira 1987a).
4 Some of the paid, private childminding is reported for taxation and regulated according to labour legislation, some is organized as 'shadow' labour (see Leira 1979; Strøm and Isachsen 1981; Sverdrup 1984b). The relative importance of legal and extra-legal private childminding arrangements is not known. For a legal review of the work environment and contracts of childminders, see Sverdrup (1984b).
5 In this study I interviewed women involved in different types of childcare careers: childminders, nannies, au pair girls, domestic servants. Some worked in their own homes, others in the home of the children minded. In the paragraphs referring to this study, I discuss only the childminders working as 'self-employed' in their own homes.
6 A Danish 1985 study concerning the combination of job and childcare found a marked preference for part-time work for both parents combined with part-time centre-based childcare (Christoffersen, Bertelsen and Vestergaard 1987).
7 Parts of the neighbourhood study have appeared previously in my 'Kvinners organisering av dagliglivet', in C. Wadel et al., eds. (1983), and in my 'Time for work, time for care. Childcare strategies in a Norwegian setting', in J. Brannen and G. Wilson, eds. (1987).

8 My analysis of processes and forms is influenced by Bateson (1965), and particularly by his *Mind and Nature* (1979), and by Wadel (1983).

7 CARER STATE AND CARER CAREERS

1 On the UK see, for example, Land (1978; 1983); Wilson (1977); Stacey and Price (1981). For Scandinavia, see Holter (1984).
2 Ruggie's analysis, however, underplays the considerable political opposition to the development of state-sponsored childcare schemes in Sweden prior to the period she examines (Kyle 1979; Kugelberg 1987).
3 Some of the activities I include under the 'informal' welfare state Wærness (1978) describes as the 'invisible' welfare state.

References

Aardal, B.O., and H. Valen (1989), *Velgere, partier og politisk avstand.* Sosiale og økonomiske studier nr 69. Oslo: Statistisk sentralbyrå.

Åström, G. (1990), 'Föräldraförsäkring och vårdnadsbidrag', *Kvinnovetenskapligt tidsskrift*, 11, no. 2: 37–48.

Acker, J. (1990), 'Hierarchies, jobs, bodies: a theory of gendered organizations', *Gender and Society*, 4, no. 2: 139–58.

Allardt, E. (1986), 'Representative government in a bureaucratic age'. In S. Graubard, ed., *Norden – The Passion for Equality*. Oslo: Norwegian University Press.

Allen, S. (1983), 'Production and reproduction: the lives of women homeworkers', *Sociological Review*, 31, no. 4: 649–65.

Andersen, B.R. (1986), 'Rationality and irrationality of the Nordic welfare state'. In S. Graubard, ed., *Norden – The Passion for Equality*. Oslo: Norwegian University Press.

Anttalainen, M. L. (1984), *Rapport om den könsuppdelade arbetsmarknaden.* Oslo: Nordisk Ministerråd.

Ariès, P. (1962), *Centuries of Childhood.* New York: Vintage Books.

Avdem, A. J. (1984), . . . *gjort ka gjerast skulde.* Oslo: Norwegian University Press.

Balbo, L. (1982a), 'The servicing work of women and the capitalist state', *Political Power and Social Theory*, 3: 251–702.

(1982b) *Crazy Quilts.* Maastricht: European Institute for Work and Society. Repr. in A. S. Sassoon, ed., (1987), *Women and the State.* London: Hutchinson.

(undated), untitled paper, concerning the historical roots of modern welfare states.

Barrett, M. (1980), *Women's Oppression Today.* London: Verso Editions and NLB.

Barrett, M., and M. McIntosh (1982), *The Anti-Social Family.* London: Verso Editions and NLB.

Bateson, G. (1965), *Naven.* Stanford: Stanford University Press.

(1979), *Mind and Nature.* New York: E.P. Dutton.

Bay, A.-H. (1988), *Penger eller barnehageplass.* Oslo: INAS-rapport 1988:7.

Beechey, V. (1978), 'Women and production: a critical analysis of some sociological theories of women's work'. In A. Kuhn and A. M. Wolpe, eds., *Feminism and Materialism.* London: Routledge and Kegan Paul.

185

Benhabib, S. (1987), 'The generalized and the concrete other'. In S. Benhabib and D. Cornell, eds., *Feminism as Critique*. Cambridge: Polity Press.

Bernard, J. (1975), *Women, Wives, Mothers*. Chicago: Aldine Publishing Company.

Besl. O. nr.57 (1974–5). Cf. Innst. O. nr 69., Stortingets forhandlinger (1974–5), part 6B.

Besl. O. nr.8 (1990–1).

Bogen, H. (1987), *Barnepass – drøm og virkelighet*. Oslo: FAFO-rapport nr R4:87.

Borchorst, A. (1987), 'Moderskab – himmel eller helvede?' In *Forskningsrapport*. Gothenburg: Sociologiska Institutionen, Göteborgs Universitet.

Borchorst, A., and B. Siim (1987), 'Women and the advanced welfare state. A new kind of patriarchal power'. In A. S. Sassoon, ed., *Women and the State*. London: Hutchinson.

Bowlby, J. (1951), *Maternal Care and Mental Health*. Geneva: World Health Organization.

Brannen, J., and P. Moss (1988), *New Mothers at Work. Employment and Childcare*. London: Unwin Hyman.

(1990), *Managing Mothers*. London: Unwin Hyman.

Brown, C. (1981), 'Mothers, fathers, and children: From private to public patriarchy'. In L. Sargent, ed., *Women and Revolution*. Boston: The South End Press.

Bryant, B., M. Harris and D. Newton (1984), *Children and Minders*. Oxford: Grant McIntyre.

Bull, E. (1979), *Norge i den rike verden 1945–1975*. Norges historie, vol. XIV. Oslo: J. W. Cappelens Forlag.

Bulmer, M. (1984), *Neighbours. The Work of Philip Abrams*. Cambridge: Cambridge University Press.

Carter, A. (1988), *The Politics of Women's Rights*. London and New York: Longman.

Central Bureau of Statistics of Norway (1980), *Educational Statistics*, Survey, 1 Oct. Oslo.

Christoffersen, M. N. (1986), 'Den usynlige private dagpleje', *Juristen*, nr 10: 390–6.

Christoffersen, M. N., O. Bertelsen and P. Vestergaard (1987), *Hvem passer vore børn?* Copenhagen: Socialforskningsinstitutet, publ. 174.

Cockburn, C. (1983), *Brothers: Male Domination and Technological Change*. London: Pluto Press.

Cohen, B. (1988), *Caring for Children. Services for Childcare and Equal Opportunities in the United Kingdom*. London: Commission of the European Communities.

Connell, R. W. (1987), *Gender and Power*. Stanford, California: Stanford University Press.

Dagens Næringsliv (8 Dec. 1988), 'Stillingsmarkedet'.

Dahl, T. S. (1976), 'Ekteskapet, den moderne husmannskontrakten'. In T. Støren and T. S. Wetlesen, eds., *Kvinnekunnskap*. Oslo: Gyldendal.

(1984), 'Women's right to money'. In H. Holter, ed., *Patriarchy in a Welfare Society*. Oslo: Universitetsforlaget.

Dahlerup, D. (1987), 'Confusing concepts – confusing reality: a theoretical discussion of the patriarchal state'. In A. S. Sassoon, ed., *Women and the State*. London: Hutchinson.

Dahlström, E., et al. (1962), *Kvinnors liv och arbete*. Stockholm: Studieförbundet Näringsliv och Samhälle.

Dahlström, E., and R. Liljeström (1981), 'Det patriarkala arvet', *Sociologisk Forskning*, 2: 12–45.

Dalla Costa, M., and S. James (1975), *The Power of Women and the Subversion of the Community*. Bristol: Falling Wall Press.

Direktoratet for arbeidstilsynet et al. (1989), *Småbarnsforeldres rettigheter*. Oslo.

Donzelot, J. (1980), *The Policing of Families*. London: Hutchinson.

Edholm, F., O. Harris and K. Young (1977), 'Conceptualizing women', *Critique of Anthropology*, 3: 101–30.

Eisenstein, Z. (1979), 'Developing a theory of capitalist patriarchy and socialist feminism'. In Z. Eisenstein, ed., *Capitalist Patriarchy and the Case for Socialist Feminism*. New York: Monthly Review Press.

(1981), *The Radical Future of Liberal Feminism*. New York: Longman.

(1983), 'The state, the patriarchal family, and working mothers'. In I. Diamond, ed., *Families, Politics and Public Policy*. New York and London: Longman.

Ellingsæter, A. L. (1987), 'Ulikhet i arbeidstidsmønstre'. In NOU 1987: 9b. Vedlegg til arbeidstidsutvalgets innstilling.

(1989), 'Holdninger til kvinners lønnsarbeid', *Søkelys på arbeidsmarkedet*. 1: 9–17.

(1990), *Fathers Working Long Hours. Trends, Causes and Consequences*. Working paper 2. Oslo: Institute for Social Research.

Ellingsæter, A. L., and G. Iversen (1984), *Endringer i kvinners arbeidsmarkedstilpasninger*. SØS nr 55. Oslo and Kongsvinger: Statistisk Sentralbyrå.

Engels, F. (1970), *Familien, privateiendommens og statens opprinnelse*. Oslo: Forlaget Ny Dag.

Equal Status Council, The, Norway (1991), *Minifacts on Equal Rights*.

Erikson, E. H. (1965), *Childhood and Society*. Harmondsworth: Penguin Books.

Erikson, R., et al., eds., (1987), *The Scandinavian Model: Welfare States and Welfare Research*. New York: M. E. Sharpe.

Esping-Andersen, G. (1987), *The Three Political Economies of the Welfare State*. Paper. Florence: European University Institute.

Esping-Andersen, G., and W. Korpi (1987), 'From poor relief to institutional welfare states: the development of Scandinavian social policy'. In R. Erikson et al., eds., *The Scandinavian Model: Welfare States and Welfare Research*. New York: M. E. Sharpe.

Finch, J. (1989), *Family Obligations and Social Change*. Cambridge: Polity Press.

Frazer, N. (1987), 'Women, welfare and the politics of need interpretation', *Hypatia: A Journal of Feminist Philosophy*, 2: 103–21.

Gershuny, J. I. (1979), 'The informal economy: its role in post-industrial society', *Futures*: 3–15.

Gershuny, J. I., and R. Pahl (1980), 'Britain in the decade of the three economies', *New Society*, 3 January.

Gilligan, C. (1982), *In a Different Voice*. Cambridge, Mass.: Harvard University Press.

Gough, I. (1979), *The Political Economy of the Welfare State*. London: Macmillan.

Gouldner, A. W. (1960), 'The norm of reciprocity: a preliminary statement', *American Sociological Review*, April, 25: 161–78.

Graham, H. (1983), 'Caring: a labour of love'. In J. Finch and D. Groves, eds., *A Labour of Love*. London: Routledge and Kegan Paul.

Grønhøj, B. (1981), *Småbørns dagpasning*. Copenhagen: Socialforskningsinstitutet publ. 103.

Grønseth, E. (1966), *Familie, seksualitet og samfunn*. Oslo: Pax Forlag.

Grude, T. (1972), 'Den historiske bakgrunn for førskolen i Norge', NOU 1972: 39, *Førskoler*, vedlegg 4.

Gulbrandsen, L., and C. U. Tønnessen (1988), 'Barnehageutbyggingens fordelingspolitiske virkninger', *Tidsskrift for samfunnsforskning*, 29, no. 6: 539–54.

Gullestad, M. (1978), 'Livet i en gammel bydel'. In C. Wadel and T. Thuen, eds., *Lokale samfunn og offentlig planlegging*. Oslo: Universitetsforlaget.

(1984), *Kitchentable Society*. Oslo: Universitetsforlaget.

Haavind, H. (1987), *Liten og stor*. Oslo: Universitetsforlaget.

Haavio-Mannila, E., et al. (1983), *Det uferdige demokratiet*. Oslo: Nordisk Ministerråd.

Habermas, J. (1980), *Borgerlig offentlighet*. Oslo: Gyldendal Norsk Forlag.

Hagen, V., and K. Skrede (1976), *Gifte kvinner, familiefase og yrkesaktivitet*. Oslo: INAS, Arbeidsrapport nr 22.

Hansen, A., and A. S. Andersen (1984), *Barns levekår*. Statistiske analyser 53. Oslo and Kongsvinger: Statistisk Sentralbyrå.

Harding, S. (1986), *The Science Question in Feminism*. Milton Keynes: Open University Press.

Hartmann, H. (1981a), 'The unhappy marriage of marxism and feminism: towards a more progressive union'. In L. Sargent, ed., *Women and Revolution*. Boston: South End Press.

(1981b), 'The family as the locus of gender, class, and political struggle, the example of housework', *Signs*, Spring, 6, no. 3: 366–94.

Hartsock, N. (1983), 'The feminist standpoint: developing the ground for a specifically feminist historical materialism'. In S. Harding and M. Hintikka, eds., *Discovering Reality: Feminist Perspectives on Epistemology, Metaphysics, Methodology and Philosophy of Science*. Dordrecht: Reidel.

Hernes, H. M. (1982), *Staten – kvinner ingen adgang* Oslo: Universitetsforlaget.

(1984), 'Women and the welfare state. The transition from private to public dependence'. In H. Holter, ed., *Patriarchy in a Welfare Society*. Oslo: Norwegian University Press.

(1987), *Welfare State and Woman Power*. Oslo: Norwegian University Press.

(1988), 'Scandinavian Citizenship', *Acta Sociologica*, 31, no. 3: 199–215.

Hirsch, F. (1977), *Social Limits to Growth*. London: Routledge and Kegan Paul.

Holter, H. (1970), *Sex Roles and Social Structure*. Oslo: Norwegian University Press.

Holter, H. et al. (1975), *Familien i klassesamfunnet*. Oslo: Pax Forlag.

Holter, H. ed. (1984), *Patriarchy in a Welfare Society*. Oslo: Norwegian University Press.

Horkheimer, M. (1936), Autorität und Familie' Transl. as 'Authority and the family'. In M. Horkheimer (1972), *Critical Theory*. New York: Continuum Publishing.

Ingelstam, L. (1980), *Arbetets värde och tidens bruk. En framtidsstudie*. Stockholm: Liber Förlag.

Innstilling fra Barnevernkomitéen I. Lov om barnevern. (1951), Sosialdepartementet.

Innstilling fra komitéen til å utrede visse spørsmål om daginstitusjoner m.v. for barn avgitt 29. mars 1961. Published with St. meld. 89, 1961–2. Departementet for familie- og forbrukersaker.

Innst. O. nr 69, 1974–5. Innstilling fra den forsterkede sosialkomité om Lov om barnehager m.v.

Innst. S. nr 11, 1962–3. Innstilling fra sosialkomitéen om retningslinjer om utbygging og drift av daginstitusjoner m.v. for barn.

Innst. S. nr. 200, 1988–9. Innstilling fra sosialkomitéen om folketrygdens økonomi og pensjonssystem.

Institute for Studies in Research and Higher Education (1987), *Students and Graduates*, Oslo: Working paper 9/87.

Jackson, B., and S. Jackson (1979), *Childminder. A Study in Action Research*. London: Routledge and Kegan Paul.

Jacobsen, K. D. (1967), 'Politisk fattigdom', *Kontrast*, 3, no. 1: 6–9.

Jensen, J. (1986), 'Gender and reproduction: Or, babies and the state', *Studies in Political Economy*, Summer 20: 9–46.

Kalleberg A. (1983), 'Foreldreskift og kjønnrolleforandring'. In C. Wadel et al., eds., *Dagliglivets organisering*. Oslo: Universitetsforlaget.

Kalleberg, A., and S. Hovde (1986), *Arbeidsdelingen i hjemmet*. Oslo: Institutt for samfunnsforskning. Rapport 1986:5.

Kaluszynska, E. (1980), 'Wiping the floor with theory – a survey of writings on housework', *Feminist Review*, 6: 27–54.

Kamerman, S. B., and A. J. Kahn (1981), *Child Care, Family Benefits and Working Parents*. New York: Columbia University Press.

Kjeldstad. R. (1988), *Inntekt over livsløpet: pensjonsgivende inntekt og alderspensjon. Forskjeller mellom kvinner og menn i fire fødselskohorter*. Oslo: INAS. Rapport 1988:2.

Knudsen, P. (1988), *The Norwegian National Insurance Scheme. The Pension System in an Equal Status Perspective*. Vienna: Paper prepared for the International Social Security Association (ISSA) Research Conference 'Equal treatment of men and women in social security'.

Knudsen, R. (1990), *Familieydelser i Norden 1989. Tekniske rapporter 52*. Stockholm: Nordisk statistisk sekretariat.

Kugelberg. C. (1987), *Allt eller inget. Barn, omsorg och förvärvsarbete*. Stockholm: Carlsson Bokförlag.

Kyle, G. (1979), *Gästarbetarska i manssamhället*. Stockholm: Liber Förlag.

Land, H. (1978), 'Who cares for the family?', *Journal of Social Policy*, 7, no. 3: 257–84.

(1983), 'Who still cares for the family? Recent developments in income maintenance, taxation and family law'. In J. Lewis, ed., *Women's Welfare, Women's Rights*. London: Croom Helm.

(1989), *The Welfare Society: Whose Welfare in Future?* Oslo: The Nordic Social Policy Research Conference, plenary paper.

Land, H., and H. Rose (1985), 'Compulsory altruisim for some or an altruistic society for all'. In P. Bean, J. Ferris and D. K. Whynes, eds., *In Defence of Welfare*. London: Tavistock.

Lasch, C. (1979), *Haven in a Heartless World*. New York: Basic Books.

Lea, J. A. (1982), *Framveksten av norsk barnehagepolitikk. En analyse av interessentene på barnehagemarkedet*. Oslo: INAS-rapport 1982:12.

Leira, A. (1976), 'Kvinner i lønnsarbeid og ulønna arbeid'. In T. Støren and T. S. Wetlesen, eds., *Kvinnekunnskap*. Oslo: Gyldendal.

(1979), 'Daglig omsorgsarbeid'. In *Lønnet og ulønnet omsorg*. Oslo: NAVFs sekretariat for kvinneforskning. Arbeidsnotat nr 4.

(1983), 'Kvinners organisering av dagliglivet. Hverdagspraksis i et eldre bystøk'. In C. Wadel et al., eds., *Dagliglivets organisering*. Oslo: Universitetsforlaget.

(1984), 'Mødre og dagmødre'. Unpubl.

(1985), *Regelmessig barnetilsyn*. Oslo: Institutt for samfunnsforskning, Arbeidsnotat 4/85.

(1987a), *Day Care for Children in Denmark, Norway and Sweden*. Oslo: Institutt for samfunnsforskning, Research report 5/87.

(1987b), 'Time for work, time for care. Childcare strategies in a Norwegian setting'. In J. Brannen and G. Wilson, eds., *Give and Take in Families*. London: Allen and Unwin.

(1988), 'Barndom i velferdsstaten', *Tidsskrift for samfunnsforskning*, 29, no. 6: 505–22.

(1989), *Models of Motherhood. Welfare State Policies and Everyday Practices*. Oslo: Institute for Social Research, 89:7.

(1990), 'Visjonen om barndommen. Den nordiske velferdsstatsmodellen'. *Norsk Pedagogisk Tidsskrift*, 74: 290–9.

(1991), 'Mor og far – stat og marked. Om den yrkesaktive mor og yngelpleien'. In R. Haukaa, ed., *Nye kvinner, nye menn*. Oslo: Ad Notam.

Leira, A., and S. Bergh (1974), *'hå har et kvinnfolk å sia, da!'* Oslo: Pax Forlag.

Leira, A., and S. Nørve (1977), 'Det skjulte markedet', *Tidsskrift for samfunnsforskning*, 18, nos. 5–6: 562–7.

Lerner, G. (1985), *The Creation of Patriarchy*. New York: Oxford University Press.

Lessing, D. (1985), *The Diaries of Jane Somers*. Harmondsworth: Penguin Books.

Lewis, J. (1980), *The Politics of Motherhood*. London: Croom Helm.

Liebach, B. (1980), *Lavindkomstproblemer blandt kvindelige servicearbejdere*. Copenhagen: Lavindkomstkommissionen. Arbejdsnotat 13.

Lien, L. (1987), *Husmødrenes barnehager 1937–1987*. Oslo: Husmødrenes barnehager.

Liljeström, R. (1984), *Våre barn, andres ungar*. Oslo: Det Norske Samlaget.

Lingsom, S. (1985), *Uformell omsorg for syke og eldre*. SØS nr 57. Oslo: Statistisk Sentralbyrå.

Lingsom, S., and A. L. Ellingsæter (1983), *Arbeid, fritid, samvær*. Statistiske analyser, Oslo and Kongsvinger: Statistisk Sentralbyrå.

Lister, R. (1990), 'Women, Economic Dependency and Citizenship'. *Journal of Social Policy*, 19, no. 4: 445–67.

Ljones, O. (1979), *Kvinners yrkesdeltaking i Norge*. SØS nr 39. Oslo and Kongsvinger: Statistisk Sentralbyrå.

(1984), 'Kvinners yrkesdeltaking i et langsiktig perspektiv'. In T. Rødseth and K. D. Titlestad, eds., *Kvinner i arbeid*. Oslo: Universitetsforlaget.

Lønnå, E. (1977), 'LO, DNA og striden om gifte kvinner i arbeidslivet'. In I. Blom and G. Hagemann, eds., *Kvinner selv . . . 7 bidrag til kvinnehistorie*. Oslo: Aschehoug.

Lov av 7. mars 1947. Om tillegg til og endringer i lov om tilsyn med pleiebarn m.v. av 29. april 1905 og i lov om forsorg for barn av 10. april 1915.

Lov om arbeidervern og arbeidsmiljø av 4. februar 1977.

Lov om barnehager av 5. juni 1975.

Lov om barnetrygd av 24. oktober 1946.

Lov om barnevern av 17. juli 1953.

Lov om enkje- og morstrygd av 20. juni 1964.

Lov om folketrygd av 17. juni 1966.

Lov om likestilling mellom kjønnene av 9. juni 1978.

Lov om social bistand (Denmark). Full title: Lov nr 33 af 19. juni 1974 om social bistand.

Lov om svangerskapsbrudd av 13. juni 1975.

McKee, L. (1987), 'Households during unemployment: the resourcefulness of the unemployed'. In J. Brannen and G. Wilson, eds., *Give and Take in Families*. London: Allen and Unwin.

Marshall, T.E. (1965), *Class, Citizenship, and Social Development*. New York: Anchor Books.

Mayall, B., and P. Petrie (1977), *Minder, Mother and Child*. London: Heinemann.

Midré, G. (1978), 'Det uformelle hjelpesystem i et nordnorsk lokalsamfunn'. In C. Wadel and T. Thuen, eds., *Lokale samfunn og offentlig planlegging*. Oslo: Universitetsforlaget.

Moen, B. (1981), *Fruktbarhetsutvikling og fruktbarhetsteorier. Norge i et internasjonalt perspektiv*. SØS nr 47. Oslo: Statistisk Sentralbyrå.

Molyneux, M. (1979), 'Beyond the domestic labour debate', *New Left Review*, 116: 3–29.

Morgan, D. H. J. (1985), *The Family, Politics and Social Theory*. London: Routledge and Kegan Paul.

Moss, P. (1988), *Childcare and Equality of Opportunity*, London: Consolidated Report to the European Commission.

(1990), *Childcare in the European Communities 1985–1990*. Women of

Europe Supplements no. 31. Brussels: Commission of the European Communities.

Myrdal, A. (1935), *Stadsbarn*. Stockholm: Kooperativt Förbund.

Myrdal, A., and V. Klein (1957), *Women's Two Roles*. London: Routledge and Kegan Paul.

Myrdal, A., and G. Myrdal (1934), *Kris i befolkningsfrågan*. Stockholm: Bonnier.

Näsman, E., K. Nordström and R. Hammarström (1983), *Föräldrars arbete och barns villkor*. Stockholm: Libertryck.

New, C., and M. David (1985), *For the Children's Sake*. Harmondsworth: Penguin Books.

Nicholson, L. (1987), 'Feminism and Marxism. Integrating kinship with the economic.' In Benhabib, S., and D. Cornell, eds., *Feminism as Critique*. Cambridge: Polity Press.

Noddings, N. (1984), *Caring*. Berkeley and Los Angeles: University of California Press.

NORD 1987:73, *Yearbook of Nordic Statistics 1987*, vol. 26, Stockholm.

NORD 1988:114, *Yearbook of Nordic Statistics 1988*, vol. 27, Stockholm.

NORD 1991:1, *Yearbook of Nordic Statistics 1991, vol. 29, Stockholm.*

Norsk Riksmålsordbok (1947), vol. II, first part. Oslo: Aschehoug and Co.

NOU 1972: 39, *Førskoler*.

  1978:6, *Arbeid for kvinner*.

  1984:26, *Befolkningsutviklingen*.

Oakley, A. (1974), *The Sociology of Housework*. London: Martin Robertson.

  (1976), *Housewife*. Harmondsworth: Penguin Books.

OECD (1981), *Women and Employment 1980*. Paris.

  (1987), *Employment Outlook*. Sept.

  (1990), *Employment Outlook*, July.

Offe, C. (1984), *Contradictions of the Welfare State*. London: Hutchinson.

Opdahl, S. (1984), *Aleneforeldres tidsbruk og levekår*. Oslo and Kongsvinger: Statistisk Sentralbyrå, Rapport 84/16.

Ot. forh. 27. mai 1975, em. *Ot. tidende*, 1974–5, vol. VIII.

Ot. prp. nr 23 (1974–5), *Lov om barnehager, m.v.*

Pahl, R. E. (1984), *Divisions of Labour*. Oxford: Basil Blackwell.

Pahl, R. E., and C. Wallace (1982), *The Restructuring of Capital, the Local Political Economy and Household Work Strategies: All Forms of Work in Context*. Paper prepared for the X World Congress of Sociology, Mexico City.

Parsons, T. (1955), 'The American family: its relations to personality and to the social structure'. In T. Parsons and R. F. Bales, eds., *Family, Socialization and Interaction Process*. Glencoe, Illinois: The Free Press.

  (1960), 'The stability of the American family system'. In N.W. Bell and E. F. Vogel, eds., *A Modern Introduction to the Family*. Glencoe, Illinois: The Free Press.

Pateman, C. (1987a), 'Feminist critiques of the public/private dichotomy'. In S. I. Benn and G. F. Gaus, eds., *Public and Private in Social Life*. London and Canberra: Croom Helm.

  (1987b), 'The patriarchal welfare state'. In A. Gutman, ed., *Democracy and the Welfare State*. Princeton: Princeton University Press.

(1988), *The Sexual Contract*. Cambridge: Polity Press.

Pichault, C. (1984), *Day-Care Facilities and Services for Children under the Age of Three in the European Community*. Luxembourg: Office for Official Publications of the European Communities.

Pinker, R. (1971), *Social Theory and Social Policy*. London: Heineman.

Piven, F. F. (1985), 'Women and the state: ideology, power and the welfare state'. In A. Rossi, ed., *Gender and the Life Course*. New York: Aldine.

Prokop, U. (1978), *Kvindelige livssammenhæng*. Kongerslev: GMT.

Rich, A. (1976), *Of Women Born: Motherhood as Experience and Institution*. New York: W. W. Norton.

Rødseth, A., and K. D. Titlestad (1984), 'Lønnsforskjeller mellom kvinner og menn'. In T. Rødseth and K. D. Titlestad, eds., *Kvinner i arbeid*. Oslo: Universitetsforlaget.

Rose, H. (1983), 'Hand, brain and heart: a feminist epistemology for the natural sciences', *Signs*, Autumn, 9, no. 1: 75–90.

Rossi, A. S. (1977), 'A biosocial perspective on parenting', *Daedalus*, Spring, 106, no. 2: 1–31.

Ruddick, S. (1980), 'Maternal thinking', *Feminist Studies*, 6, no. 3: 343–67.

Ruggie, M. (1984), *The State and Working Women*. Princeton, New Jersey: Princeton University Press.

Rutter, M. (1972), *Maternal Deprivation Reassessed*. Harmondsworth: Penguin.

Sahlins, M. (1969), 'On the sociology of primitive exchange'. In M. Banton, ed., *The Relevance of Models for Social Anthropology*. Association of Social Anthropologists Monograph no. 1.

Samordningsnemnda for skoleverket, oppnevnt ved kongelig resolusjon 7. mars 1947. (1951), *Tilråding XV om barnehager og utdanning av barnehagelærerinner*. Kirke- og undervisningsdepartementet.

Sande, R. (1984), 'Frå førskole til barnehage. Utviklinga av tilbod for barn under skolepliktig alder 1949–1975 i politisk perspektiv'. Oslo: Barnevernsakademiet. Hovudoppgåve (Dissertation).

Saraceno, C. (1984), 'The social construction of childhood: child care and education policies in Italy and the United States', *Social Problems*, 31, no. 3: 351–63.

Sassoon, A. S. (1987), 'Introduction: the personal and the intellectual, fragments and order, international trends and national specificities'. In A. S. Sassoon, ed., *Women and the State*. London: Hutchinson.

Schaffer, R. (1977), *Mothering*. London: Fontana/Open Book.

Scott, J. (1988), *Gender and the Politics of History*. New York: Columbia University Press.

Seccombe, W. (1974), 'The housewife and her labour under capitalism', *New Left Review*, no. 83.

Seip, A.-L. (1977), *Om velferdsstatens framvekst*. Oslo: Universitetsforlaget.

(1984), *Sosialhjelpstaten blir til: Norsk sosialpolitikk 1740–1920*. Oslo: Gyldendal Norsk Forlag.

(1987), 'Who cares? Child, family and social policy in twentieth century Norway'. In K. Ekberg and P. E. Mjaavatn, eds., *Growing into a Modern World*. Proceedings, vol. I. Trondheim: The Norwegian Centre for Child Research.

Selid, B. (1968), *Kvinner i yrke, hjem og samfunn*. Oslo: Fabritius and Sønners forlag.

Shinman, S. M. (1981), *A Chance for Every Child*. London: Tavistock Publications.

Siim, B. (1984), *Women and the Welfare State – Between Private and Public Dependence*. Paper presented at the Center for Research on Women, Stanford University.

(1987), 'The Scandinavian welfare states. Towards sexual equality or a new kind of male domination?' *Acta Sociologica*, 30, nos 3–4: 255–70.

Skaara, A. (1979), 'Omsorgens sosiologi', *Sykepleien*, 3: 12–17.

Skrede, K. (1984a), 'Familieøkonomi og forsørgerlønn', *Tidsskrift for samfunnsforskning*, 25, no. 4: 539–54.

(1984b), *Occupational and Industrial Distribution in the ECE Region*. Paper prepared for The Economic Commission for Europe.

(1986), 'Kvinner, familien og velferdsstaten'. In K. Skrede and K. Tornes, eds., *Kan vi planlegge oss til likestilling i år 2010?* Oslo: Universitetsforlaget.

Skrede, K., and K. Tornes, eds. (1986), *Den norske kvinnerevolusjonen*. Oslo: Universitetsforlaget.

Slagstad, R. (1981), 'Velferdsstaten'. In *Pax Leksikon*, 6. Oslo: Pax Forlag.

Smith, D. (1988), *The Everyday World as Problematics*. Milton Keynes: Open University Press.

Socialtjänstlagen (1980:620), coming into effect as of 1 January 1982.

Social tryghed i de nordiske lande (1989), Nordisk statistisk skriftserie 50. Copenhagen: Nordisk statistisk sekretariat.

Solberg, A., and G. M. Vestby (1987), *Barns arbeidsliv*. Oslo: NIBR.

Sosialdepartementet (1954), *Forskrifter for daginstitusjoner for barn*.

Søsveen, R. (1974), 'Barnehagene i Norge. En historikk'. Oslo: Universitetet i Oslo. Hovedoppgave i pedagogikk (Dissertation).

Stacey, M. (1983), 'The division of labour revisited or overcoming the two Adams'. In P. Abrams et al., eds. *Practice and Progress: British Sociology 1950–1980*. London: Allen and Unwin.

Stacey, M., and M. Price (1981), *Women, Power and Politics*. London: Tavistock.

Stack, C. B. (1974), *All Our Kin. Strategies for Survival in a Black Community*. New York: Harper and Row.

Statistisk Sentralbyrå (1969), *Ønsker om og behov for sysselsetting blant gifte kvinner*. Rapport fra kontoret for intervjuundersøkelser, nr 7.

(1973), *Boforholdsundersøkelsen*. NOS A 673.

(1976), *Undersøkelsen om barnetilsyn 1975*. Rapport nr 39 fra underavdelingen for intervjuundersøkelser. Oslo.

(1977), *Barneomsorg 1976*. NOS A 978.

(1981), *Kvinners arbeid 1980*, NOS B 242.

(1987), *Barnehager og fritidshjem 1986*. NOS B 804.

(1991), *Statistisk ukehefte*, 23/91.

Statistiska Centralbyrån (1986), *Barnomsorgsundersökningen 1986*. Stat. Meddelanden S 10 SM 8601.

(1990), *På tal om kvinnor och män*.

St. meld. 89, 1961–2, *Om retningslinjer for utbygging og drift av daginstitu-sjoner m.v. for barn.*

45, 1968–9, *Om arbeidsmarkedspolitikken.*

55, 1969–70, *Langtidsprogram for 1970–3.*

25, 1973–4, *Petroleumsvirksomhetens plass i det norske samfunn.*

93, 1980–1, *Barnehager i 80-årene.*

50, 1984–5, *Om familiepolitikken.*

8, 1987–8, *Barnehager mot år 2000.*

4, 1988–9, *Langtidsprogrammet 1990–3.*

12, 1988–9, *Folketrygdens økonomi og pensjonssystem.*

Stoltenberg, Aa. (1962), 'Husmødrenes barnehager 1937–1962, 25-års beret-ning'. In *Husmødrenes barnehager, Årsberetning 1/1 – 31/12 1962.* Oslo.

Stoltenberg, L. (1937), 'Hvor skal vi anbringe barna?' *Tidsskrift for Hjemmenes Vel*, 7: 77–9; 8: 83–9.

Strøm, S., and A. J. Isachsen (1981), *Skattefritt. Svart sektor i vekst.* Oslo: Universitetsforlaget.

Strømsheim, G. (1983), *Working Hours and Segmentation in the Norwegian Labour Market.* Oslo: Institute for Social Research. Working paper 4/83.

Sverdrup, T. (1984a), 'Folketrygdloven i et kvinneperspektiv'. In A. Kjønstad, ed., *Folketrygden i støpeskjeen.* Oslo: Universitetsforlaget.

(1984b), *Lovvern for arbeidstakere i andres hjem.* Kvinnerettslige arbeidsno-tater nr 31. Oslo: Universitetet i Oslo, Kvinneretten.

Thayer, P. P., et al. (1988), *Forms of Child Care.* Strasbourg: Council of Europe.

Thorne, B. (1983), 'Feminist rethinking of the family: an overview'. In B. Thorne and M. Yalom, eds., *Rethinking the Family.* New York: Longman.

Titmuss, R. M. (1968), *Commitment to Welfare.* London: Allen and Unwin.

(1969), *Essays on 'the Welfare State'.* London: Unwin University Books.

Tornes, K. (1986), 'Kvinners plass i offentlig arbeidsmarkedpolitikk'. In K. Skrede and K. Tornes, eds., *Den norske kvinnerevolusjonen.* Oslo: Univer-sitetsforlaget.

Ungerson, C. (1987), *Policy is Personal. Sex, Gender and Informal Care.* London and New York: Tavistock Publications.

(1990), 'The Language of Care: Crossing the Boundaries'. In C. Ungerson, ed., *Gender and Caring. Work and Welfare in Britain and Scandinavia.* London: Harvester Wheatsheaf.

Unwin, C. (1985), 'Constructing motherhood: the persuasion of normal devel-opment'. In C. Steadman, C. Unwin and V. Walkerdine, eds., *Language, Gender and Childhood.* London: Routledge and Kegan Paul.

Ve, H. (1984), 'Women's mutual alliances. Altruism as a premise for inter-action'. In H. Holter, ed., *Patriarchy in a Welfare Society.* Oslo: Univer-sitetsforlaget.

Wadel, C. (1977), 'Hva er arbeid? Noen refleksjoner om arbeid som aktivitet og begrep', *Tidsskrift for samfunnsforskning*, 18, nos. 5–6: 387–411.

(1983), 'Dagliglivet som forskningsfelt'. In C. Wadel et al., eds., *Dagliglivets organisering.* Oslo: Universitetsforlaget.

Wadel, C., et al., eds. (1983), *Dagliglivets organisering.* Oslo: Universitetsfor-laget.

Wærness, K. (1978), 'The Invisible Welfare State; Women's Work at Home', *Acta Sociologica*, supplement.

(1979), 'Kvinners omsorgsarbeid i den ulønnede produksjon'. In *Lønnet og ulønnet omsorg*. Oslo: NAVFs sekretariat for kvinneforskning. Arbeidsnotat nr 5.

(1982), *Kvinneperspektiver på sosialpolitikken*. Oslo: Universitetsforlaget.

(1984), 'Caring as women's work in the welfare state'. In H. Holter, ed., *Patriarchy in a Welfare Society*. Oslo: Norwegian University Press.

(1987), 'On the rationality of caring'. In A. S. Sassoon, ed., *Women and the State*. London: Hutchinson.

Wearing, B. (1985), *Ideology of Motherhood. A Study of Sydney Suburban Mothers*. Sydney: Allen and Unwin.

Wilensky, H. L., and C. N. Lebeaux (1958), *Industrial Society and Social Welfare*. New York: The Free Press.

Wilson, A. (1980), 'The infancy of the history of childhood: an appraisal of Philippe Ariès', *History Theory*. 19, no. 2: 132–53.

Wilson, E. (1977), *Women and the Welfare State*. London: Tavistock Publications.

Wolfe, A. (1989), *Whose Keeper? Social Science and Moral Obligation*. Berkeley: University of California Press.

Zelditch, M. (1956), 'Role differentiation in the nuclear family'. In T. Parsons and R. F. Bales, eds., *Family Socialization and Interaction Process*. London: Routledge and Kegan Paul.

Zetterberg, H. (1986), 'The rational humanitarians'. In S. Graubard, ed., *Norden – The Passion for Equality*. Oslo: Norwegian University Press.

Index

abortion 42
 on demand 97
 law 78
Acker, J. 121
Act governing day care 70, 77, 79, 83, 87,
 92, 133, 163; *see also* Day Care Act
Allardt, E. 20, 41
Andersen, B.R. 20, 41
Aström, G. 44

Balbo, L. 19–21, 30, 142, 167, 176
Barrett, M. 14, 29, 77
Bay, A.-H. 75
Beechey, V. 14, 15
benefits
 caring-related 23
 employment-related 21, 24, 27, 106
birth/s 15, 16, 23, 42–4, 50, 97, 119, 138,
 164
Borchorst, A. 26, 37, 57, 58, 61, 77, 95,
 125, 167 168
Brannen, J. 134, 138, 141
Britain 4, 24, 27, 45, 55, 67, 134, 138, 141,
 168, 169; *see also* UK
Bulmer, M. 144, 157
bureaucracy 32–4

care
 cash for 37, 39, 102, 140
 concepts of 3, 4, 27, 30, 34, 40, 47, 87,
 88, 174
 rationality of 34
care-giving/care-giving work 31, 37, 151,
 154, 158, 171
care-providing systems 41
 recipient 32
carer careers 28, 34, 38, 39, 157, 161, 170–3
 state 19, 21, 26, 34, 125, 161, 170, 171
caring wage 24, 39, 118, 171
Carter, A. 167
child benefit 23, 68, 102
Child Benefit Act 102

childcare
 class-divided 49, 66, 81
 collectivization of 6, 36, 42, 45, 64, 66,
 68, 118–20, 129, 168
 equity of access to 49, 52–4, 93
 informal economy of 10–11, 100, 121,
 123–4, 126, 142, 159, 165
 informal labour markets in 82, 101,
 122–4
 institutional differentiation of 29, 34–9,
 58, 65, 100, 132, 133, 135, 165, 167,
 171, 173, 174
 professional 28, 36, 47–9, 57, 68, 70, 76,
 83, 85, 86, 92, 132, 139, 157
childminders, licensing of 85, 87, 90, 116
child protection 65, 71, 72, 74, 75
Child Protection Act 71, 72, 74, 75
citizen 18, 19, 22, 25–7, 98, 167–9, 171–3
 as carer 5,6, 26, 162, 170–4
 mothers 5, 170, 177
 and state 2, 3, 5, 8, 12
 as wage-worker/earner 5, 6, 12, 22, 25,
 26, 45, 103, 162, 170, 171, 173
citizenship 5, 6, 8, 12, 24–7, 77, 162, 170–2
 gendering of 6, 12, 22, 24–6, 162, 171,
 172
 Scandinavian 25, 27
class (*see* social class)
class differences 101, 137; *see also* social
 class
community care 154, 157

Dahl, T.S. 23, 26, 124, 167
Dahlerup, D. 125, 168
Dahlström, E. 39, 108
Day Care Act 9, 77–80, 85, 90, 94, 115,
 116, 118, 121, 126, 129, 130, 164; *see
 also* Act governing day care
day-care
 attendance 53, 82, 114
 legislation 9, 68, 80, 82, 84, 85, 93–5,
 126, 128, 162–4

197

day-care (*cont.*)
  parent co-operative 38, 50, 74
  part-time 37, 66, 92, 117, 167
Denmark 1, 7–9, 18, 23, 24, 41–52, 54–8,
  60–2, 125, 130, 162, 163, 168
distributive justice 46, 51–3
division of labour 24, 70, 88
  in childcare 35, 141, 167, 177
  by gender 5, 6, 11, 14–17, 22, 26, 27, 29,
    34, 46, 104, 105, 118, 124, 133, 145,
    148, 151, 155, 158, 161, 162, 167,
    171–3, 175, 177,
  between parents 13, 17
  between the public and the private 9, 51,
    69, 81, 84, 187
  in society 7, 25, 40, 175
divorce/d 97, 102, 140
domestic labour 29, 30, 108, 112, 117 155,
  164
  debate 4, 13, 29, 30, 34, 36, 38, 39, 42,
    66, 107, 108, 110–12, 117, 121, 133,
    134, 137, 142, 155, 156, 164, 168, 170,
    172
domesticity of mothers 10, 73, 77, 95, 104,
  128
dominance 29, 142
  gendered division of 29
  male 29, 42, 167, 169
dual-earner/family 53, 93, 97, 110–11,
  113–16, 118, 120, 122–3, 132–4, 137,
  142, 144, 160

Eisenstein, Z. 1, 16, 20, 29, 42, 167
Ellingsæter, A.L. 98, 107–9, 134
employed-mother family/ies 2, 7, 12, 13,
  17, 18, 42, 57–60, 62, 78, 83, 95,
  99–100, 111–13, 116, 118–20, 127–30,
  133–6, 138, 145, 162, 165, 170
Engels, F. 29
equal status 18, 113; *see also* gender
  equality, social equality
Equal Status Act 78, 106, 129
Equal Status Council 78, 89, 109
equal status legislation 131
  policies 42, 79, 108, 120
Esping-Andersen, G. 20, 25, 41, 46, 169

family
  domesticated mother 104, 128
  gender-differentiated 3, 27, 69, 77, 104,
    118
  nuclear 13, 14, 17, 42, 61, 73, 95, 96,
    103–5, 118, 133, 158, 170
  role-differentiated 13
  traditional 17, 61, 103, 117, 118, 123,
    129, 130, 132, 157, 160

  see also dual-earner and single-parent
    family
family day care 55, 56
family wage 101, 106
father/-hood 15, 44, 53, 59, 78, 111, 112,
  134, 141, 145, 146, 164, 165, 168
  as economic provider/breadwinner
    13–15, 17, 18, 46, 102, 104, 123, 141,
    145
  as employed 6, 10, 23, 43, 116, 119, 134,
    172
feminism 169
feminist research 1, 5, 14–16, 20, 25, 29,
  30, 104, 125, 166–8, 173
feminization of poverty 23, 102
Finch, J. 4
functionalism 4, 13, 14, 29

gender equality 44, 52, 78, 80, 83, 106, 111,
  113, 117, 133, 156
  hierarchy 29, 169
  inequality 44, 107, 108
Gough, I. 18, 25
government
  central and local 46, 48, 49, 51, 60, 75,
    81, 84, 120, 131
  coalition 69, 77, 79, 88
  committees appointed by 9, 47, 69, 71,
    111, 127, 128
  Labour 67, 73, 77, 79, 88, 89, 116, 123,
    126 129, 130
Graham, H. 4, 28
Gullestad, M. 143, 145

Haavind, H. 1, 16, 37
Hartmann, H. 29
Hernes, H.M. 1, 5, 20, 25, 58, 95, 108, 125,
  166–9
hierarchy 5, 27, 30, 171, 173, 176; *see also*
  gender hierarchy
Holter, H. 104, 108, 139
home-maker 13, 46, 104, 123
household 6, 8, 17, 28, 35–9, 46, 104, 107,
  110, 113, 124, 132–4, 140, 142–8,
  150–2, 154–60
  modern 146, 150, 155, 157, 158
  traditional 146–8, 150–8
housewife/ves 50, 67, 74, 89, 103, 140, 107,
  128, 148, 150
housewives' association 67, 89

ideology 27, 68, 77, 89, 99, 104, 117,
  128–31, 163, 176
income maintenance 21–3, 41, 124
inequality (*see* gender inequality and social
  inequality)

institutional differentiation, typology of 13
insurance 22–4, 43, 102, 152

kinship 21, 38, 56, 86, 121, 139, 144, 151
Knudsen, P. 22, 26, 102
Knudsen, R. 23, 44
Korpi, W. 20, 25, 41, 46
Kugelberg, C. 37, 57, 62

labour market
   institutional differentiation of 120, 122,
      133
   participation rates 112, 134
   policies 59, 62, 112, 114, 119, 126, 164
   segregation 106
Labour government (see government,
   Labour)
Labour party 41, 68, 69, 73, 77, 95, 101,
   117, 127–30; see also Social
   Democratic party
Land, H. 27, 147
leave of absence 23, 42–5, 119, 139, 164;
   see also maternity leave, paternity
   leave, parental leave
Lewis, J. 77, 154
liberal policies 84, 88, 92
Lingsom, S. 98, 107, 134
Liljeström, R. 16, 39, 98
Lister, R. 5, 27

marriage 32, 97, 101, 103, 124
Marshall, T.H. 5, 18, 24, 25, 47, 162
Marxist 29
maternal deprivation 15
maternity leave 15–17, 43, 45, 119, 121, 134
   rights 23, 43
middle-class 52, 101, 118, 137, 139, 140,
   173
Morgan, D.H.J. 14
Moss, P. 1, 20, 45, 49, 55, 57, 59, 134, 138,
   141
mother–child relationship 3, 15, 61, 110,
   163
mother–minder relationship 11, 140
motherhood
   biological 16, 42, 108
   carer aspects of 9, 11, 28, 35, 64, 65, 101,
      102, 121, 126, 136
   earner aspects of 5, 6, 10, 17, 58, 65, 66,
      100, 102, 119, 120, 133
   making of 5–7, 11, 132, 161, 166, 174, 176
   models of 2, 9, 10, 12, 42, 43, 46, 64, 69,
      94, 95, 99, 100, 110, 126, 129, 132,
      136, 165
   modernization of 6, 28, 42, 57, 97, 100,
      102, 118, 135, 159

political 16, 42, 59, 173, 175
   social construction of 1, 4, 7, 27
   traditional 128
motherhood policies 1, 8, 42, 55, 77, 110,
   126, 162, 165
mothering 2, 108, 110, 132, 139, 141,
   145–7, 150, 155, 156
Myrdal, A. 67, 77, 107

National Insurance Act 22, 24
National Insurance Scheme 22–4, 43, 102
Norway 8–10, 17, 18, 23, 24, 41–64, 66–8,
   74, 77, 78, 87, 89, 94, 95, 97, 99–110,
   118, 125, 130, 132, 133, 138, 139, 142,
   143, 162–5, 167, 169, 174

Oakley, A. 14, 16
Ot. prp. nr. 23 (Day Care Act) 82, 85, 86, 90

Pahl, R.E. 4, 39, 132
parental leave 23, 43–5, 55, 164
parenthood 3, 13, 43, 46, 47, 110, 123
Parsons, T. 4, 13–15, 17, 18, 20, 104
partnership 1, 2, 24, 58, 59, 125, 162, 164,
   166–70
part-time day care (see day-care part-time)
part-time work 103, 105, 107, 108, 127,
   145, 147, 150, 152, 155, 172
patchwork quilting 174
Pateman, C. 5, 25, 34
paternity leave 44, 45, 119
patriarchy 1, 2, 11, 16, 29, 162, 166–9, 170,
   173
political parties 53, 61, 65, 68, 69, 78, 79,
   89, 98, 131
   bourgeois 66, 83, 117, 118, 129, 130
   centre and conservative 65, 117, 129
   to the left 75, 129
   see also Labour party
pregnancy/ies 15, 16, 97
pre-school teachers, 67, 70, 72, 79, 90, 91,
   139
profession 34, 56, 78, 89, 90, 91, 103, 111,
   130, 132
professional childcare (see childcare)

reproductive capacity 14, 17
   control 97
Rose, H. 32, 147
Ruggie, M. 1, 59, 168

Sassoon, A.S. 1, 34
Scandinavia 7, 8, 16, 18, 20, 22–4, 28, 32,
   34, 38, 44–7, 50, 51, 54, 55, 57, 58, 60,
   62, 66, 102, 129, 161, 163, 164, 166
   family in 13, 17

Scandinavia (*cont.*)
  motherhood in 1, 4–6, 12, 42, 43, 45, 57,
    59, 161
  research in 1, 4, 14, 20, 30, 37, 41, 109,
    125, 168, 173
Scandinavian welfare state (*see* welfare
    state in Scandinavia)
segregation 106, 165
Seip, A.-L. 19, 24, 64
sex discrimination 107
sex role 14, 145, 170
Siim, B. 1, 19, 26, 37, 57, 58, 61, 77, 95,
    125, 167, 168
single mothers 3, 102, 103
  providers/earners 23, 43, 44, 83, 94, 102,
    112, 117, 122
single-parent family 74, 75, 85, 115
Skrede, K. 23, 103, 104, 106, 108
Slagstad, R. 18
social class 3, 25, 93, 138; *see also* middle,
    upper, working class/es
Social Democratic party 41, 129; *see also*
    Labour party
social equality 5, 19, 25, 129
social inequality 5, 25
social security 18, 21, 23, 102, 124, 125, 140
Stacey, M. 34
St. meld. 4, 1987–8 (The long-term plan
    1990–3) 44
St. meld. 50, 1984–5 (On family policy) 87
St. meld. 89, 1961–2 (On day-care
    institutions for children) 75, 111
St. meld. 93, 1980–1 (Day care for children
    in the 1980s) 87, 122
subordination of women 14, 29, 42, 167, 169
Sweden 1, 7–9, 18, 23, 24, 41–62, 125, 130,
    162, 163, 168

Titmuss, R.M. 18, 47, 69
Tornes, K. 61, 104, 108, 127, 128

UK 59, 67, 101, 105, 106, 128, 167; *see also*
    Britain
unemployment 22, 101, 106, 108, 123

Ungerson, C. 4, 31
upper classes 66, 67, 101

Ve, H. 147

Wadel, C. 4, 37, 132
Wærness, K. 4, 31, 34
wage 27, 32, 44, 106, 107, 111, 171
  for care (*see* caring wage)
  compensation 23, 43, 44, 119
  family (*see* family wage)
wage-work 1, 5, 6, 25–7, 29, 32, 42, 66, 68,
    99, 107, 111, 115, 121, 125, 137, 147,
    149, 151, 171, 175
welfare state benefits/entitlements 5–6, 21,
    24–7, 48, 102, 162, 170–2
welfare state
  in Denmark 1, 7, 25, 58, 125
  informal 98, 171, 175
  as institutional 19–21, 41, 95, 163, 168
  as liberal 59, 168
  in Norway 7, 22, 63, 69, 93, 95, 96, 110,
    129, 166, 170, 171, 173
  as patriarchal 167, 169, 170
  as residual 19–21, 41, 64, 163, 168
  in Scandinavia 2, 6–8, 12, 13, 17–19, 21,
    25, 26, 41, 42, 48, 52, 53, 58, 59, 125,
    162, 163, 166, 168–70
  as Social Democratic 41, 168, 169
  in Sweden 1, 7, 44, 58, 169
Wilensky, H.L. 19, 20
womanhood 8, 125
Women's Movement 78, 108
Work Environment Act 22, 119
worker-parent 119
working-class 19, 52, 101, 117, 139, 140
  interests 59, 129, 169
  mothers 66, 114, 139, 140
  reforms 59
working hours 22, 66, 105–7, 111, 114, 115,
    117, 119, 122, 135, 174
working part-time (*see* part-time work)

Zetterberg, H. 33, 34